Parish life troubled vicar

Crich
1875–1900

Schools' history
Church & Chapel conflict
Court cases galore
Village scandal
Drunkenness
Fascinating residents
and much more...

as reported in newspapers, letters and logbooks
with photographs to set the scene

Peter Patilla

Published by Crich Area Community News

ISBN 978-0-9562271-0-2

Designed by Peter Patilla
Edited by Louise Maskill
http://lmaskill.wordpress.com

Printed by Higham Press

For
more recent
happenings in Crich
visit –
www.cacn.org.uk

CRICH

Contents

Views of Crich as it must have looked during the latter part of the 1800s

Crich from the quarry to Town End and St. Mary's Church.

Crich from the Queen Victoria Jubilee Gardens; St. Mary's Church and the 1854 Crich Stand can be seen in the distance.

Foreword

Why write a story about Crich parish life between the years 1875 and 1900? Being involved in education all my working life I was naturally interested in how the schools came to be in the village where I live. An article by Sylvia Taylor about *Early Education in Crich*, on Alan Flint's Crich Parish website, intrigued me and I wanted to find out more about the breakaway school headed by Mr Scott. Then, after reading a newspaper article which recorded how several hundred parishioners paraded the vicar's effigy through the village and burnt it outside the vicarage, I was hooked. The more I researched the more amazing the saga of this vicar became. Many court cases, scandals, good deeds, sexual shenanigans and tragedies made it too good a story not to tell.

I have included transcripts of the actual newspaper reports – the Victorians certainly liked the tittle-tattle and scandalous detail. They do make good reading.

I hope the story will be of interest to anyone with Crich connections, either past or present.

Although written about the parish of Crich 1875–1900 the story will be relevant to anyone with an interest in social history, how schools developed in villages, and the rise of nonconformist religion in a small community.

Peter Patilla

Acknowledgements

Firstly, thank you to Ron Howe for lots of initial information about the Acraman family and for putting me in contact with his son, Alan Howe. His kind words and support have been most appreciated.

Without Alan Howe I do not think this book would have been produced. Alan has shared with me and allowed me to use any part of his (as yet) unpublished book into the fascinating Acraman family. The story of William Acraman, one-time vicar of Crich, is only part of the much wider tale of this amazing family. Alan has been most generous with his knowledge, information and enthusiasm. As he has said, "You cannot choose your relatives!"

I would like to record my gratitude to the Derbyshire Library Service who have placed INFOTRAC® – a collection of old newspapers – on their website; this proved invaluable in the research. Also, thanks to the Local Studies Library and County Archives in Matlock for their help in researching old newspapers, logbooks and reports.

Several people read the book before publication and gave me feedback; thanks to you all. In particular: Brian Gibbons, who read every comma and full stop as well as finding "howlers" that had passed me by; Ken Rickwood, late of Essex University, was also most helpful in his detailed comments and helpful advice; Louise Maskill for the many hours of final editing above and beyond the call of duty.

Thank you to Sylvia Taylor's informal Family History Group for their enthusiasm, good company and willingness to listen to ramblings about "my friend the vicar." Also to my friends and colleagues on the Crich Area Community News committee who have, as always, encouraged and supported me.

Acknowledgements

I am grateful to Alan Flint for information about the history of the Crich Baptists, and Rosemary Hall for some fascinating family documents.

I must mention the late Dr J. G. Dawes whose boundless enthusiasm for Crich and its history regaled during our bell-ringing days helped sow the seeds of my own interest.

In reproducing the old photographs I do hope I have not inadvertently infringed anyone's copyright, especially as some of the photographs are from unknown sources and their provenance is lost. In particular I must thank Beryl Calladine for the loan of her album and Stan Smith for photographs from the George Smith collection. Several photographs are from a family album, the owner of which would prefer to be unnamed. I have included other photographs courtesy of: Rosemary Hall, Rosemary Bower, Hugh Potter, Les Barber.

Finally, thanks to my wife, Janet, who has had to endure repeats of the story told so often she could have written the book herself.

Introduction

This book is about the parish of Crich between 1875 and 1900, in particular the life and times of its vicar, William Acraman – a troubled and troublesome priest.

It is an account of the turmoil in the village through the ministry of Revd William Acraman. The saga as it unfolds gives a wonderful insight into the tensions, rivalries, bigotry and power struggles in a small village community during the last quarter of the nineteenth century.

It was a time when the power of the vicar was under attack from the Nonconformists and the powerful overseers in the mills and factories.

Nationally, School Boards were being formed to provide local education. This was highly unpopular with the church and many ratepayers in the community. The church would lose the control it had in church, or parochial, schools, whilst the ratepayers would have to fund the Board Schools. Managers of Board Schools were elected, so the schools were popular with many Nonconformists.

Chapels were being built, the railway system developed, roads were being improved, mills were thriving – it was a time of rapid change for a small community.

It was also a period that took in Queen Victoria's Golden and Diamond Jubilees. Crich did not have piped water, nor street lighting. Illnesses, such as scarlatina and measles, would sweep through the parish with tragic effect. Quarrying was a common and dangerous occupation – the quarry owners seemed very hard and uncaring.

The parish vicar, William Acraman, was a complex man. He clearly had trouble with relationships and could not handle any conflict of opinion or challenge to his authority.

On several occasions he was on trial both legally and ecumenically. His handling of school affairs split the village.

During his ministry –

Parishioners wanted him sacked.

His effigy was paraded through the village and set on fire.

A mock funeral was held outside the vicarage.

There were scuffles and fights in the church, vicarage and school.

A breakaway school was formed.

He arbitrarily sacked several head teachers.

He was imprisoned.

Scandalous stories of his conduct were commonplace.

Eventually he was imprisoned for two years and unfrocked as a vicar.

He was a spiteful and vindictive opponent who would go to extraordinary lengths to try and "bring people to heel." However, he was responsible for stopping an unpopular School Board coming to Crich and for shaping the schools in the parish. He was generous with his own money in supporting the development of the parochial schools in Crich and Crich Carr. His legacy has left us with four flourishing schools to this very day. He was a skilled cantata writer whose music was sung in churches far beyond the parish. William Acraman was popular with Florence Nightingale, whose servants told her about his sermons. His support for temperance in the parish, fully encouraged by his sisters, was particularly welcomed by Florence.

The story is mainly told through newspaper reports and school logbook entries, supported by correspondence between some of the key players.

Introduction

In transcribing the letters, logbooks and newspapers I have tried to keep what was written as accurate as possible. You will find spelling errors, strange punctuation, some wonderful local dialect and grammatical inaccuracies. They also liked terms such as "ult" (meaning last month), "inst" (meaning this month) and "prox" (meaning next month). Shorthand was commonly used – such as &c. for "and so on." People and place names could be spelt differently in the same article. So, when reading the transcripts any errors are not of the author's or editor's making!

Newspapers of the time did not withhold children's names from what they wrote. There was no right to anonymity. This caused me a little concern when transcribing articles about certain events that happened. As a result I took the decision to withhold two children's names and replace them with *Child A* and *Child B*. As these terms were not in the original articles I have set them in italics whenever they are used.

You may pick up on the fact that the Sunday School was a vital part of the vicar's life. During the period of this story Sunday Schools were concerned with free education of the poor, and teaching the values of the 'respectable' working class, stressing self-discipline, industry and thrift. Reading was taught so that access to the Bible was possible. Headmasters of the Parochial School in Crich were expected to fully participate in teaching at the Sunday School. Sunday was not a day off for them. There was another "hidden agenda" in having an active Sunday School. It was a time when the Nonconformists were seen to be more inviting to the young. Chapels had better music and they seemed to have a richer social life. The vicar needed to keep the young from the clutches of the Nonconformists.

Key Players

Here are some of the villagers who took an important part in the following history. There were of course a great many more who also influenced the course of events.

Acraman William – Vicar of Crich 1875 to 1900

Acraman Essie – Vicar's daughter

Acraman Julia – Vicar's sister and church worker

Acraman Laura – Vicar's sister and church worker

Barnes J H – Teacher, Crich Parochial School

Bennett Samuel – Framework knitter, supporter of Mr Scott

Blair Andrew – Curate at Crich

Boag Robert – Lime kilns manager, supporter of Mr Scott; Overseer

Bower Samuel – Highway Surveyor, supporter of Mr Scott

Brumwell Miria – Teacher, Crich Parochial School

Bryan Richard – Senior Guardian

Burrough J – Diocesan Registrar, Belper

Cosgrove Patrick – Village policeman

Cousens R W – Curate at Crich

Cowlishaw A C – Guardian of Crich, Architect

Curzon George – Farmer and 'prominent' ratepayer

Dawes George – Parish Clerk

Dawes John – Rate collector

Dawes Thomas – Shopkeeper

Dronfield Joseph – Publican, Jovial Dutchman

Dunn Christopher Blans Noble – Village doctor and Medical Officer for Belper Area

Dyson Heyworth – Master, British School

Ellis C J B – Master, Crich Parochial School

Frost George – Resident

Glossop Walter – Church pianist

Greenhough E – Secretary, British School Managers

Greenhough John – Resident

Greenhough Johnny – Messenger for the Vicar

Griffiths Mr – Master, Crich Carr School

Hallsworth Thomas B – Publican, Bulls Head

Hawkes Nathaniel I – Churchwarden

Higton John – Butcher

Holmes Annie – Friend of *child A*

Hurt Francis – Chairman of Parochial School Managers

Hurt (Misses) Elizabeth, Emma, Selina – Benefactors of the parish of Crich

Iveson Thomas Gill – Civil Engineer and supporter of Mr Scott

Jacoby J A – Member of Parliament

Kent George Henry – Master, Crich Parochial School

Kirk Elijah – Draper, supporter of Mr Scott

Knighton Job – Druggist and prominent Baptist

Key Players

Knighton Robert – Master, Crich Parochial School

Layton J – Parochial School Secretary to the Managers

Lee John – Churchwarden

Lee James Thomas – People's warden

Lee Mary – Wife of John

Lloyd M L – Teacher, Crich Parochial School

Macdonald George G – Village doctor

Macdonald Supt. – Belper Police Superintendant

Milward Martha – Friend of *child A*

Moody A W – Master, Crich Parochial School

Mulkerns J – Vicar of Wessington

Neville J P – Curate at Crich

Nightingale Florence – Church supporter

Perry Walter – Scholar

Petts Isaac – Builder and prominent Baptist, Overseer

Potter James – Solicitor of Matlock

Poyzer James – Scholar

Radford Joseph – Overseer

Saxton John – Churchwarden, secretary to Parochial School Managers

Scarffe Inez – Teacher at Crich Parochial School

Scott Henry Stephen – Master, Crich Parochial School, then the British School (also called Scott's School)

Slack Albert E – Publican, Black Swan

Slack Edward – Grocer

Slack Joseph – Resident

Slack Mary – Wife of Edward, carer of Vicar's daughter Essie

Smith Joseph – Blacksmith

Stocks John – Baker

Stocks Samuel – Publican, Royal Oak

Strutt Herbert – Mill owner and magistrate

Sumner William Thomas – Master, Crich Parochial School

Walker Charles – Resident

Wetton John – Parish Clerk

Wetton Mary – Housekeeper at the vicarage

Wharmby Samuel – Builder of British School

Wheatcroft Henry – Solicitor and Secretary to the School Managers

Wildgoose John – Landlord of the Rising Sun

Wildgoose Robert – Lea Mills, supporter of British School

Wilson J G – Solicitor at Alfreton

Wilson Mortimer – Solicitor at Alfreton

Woolley Elizabeth – Resident

Child A – Friend of Vicar's daughter
Child B – Scholar
Mrs A – *Child A's* mother

Chapter 1
School problems

This story starts in 1875 with the arrival in Crich of the Revd William Acraman. He was born in Bristol on the 12th November 1837, the son of a very wealthy family – the Acramans. They were by the 1830s the owners of a big firm, with three Bristol works where they built bridges and cranes, made anchors and, later, locomotives and iron ships. Brunel was a friend of the family. To this day there are bridges that bear the name *Acraman*. They helped build the *s.s. Great Western*, and finally had a spectacular bankruptcy in 1842, with debts of £75,000.

William Acraman decided to become a vicar and was ordained in Hereford during 1865, becoming curate there at St. Peter's. He was a curate at: Oakham, 1866 to 1868; Aberdeen, 1868 to 1870; and Paston in Northamptonshire, 1870 to 1872. He was vicar at Appleton-le-Moors in Yorkshire from 1872 until 1875, after which he moved to become vicar of St. Mary's, Crich.

TIMES: 25 December 1875

𝕰𝖈𝖈𝖑𝖊𝖘𝖎𝖆𝖘𝖙𝖎𝖈𝖆𝖑

PREFERMENTS AND APPOINTMENTS,
Rev. W. Acraman to Vicarage of Crich, Derbyshire.

He had four sisters, Sarah, Julia, Laura Elizabeth and Mary Jane. Two of these, Laura and Julia, lived with the vicar in Crich for a number of years. They took an active part in church affairs and were involved in the local temperance movement. They were of great support and comfort to him in times of trouble.

Early education in Crich

The vicar arrived in the village to find that the education being received by the children in his parochial school was rather poor. It is worth a brief look at the history of schools in the village to see how this state of affairs had arisen. Sylvia Taylor, on the Crich Parish website, writes:

There is little record of early educational provision in Crich. However, a prospectus does exist for "Crich School" for the year 1805 under the direction of J. Walker and "able assistants" but this was a boarding establishment for the boys of comparatively rich families. As well as a general education, "Young Gentlemen of proper age and abilities" could be instructed in "the Law and practical conveyancing" for an extra £2 2s 0d per annum.

The educational provision for poorer children was investigated by a select committee on Education for the Poor in 1818. They found that within the Parish of Crich there were three day schools for boys and the same number for girls, containing together from 140 to 160 children, and four dame schools consisting of 20 to 30 children each. This was inadequate for the number of children of school age; "The poor have not sufficient means but appear desirous of education."

Bagshaw's History (1846) recorded four academies in Crich, conducted by Mr. W. B. A. Walker, Sarah Wigley, Joseph Witham and Joseph Daykin at Fritchley.

While there was a growing feeling throughout this time of the desirability of an elementary education for the children of the poor, the Government was unwilling either to take the initiative or to produce the finance to provide this single-handed; instead sums of money were made available to be used by the Religious Educational Charities.

A Parochial School was erected in Crich in 1848. The cost was met by £600 raised by public subscription and a grant of £250 from the Government. This church school was enlarged by the addition of an infant classroom in 1855.

In 1862 the system of payment by results was instituted so that the full grant to a school was dependent on a satisfactory report by the H.M.I. (Her Majesty's Inspectors) following their annual inspection. Unfortunately the Parochial Academy was sometimes found wanting; in 1864 the H.M.I. found the children "deficient in arithmetic and the lower classes have not been adequately taught." Consequently they lost two tenths of the grant. It cannot have been easy for the schoolmaster and his assistants, education was not compulsory at this time; absenteeism and unpunctuality were very common.

There were many absences throughout the winter months due to the bad weather and sickness. Then the annual pattern of absences developed as many children stayed at home to help prepare for Christmas and then Easter; later came haymaking, gleaning and the blackberry season, culminating in preparation for Crich Fair in October.

There was competition for the sometimes unwilling pupils. In August 1868, the Parochial Schoolmaster recorded that "a great number, mostly infants, have left to go to one lately opened by the Reformers." In January 1870 some left to go to the new National School at Fritchley. This school, built in 1869, was extended in 1875 and again in 1894. The fees when it opened were 4d per week. At Crich Parochial School there was a more flexible scheme of charges in 1883. These were:

Infants	*2d per week*
Standards I and II	*3d per week*
Standards III and Above	*4d per week*

The fourth child in every family free and 1d off for the third child if three are coming regularly.

Sometimes a local benefactor would undertake to pay the 'school pence' for one or more children in a poor family.

The Parochial School gained pupils when a 'venture' school closed down in 1873, but the battle for pupils was not over. The Education Act of 1870 had provided for the establishment of local school boards to make good a shortage of school places in their area.

A dame school was an early form of a private elementary school. They were usually taught by women and were often located in the home of the teacher. They were quite varied – some were day care facilities, overseen by illiterate women, while others provided their students with a good foundation in the basics. Dame schools became less common after the introduction of compulsory education in 1880, when schools that were found to be below government-specified standards of tuition could be closed.

Competition from South Wingfield

In 1876 Crich Parochial School lost all the pupils who lived in South Wingfield. A Board School had just opened there and all the children obviously stopped coming to Crich. To make matters worse the new Wingfield school tried to entice Crich pupils by undercutting the charges. Thirty children left for the new school.

Parochial School logbook: 1876

Many children absent this morning. All the children from Wingfield being absent. The Board Schools of this place being opened and they liberally posted this place with bills gratuitously offering to take children for about half our prices or charges. Even posted one close to the school walls.

The opposition to Board Schools was to play a major part in the events that unfolded in the village during the coming years. It was to result in confrontation between church and chapel, in victory for the vicar and in accusations that it was partly responsible for his disgrace and downfall. Unlike the neighbouring parishes of South Wingfield and, eventually, Lea and Holloway, Crich would not have a Board School.

Market Place.
Note the mineral railway bridge and grassed area.

Crich Parochial School had problems. The records show poor standards, absenteeism and a weak head in Mr Knighton. The staff was Mr Knighton, his wife, a pupil teacher and a monitor. The reports from the School Inspectors were uniformly bad and, because they were paid by results, the grants to the school were often cut. According to the records the only thing the pupils excelled in was copying from each other. The following extracts are from the logbooks reporting what the Inspectors found.

Parochial School logbook: 2 May 1877
Arithmetic is still in an unsatisfactory state, discipline somewhat improved but not what it should be. Grant to be reduced one-tenth under Article 32 (b) for defective teaching in Arithmetic.

The school logbook was most important. It was bound with hasp and lock to keep its contents private. The Inspectors, vicar and other official visitors recorded their visits and comments. Staff admonishments and attendance were also recorded. It was a diary of the school, and gives excellent reports of critical happenings in the school.

Note: See the Appendices for more about Board Schools

Poor school reports

Parochial School logbook: 24 May 1878

The school has increased in numbers but otherwise it is in a very unsatisfactory state. The spelling and particularly Arithmetic are bad. The classes require to be constantly watched in order to prevent copying. A Monitor, fourteen years of age, prompted several children in the Infant Department. The master would do better in a smaller school. A deduction of one tenth is made for faults of instruction in spelling and Arithmetic. It is with great hesitation that my Lords have allowed the payments of grants for music, discipline and organisation under Article 19 (G). I, as HM Inspector, report it is most unsatisfactory in these points. I am to inform you for the future such a lenient decision must not be looked for.

Grant	
Attendance 118 @ 6/-	£35 8s 0d
Inf. Presented 24 @ 8/-	£9 12s 0d
In standards 105 passes @ 3/-	£15 15s 0d
Gross total	£60 15s 0d
Reduction one-tenth	£6 1s 6d
Balance	£54 13s 6d

Victorian lessons were not an exciting form of learning, concentrating on the "three Rs". Children learnt by reciting things by rote, until they were word-perfect. Science was taught by "object lesson". For example, pictures of flowers, elephants or camels were placed on each pupil's desk as the subject for the lesson. They then had to talk about what the picture showed them. Unfortunately, many teachers found it easier to chalk up lists describing the object, for the class to copy. Geography meant yet more copying and reciting, listing the countries on a globe or wall map. Because classes were so large, pupils all had to do the same thing at the same time. When pupils found their work boring, teachers found their pupils difficult to control!

6

Parochial School logbook: December 1879

The number has increased and there is some slight improvement in the standard of work but the attainments are still far from satisfactory. The grammar above the second standard was badly done, and very few answered with any intelligence in the Geography. Two children were struck off for copying and a large number required constant watching. The needlework is very fair. The Pupil Teacher has passed an unsatisfactory examination: he has been in the habit of receiving instruction between morning and afternoon school. My Lords have had much hesitation in sanctioning the payment of grant for discipline and organisation in consequence of the prevalence of copying amongst the children. J. J. Parkins should improve very greatly.

Robert Knighton	*First class*
Maria Knighton	*Second Class*
J. J. Parkins	*Pupil Teacher*
Hannah Ruth Holmes	*Paid monitor*

Children as young as thirteen helped the teacher to control the class. They were called "pupil teachers" and received certificates which helped them qualify as teachers when they were older. Sometimes a single teacher instructing a large class had the help of pupils called "monitors". The head teacher quickly taught these monitors, some of them as young as twelve, who then tried to teach their schoolmates. After 1870, all children from five to thirteen had to attend school by law. A large number didn't turn up. Lessons typically lasted from 9a.m. to 5p.m., with a two hour lunch break.

Chapter 2
Nonconformists increase in influence

In the middle of the 1870s the development of the various nonconformist religions in the parish was to be significant in the troubles that followed over education in the village. Revd Acraman arrived just in time to be involved in the social and religious upheaval that followed.

The Baptists had a Meeting Place on Roes Lane, built in 1839. In 1875, because of increased numbers, it was decided that they needed larger premises. Right in the centre of the village the old Manor House and grounds were up for sale. With great vision and faith, the members decided that these should be purchased. The cost proved to be just over £600. It would appear that in some measure the 'wrath' of some local people was encountered, because in order to build the present church, it proved necessary to demolish the Manor House.

Of course there had been Nonconformist chapels in the parish for some time. The first was the Wesleyan Chapel (1765), but others included - Crich Primitive Methodists (1855); Fritchley Primitive Methodists (1829); Crich Carr Primitive Methodists (1877); United Methodists at Mount Tabor (1864); and the Congregational Chapel in Fritchley (1841).

There was some rancour with the vicar because the Nonconformist's children attended the Parochial School but did little to support the fabric of the school.

As the story unfolds the involvement of the Nonconformists, the Baptists in particular, becomes significant, as does the Mount Tabor Chapel.

The Baptist Church is located on a very historic site. The 14th century Manor House of Sir Roger Beler was on this very spot. By the time the Baptists purchased it at auction in the mid 1870s it was called *Wheeldon House* and was in need of substantial repair.

The foundation stone was laid in July 1877.

Mount Tabor United Methodists Chapel, on Bowns Hill, was built in 1864.

This was to become a school during the troubles that lay ahead. It was largely built by quarrymen in their spare time.

Wesleyan Chapel, on Chapel Lane, the oldest in Crich, was built in 1765.

Charles Wesley preached here.

9

Crich chapels

Crich Primitive Methodist Chapel, on Sun Lane, was built about 1855.
The Primitive Methodists had already built a chapel at Fritchley in 1829, which was rebuilt in 1852. Crich Carr Primitive Methodist Chapel was built in 1877.

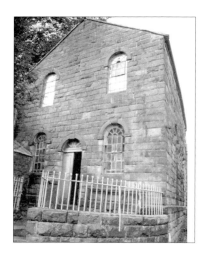

Fritchley Congregational Chapel, Fritchley Green, was founded in 1841.

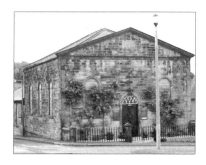

Fritchley Meeting House, Chapel Lane Fritchley, was built in 1897.
For many years before that they met at "Fernside" on Bobbin-Mill Lane. The Society of Friends became prominent in Fritchley during 1863. and had quite an influence in the parish.

The new Baptist Chapel, the construction of which began in 1877, was in prime position, right in the centre of the Market Place. There were rumours that the site had been bought under "strange circumstances", with a bit of manipulation being applied for its purchase. What is certain is that the Chapel was built very rapidly. Within the year the building was up to the first floor windows. Stone to build it came from the demolished Manor House, the nearby parish quarry and Duke's Quarry in Whatstandwell.

The pipe organ came from Derby and lessons were paid for so that it could be played during the services. The pulpit was specially designed and built for the Chapel. The clock cost £50, the money being raised by public subscription. However, the clock on the building today is not the original.

The Baptists of 1878 received the princely sum of £50 following the sale of the old Meeting House on Roes Lane, now a private house, but before that a joinery workshop.

George Smith Collection

Baptist Chapel before the Market Place was developed. Date unknown.

New Baptist Chapel

Derby Mercury: Wed 18 July 1877

CRICH

THE NEW BAPTIST CHAPEL – The ceremonial of laying the foundation-stone of this new chapel was on Wednesday the occasion of a large and influential gathering at Crich, which overlooks some of the loveliest scenery in England. The new chapel will seat some 250 people, and the estimated cost is £1,400, towards which £600 had been given or promised before the day of opening. It has been designed by Mr Isaac Petts of Crich, who is also the builder. The proceedings commenced by a procession from the old Baptist Chapel, which, preceded by the South Wingfield brass band, went round the village, the Sunday scholars singing at intervals on the route. Lunch was provided in the Mount Tabor Schoolroom. The central principal memorial stone was laid by Mr J. C. Jones, of Manchester, who is a donor of 50 guineas to the fund. A devotional service was conducted in the front of the site of the new chapel by the Rev. W. Underwood, D.D. of Derby. The introductory discourse was delivered by the Rev. T. Goadby,

B.A., president of Chilwell College, and formerly of Derby. Mr W. B. Bembridge, of Ripley, then presented Mr Jones with a silver trowel and mallet, with which he laid the central memorial stone, and the Rev. W. Underwood delivered an address. A collection was then made in aid of the chapel memorial fund. The remaining memorial stones were laid by Mrs J. Willn, of Cromford; Mrs W. B. Bembridge, of Ripley; Mr Samuel Bennett, of Derby; Mr R. Wildgoose, of Holloway; Mr George Slack, of Derby; and Mr Richard Bryan, of Crich Carr. Several brief addresses followed. Subsequently Councillor James Hill, of Derby, opened a bazaar of useful and fancy articles in a large marquee in the Market-place. Afterwards a public tea took place in the Mount Tabor schoolroom. The weather was very favourable, and there was a large number of visitors including Mr Abraham Woodiwiss and family, Mr Councillor Bowmer, Mr Embery, Mr Cholerton, and Mr Lamb of Derby. The amount realised by the day's proceedings was £300.

A report to the Local Association in 1879 observed: *"The past year has witnessed the opening of our new, commodious and beautiful chapel, situated in the centre of the Market Place. The interior of the chapel is very compact and is pronounced the nicest country chapel in the county. It contains a good organ. The congregation is much improved since we left the old chapel. There is a new clock put in the front elevation, which cost £50. The funds for the clock were subscribed by the public."*

The Baptists were to play a vital role in the events that were about to unfold.

Although the Baptists were very prominent because of their building project, the Primitive and Wesleyan Methodists were also still very active. The Primitive Methodists in Whatstandwell and Crich Carr were anxious to try and have their new chapel built before that of the Crich Baptists. A race was on.

Derby Mercury: Wed 23 October 1877

CRICH

A temperance meeting was held in the new Infants schoolroom in the "Carr" on Thursday evening last. The meeting was addressed by the vicar, and the Rev. Mr Smith, lately curate at Matlock Bath, gave a reading.

The Wesleyan Methodists held a missionary meeting in their chapel on the evening of the 23rd. The attendance was very small. The Rev. Drummond, one of the circuit ministers, and Mr Selvey, a Wesleyan student, at present allocated at Belper, addressed the meeting. The chairman was Mr John Storer, a local preacher of the place.

The rather imposing building now in course of erection by the Baptists seemed to have received an increased fillip towards completion lately. We notice a popular lecture announced to be delivered this week in aid of the building fund, the lecturer being the Rev. W. Jamieson, of Riddings.

The even more ecclesiastical looking building now in course of erection in the "Carr" under the auspices of the Primitive Methodists, is being pushed on with spirit.

Whatstandwell Chapel, at the end of Middle Lane. Date unknown.

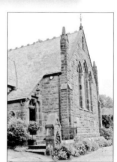

Primitive Methodists Chapel, Crich Carr, was built in 1877.

Chapter 3
Florence Nightingale and the shipwreck

Florence Nightingale occasionally worshipped at Crich, her home being nearby at Lea Hurst. The following letter, sent to Revd Acraman in 1878 about the brave rescue of four of her nurses, is a fascinating one. The nurses were shipwrecked two days out of Montreal and marooned for a week on an island. They were rescued thanks to the heroic efforts of an officer who swam two icy rivers to reach a lighthouse and raise the alarm. They were taken aboard the *ss Erl King*, captained by Ed. Scott, and landed in Glasgow on August 9th 1878 some three weeks after originally setting out.

Florence wrote asking the vicar for a mention of her nurses at the church service. Below is a transcript of her letter; see Appendix 1a for a copy of the original.

Lea Hurst
Cromford Derby
Aug 16/78

Dear Sir

Four of our trained Nurses have been wrecked on their way home from Canada, where they had been nursing for us at the Montreal General Hospital & were returning for further Nursing employment under us.

The steamer was wrecked upon a reef two days out from Canada, on July 21. All night she was beaten about & in danger of going to pieces. At day break the Captain lowered the passengers into a life boat, but she drifted out to sea & again they were with difficulty saved. For a whole week till the 28th they were on an island, whence an officer made his way to the nearest light house, swimming two rivers, (which the crew would not cross) or battened down in the hold of a small fish schooner, without food or air, in a terrific storm. On July 28 they were rescued by the Erl Kïng, Capt. Ed. Scott, whose kindness we can never forget, bound for Glasgow where they landed safe on Aug 9.

Would you allow me to return thanks for ~~them~~ our four Nurses in your church next Sunday?

Their names are: Nurse Styring
     Nurse Wilson
      " *Cross*
      " *Webb*

Might I say, in any terms you would be good enough to use:

 Florence Nightingale desires to return the most humble & hearty thanks to Almighty God for four trained Nurses returning home (on duty) from Canada who were wrecked on July 21, were saved three times from a watery grave, & after severe sufferings for a week from exposure & hardship, were rescued on the 28th by a vessel bound for Glasgow & safely landed on August 9 thro' a merciful Providence.

      Pray believe me, Sir,
      ever your faithful servt
      Florence Nightingale

The Revd
W. Acraman

             Letter courtesy of Alan Howe

The rescue ship the *ss Erl Kïng* was not a particularly "lucky" ship. She hit an iceberg on 5th August 1885 on the way from Montreal to London, limping into St. John's with a hole in her starboard bow. Eventually she sank in heavy seas at Caesar's Creek, Long Reef, Florida, in December 1891.

 This story of shipwrecks must have cheered the vicar up, as he was shortly to set off on his world tour.

Chapter 4
The vicar's world tour 1880

It was in January of 1880 that the Revd Acraman left Crich for a "World Tour". This took in America and Australia, where he had relatives. He left because he had suffered a family bereavement and needed a rest. It was recorded in the school logbook.

Parochial School logbook: January 1880

Rev. C. D. Richardson took over the parish - vicar having left for Australia on the 10th.

During his absence difficulties at the school continued with unfavourable Inspector's reports.

Parochial School logbook: 9 June 1880

The order is not satisfactory, the children were inclined to prompt one another and they were noisy. A large proportion of the children were presented in the first and second standards. The spelling and the Arithmetic of the upper standards were poor; the Arithmetic very poor. The infants are backward. The school is a large one. The present staff in my opinion wanting in the power necessary to control the number of children assembled.

The vicar returned early owing to health problems.

Parochial School logbook: 19th November 1880

Vicar returned from his voyage to Australia and America for the benefit of his health.
22 November 1880
Welcome Home meeting in the schoolroom.

The vicar's tour was reported fully in the newspapers. At this time it appeared that he was quite popular with few signs of the problems that lay ahead.

Derby Mercury: Wed 1 December 1880

CRICH.

The parish of Crich has recently been in a state of considerable excitement owing to the return of the vicar, the Rev. Wm. Acraman from a voyage round the world. The rev. gentleman had been recommended change and rest, as his health had given way through domestic bereavement and the hard work of a large and arduous parish, and took the opportunity thus given to visit relations in Australia. On his return it was determined by some of the parishioners to give a public welcome which took place on Monday week at the large and commodious National Schoolroom. The bells of the fine old parish church rang out merry during the afternoon and evening, and, had time permitted, a triumphal arch would have been erected. As it was the gateway of the schoolroom was adorned with evergreens. On entering the building, which was tastefully decorated for the occasion, an interesting sight presented itself, the room having a festive appearance, while over the platform were placed, in letters worked in laurel leaves on a white ground, the words "Welcome Home." A very large assembly was gathered together, nearly 400 (inclusive of the scholars) sitting down to an excellent tea provided by Mr. John Stocks, the tables being presided over by lady members of the congregation. The children attending the Church Sunday schools of Crich, Fritchley and Crich Carr were first entertained at a free tea, kindly given in honour of the event by one of the congregation. – After tea the chair was taken by the Rev. G. D. Richardson, curate in charge, who, in a few well turned phrases, in the name of the people bade Mr. Acraman in a hearty welcome. After some glees and songs, which were well rendered by members of the church choir, and ably accompanied on the piano by Mrs. Dunn, the Chairman called upon the Rev. William Rowthorne, of Wessington, as a neighbour to say a few words, and then requested Mr. Acraman to give some account of his travels. – In an address of one hour's duration, which was listened to with the deepest attention, the Vicar eloquently brought before his people pictures of travel, life, and society in Australia and America, and in a few touching words expressed his thankfulness for the kind and hearty reception he had met with, and the gratitude he felt at being once more safe home to live and labour amongst them. – The congregations on Sunday were remarkably good, that in the evening being the largest seen in Crich for many years. The Vicar took for his text Acts viii. verses 5 and 8 "Then Philip went down to the city of Samaria and preached Christ unto them. And there was great joy in that city." And in a sermon marked by his usual earnestness ably impressed the truths of Scripture on his people, the service being brought to a close by the appropriate hymn "Safe, home, safe home in port." We understand that Mr. Acraman promises to give a further account of the countries he has passed through in his journey round the world when time permits.

St Mary's Church as it looked when Revd Acraman was vicar.

Chapter 5
Crich poem of 1880

In the May of 1880 an anonymous poem, penned by someone with the initial W.H., was written about the trades people of Crich. Although obviously a very home-spun piece of work it does give quite a bit of information about the tradesmen and women of Crich and sometimes an insight into what they might have been like. Several of the people mentioned have starring roles in the events that happen later on in this account.

THE TRADES PEOPLE OF CRICH

With our worthy Vicar I must begin,
His duty is to save from sin;
His sermons and his prayers should raise,
Our hearts to God in thankful praise.

Our Doctor next comes into view,
In cleverness he's beat by few;
His skill and talent gain renown,
The finest man in all the town.

Of Lawyer Harris not much is known,
The less the better you all will own;
For if from him you want advice,
You'll have to pay a heavy price.

In Mr. Boag you'll see combined,
Largeness of heart and soul and mind;
He's shrewd of thought, in words polite,
His life with all his acts unite.

Of Mr. Coupe, there's no offence ,
In saying he's a man of sense;
To ought that's good his hand he'll lend.
The poor in him possess a friend.

Joseph Howitt is a decent man,
Most of his workmen say;
And for their sake we'll hope he'll live
Their wages long to pay.

Above him lives his brother Harry,
A gun he used to love to carry;
But now he's got a shop and wife,
He has to lead a steadier life.

Mr. Burton has only one arm,
But to make up for this he's got a large farm;
He's also got three servant chaps,
And so he takes no harm perhaps.

Mr. Cowlishaw's an upright man
In all his ways and dealings;
He studies business while he can,
And is possessed of proper feelings.

Mr. Storer is a very good man,
Who works for God below:
And when he's done what good he can,
To heaven I'm sure he'll go.

19

Trades people of Crich

Mr. Wightman's just and true,
To all he'll do or say;
Of such as him we have but few,
He's honest as the day.

Miss Walker keeps the Kings Arms Inn,
In order and control;
Sells Whisky, Brandy, rum and gin,
And ale to make men roll.

Joseph Rollinson he works hard,
He also keeps a shop;
But, as I've many more to name,
With him I must not stop.

Thomas Dawes he keeps a grocer's
shop,
Sells all you may require;
But if you say too much to him;
The fat is in the fire.

Another upright man I reach,
Whose name I mean to mention;
Joseph Whittaker, (I've heard him
preach,)
To do good is his intention.

George Stocks works at the frame,
And he contrives to do what's right;
Joseph Slack he does the same,
They both work hard from morn till
night.

Charley Walter lives above,
A barber and hair-cutter;
Scissor-grinder too is he,
Sells hair oil rich as butter.

There's Joseph Brown I won't forget
A framesmith very good;
And if his work I meant to blame,
I could not if I would.

There's Edward Bown, a neighbour
good,
As all around will say;
T'would cheer you up to see his face,
If you should pass that way.

Samuel Stocks works very hard,
His children do as well;
But which brings home of money most
There is no need to tell.

John Haynes, our only joiner here,
Makes aught you may require;
In shape of tables, box, or drawers,
He'll suit a small desire.

Ralph Smith, who lives at Dimple
House,
A butcher used to be;
He leads a very easy life,
For retired now is he.

A respectable draper is Mr. James Lee,
Candles he makes and keeps a farm;
He also deals in sugar and tea
Churchwarden too, and does no harm.

Near him lives our friend John Perry
Who deals in apples, pears, and
cherries;
Potatoes, oranges, (and fish,
Which many think a dainty dish).

John Dawes he does the rates collect,
Also a shop he keeps of toys;
He penny pipes and 'bacca' sells,
for naughty little boys.

Frederick Curzon a tailor is,
That does his work right well;
Caleb Gratten lives next door,
Who cakes and pies does sell.

A druggist shop we now have got,
Which some think very handy;
To get laudanum, snuff and pillruff,
And also sugar candy.

Mrs Howitt and Miss Poyser
Dressmakers are first class;
For style and fit it well is known,
There's none them can surpass.

John Stocks is a very good baker,
Pork pie and sausage maker;
His flour is good, his bread is clean,
The sweetest and freshest that ever was
seen.

Vaughan Taylor he in beef doth deal,
Mutton also lamb and veal;
His weight is just his price is fair,
His customers this all declare.

John Higton is a butcher too,
On cutting up he's beat by few;
His quality and quantity both are good,
So buy a pound or two off him, if want
you ever should.

Arthur Smith another butcher is,
Fred Cheetham would be the same;
But he so very oft gets drunk,
For which he's much to blame.

Robert Foster is a very real English man,
One of the oldern kind;
Honest, straightforward and upright,
He always speaks his mind.

William Thorpe lives just above,
He is a man of taste and sense;
For flowers and snuff there's lots will
own,
He spares no trouble or expense.

John Saxton a churchwarden is,
A lawyer's clerk besides;
And if you want your will to make,
In him you must confide.

Joseph Ash goes to the mill,
A shop he also keeps;
And straight to see Miss Fanny Dear,
Will Petts he often peeps.

Richard Young he is a farmer,
A plumber and a glazer too;
He is a tidy sort of fellow,
But alas he is a blue.

Mr Kirk who lives on Bown's Hill,
A very good draper's shop does keep;
And when he is selling off his things,
You'll get your clothing very cheap.

Mrs Wigley sells bulls eyes,
A school she also teaches;
Of little girls, and also boys
Not yet put in their breeches.

A blacksmith William Poyser is,
The same is Ralph his son;
And if your horse would want a shoe,
He'll slowly put it on.

There's Greenhough, Prince and Shipton
too,
All three a shop possess;
But Prince has lately bankrupt turned,
Which is no pretty mess.

George Smith a man of principle,
His son the same may be;
A wheelwright that none can beat,
A farmer too is he.

Trades people of Crich

Another blacksmith we have got,
Thomas Taylor is his name;
And if I say he nothing knows,
I shall be much to blame.

Mr Twigg's the parish guardian,
And reliever of the poor;
With his smashing trap and pony,
Rides the parish o'er and o'er.

A toyshop Mrs Wetton's got,
Sells dolls the child to please;
And lollipops and ginger beer,
So strong it makes you sneeze.

Mr Hunt he saddles makes,
His work he well doth do;
And if you want your harness good,
You'll get it strong and new.

Mrs England keeps a shop,
Sells sugar tea and balm;
Samuel Holmes he does the same,
He also has a farm.

Of publicans I've not said much,
But we have a lot;
The stuff they sell is nothing worth,
Makes man a brutish sot.

John Wetton is the parish clerk,
'Amen' he shouts on Sunday;
In earnestness he does his work,
Though he be hoarse on Monday.

But he's a still more solemn charge,
The graves are in his trust;
Which holds the wicked and the good,
The righteous and the just.

Long life and prosperity,
To all my friends around;
And may you ever while you live,
With noble works abound.

My story now is finished,
My yarn I now have spun;
Adieu my fellow brethren,
My criticising's done.

W.H.
CRICH, May 1880

Poem courtesy of Beryl Calladine

Kings Arms, on the
Common.
Miss Walker was publican
here in 1880.

Chapter 6
Florence Nightingale and temperance

Florence Nightingale wrote to support the vicar's stance on temperance. She enclosed three guineas for his good works, wishing it could be more. In the letter she has a goodly rant about the poor dress, living conditions and drinking habits of the people of Crich.

Lea Hurst
Nov 26 1881

Dear Sir
I beg your acceptance of £3. 3 for any of your works that require it most. Temperance or Lay Reader.
I wish it were more, but the claims upon me are far beyond my means.
I trust that your fight in favour of temperance will be crowned with success as I am sure you will also pray for ours.
Drink & dress seem to be the great barriers against civilization, against God's work in these parts. The people do not even understand their own interests: they will live in wretched quarters, perhaps 7 in family <u>and</u> a lodger, in two miserable bed rooms – happy too if grown up sons & daughters are not in the <u>same</u> bed room & even (up into the teens) in the same bed. While they spend more on eating & drinking & dressing (with <u>no</u> mending) than we do – and mend their clothes less than we do. There are people earning (parents, sons & daughters included) considerably more than a London Government clerk, who has to appear like a gentleman. What wonder if immorality is rampant!
I have to thank you for a sermon preached the Sunday before last against <u>profanity</u>, & against drinking, repeated to me, as far as I could guess almost word for word, by my maid. I always make them tell me the Sermons they hear.
I pray God to bless your work
> *Excuse pencil*
> *I pray believe me*
> *ever your faithful serv^t*
> *Florence Nightingale*
Revd W. Acraman

Letter courtesy of Alan Howe

Temperance in Crich

The vicar wrote several musical pieces in support of the Band of Hope temperance movement. His sister Julia was also very active in temperance movements.

It is interesting to note that the papers of the time had many reports of drunkenness in Crich. One group of drinkers had to travel to Wirksworth as it seemed they had been banned from every pub in Crich.

Florence Nightingale obviously took a great interest in happenings at Crich, living as she did so close at Lea Hurst.

Postcard of Florence Nightingale's home at Lea Hurst by Harold Burkinshaw of Belper, taken in the early 1900s.

One source of information states that the Directors of the Midland Railway ordered a railway station to be built especially for her. It was built just behind the Derwent Hotel in 1853. It is said the Directors did not like the idea of Florence having to travel to Cromford station and then on to her family home at Lea. It was much more convenient for her to alight at Whatstandwell and travel up Robin Hood to Lea Hurst. Let us take a closer look at this claim.

The first station at Whatstandwell was officially opened for passenger traffic in 1853, and officially closed for passenger traffic from 11th November 1894 when the second station was opened and remains open today. The first station was located behind the Derwent Hotel at the north end of the Whatstandwell tunnel and later became the location of goods operations when the new station was opened. The stations were originally called Whatstandwell Bridge, but became plain Whatstandwell from July 1896.

Cromford station, originally Cromford Bridge, was officially opened for passenger traffic on 20th August 1849, the same date as Matlock Bath, Matlock, Darley and Rowsley. The line between Ambergate and Rowsley was officially opened on 4th June 1849 although neither passenger nor coal traffic commenced until 20th August 1849.

This factual account does not offer any reasons as to why Whatstandwell was opened after the other stations on the line. Railway author Bill Hudson makes no reference to Florence Nightingale, but states: "In planning the railway the directors of the Manchester, Buxton, Matlock & Midlands Junction Railway (MBM&MJR) saw no reason to build a station at this point (Whatstandwell), but later, the success of the line, plus pressure from local residents, induced a change of heart."

Florence Nightingale did not leave home until August 1853 when she took up nursing in London, so she would presumably not have travelled by train to Lea Hurst very much between 1849 and 1853. The Crimean War finished in February 1856. She was one of the last to return and by then the station was open in Whatstandwell, so if there was pressure on behalf of Florence Nightingale it was certainly in her absence.

So, it is possible that the station was built for Florence Nightingale, but the evidence is somewhat inconclusive – it is a nice thought though.

(Thanks to Stan Smith)

Courtesy Peter Taylor

The 1894 Whatstandwell station.

Chapter 7
New schoolmaster, troublesome teacher

In March 1881 the schoolmaster Robert Knighton resigned and moved, with his wife Maria, to a new school in Grantham. The struggling pupil teacher J. J. Parkins left to become a bookkeeper at Butterley Ironworks.

A new head was appointed – Mr Henry Stephen Scott. His family were also employed in the school: his wife, Laura Scott, as sewing mistress; daughter Beatrice as a pupil teacher; and daughter Florence as monitress. Although born in Wiltshire Mr Scott had spent some time in Canada, most of his children having been born there.

Mr Scott's initial troubles came in two forms. Firstly, although the staff comprised mostly of his family he had a very troublesome assistant teacher in Miss M. L. Lloyd, who was, apparently, a friend of the vicar. Secondly, there was chronic overcrowding.

Parochial School logbook: 21 April 1882

A managers meeting having been held during the holiday a complaint was made by the assistant that the master had insisted on her being in school at 1/4 to 9 to see to the ringing of the bell and that the room was ready for work, also that the master had directed her to see to the school being locked at 4 o'clock in preference to the monitors. The matter was then taken into consideration when it was decided that the assistant was to perform these duties until such time that another assistant was appointed (pending receipt of report) when they (the two assistants) are to perform these duties between them.

Mr Scott arrives

The Inspector's report of April 1882 confirmed the overcrowding and inadequate staffing.

Parochial School logbook: 29 April 1882

The school has increased in numbers and the programme that has been made towards order and efficiency is creditable to the master. Satisfactory results cannot be expected unless the teaching staff is increased. All children should be present on the day of inspection. A number of younger children were absent. I have some hesitation in recommending the grant under Article 19 (B). There is hardly suitable accommodation for the number of infants at present on the books of the school.

A qualified assistant teacher should be at once engaged and a pupil teacher transferred from another school.

The requirements for the report must be carefully attended to.

Staff -

H S Scott	master
Mrs Scott	sewing mistress
M L Lloyd	assistant
B H Scott	PT 3rd year
H R Holmes	monitor
F A Scott	monitor

It was, of course, the vicar's duty to see that the Inspector's report was acted upon. This he did not do, despite there being about 350 children in the school and only two qualified teachers – Mr Scott and Miss Lloyd – who were at loggerheads. The pressure was building up.

The problems with the assistant teacher, Miss Lloyd, continued through the year.

> *Parochial School logbook: 29 April 1882*
>
> Mrs Ash complained of assistant ill treating her child by throwing a slate in her face also, the girl, H. Stocks, complained of her pinching and beating her.
>
> *6 May 1882*
>
> I find the assistant very careless and lazy.
>
> *10 June 1882*
>
> 187 present and 153 absent, very wet day was no doubt the cause.
>
> *w/e 30 June 1882*
>
> Cautioned Miss Lloyd, assistant, as to carelessness in marking registers, general slackness in relation to her duties, writing letters in school and sending them with children, and beating children (Thurs).
>
> On Friday again cautioned Miss Lloyd for slapping R Thorley on the back, her mother having complained, also 2 marked incorrectly in the register.
>
> *w/e 24 November 1882*
>
> Miss Lloyd (assistant) having knocked the girl Ellen Crowder down on the ground near the stove, have for the protection of the children removed her class, also order the curtains not to be drawn (Thursday). The assistant in defiance of the master is giving H. Holmes lessons.

Miss Lloyd's carelessness with the register was quite a crime. Accurate register keeping was vital because spot checks were made and it was very serious if errors were found. Part of the school's grant was based on attendance figures.

Chapter 8
The school conflict blows up

It was in January 1883 that the problems at school blew up in such a dramatic fashion for the master, Mr Scott, and Revd Acraman. It was bitterly cold, and the school was dirty and understaffed. What made the problem a crisis was that several staff were off ill, leaving the master and his daughter in charge of several hundred children on their own. There was no sympathy or help forthcoming from the vicar. Mr Scott's despair showed in the writing of the school log.

Parochial School logbook: w/e 13 January 1883

School is only supplied with master, 1 pupil teacher and 1 monitor. School very full this week, difficulty to find seats for all. Only one fire. School is very cold.

w/e 20 January 1883

Found school on Monday in a very dirty state also the out offices. Sent word to the cleaner respecting it.

Tuesday, H. Holmes monitress ill, school now in charge of master and P.T. and sewing mistress afternoons. Four admitted.

Sent to vicar respecting help. Closed on Tuesday at 1/4 to 4. Mr. Blair visited. Holiday on Wednesday afternoon to rest the teachers. Still left to do the work. Received reply respecting help from Mr. Saxton on 18th dated 16th.

Mr Blair was curate and was to play a significant part in the brewing storm. The logbook shows a copy of letters written to and from Mr Scott.

The school logbook contained a copy of the letter written by Mr Scott to the vicar stating his complaint. It was recorded in the logbook as an "official" record. He was perhaps afraid that his letters to the vicar might become mislaid!

Parochial School logbook: January 16th 1883

Rev. Sir,

The school is now left to myself and daughter. I wish to know if you are going to supply me with help or am I to take the responsibility of supplying myself.

Last week 3 teachers did the work of 6 teachers and now this week 2 teachers have to do it. I shall give half holiday tomorrow to rest ourselves

I am sir,

Yours obediently,

H. S. Scott

The vicar did not reply personally to this letter. That was left to Mr J. Layton who was secretary to the school managers. The reply was also copied out into the school logbook.

From the reply it seems that one of Mr Scott's daughters had left the school to work elsewhere, and this upset the vicar. It may have had something to do with his not rushing to help with the short staffing. As later events show, the vicar went to extraordinary lengths to vent his displeasure at those who upset him. Mr Scott was to find this out.

Vicar's response

Parochial School logbook: January 16th 1883
Reply –

The Hollies, Crich 16th January 1883

Dear Sir,

Crich Parochial School

I have already mentioned to you that steps are being taken to endeavour to supply the gap caused by the sudden removal by you of your daughter and that a letter is expected daily to settle the matter.

I may add that steps are also taken to provide additional temporary help which seems needed through illness of some of the school staff. You had better address any future communication direct to myself, which is preferable, and I can then as secry (sic) bring any matters, if necessary, before the school committee.

Yours truly

J. Layton

It was clear from the reply that the vicar did not want to communicate directly with Mr Scott.

This breakdown in the relationship between vicar and headmaster was to have dramatic and far-reaching consequences.

When the monitor, Miss Holmes, returned after her illness Mr Scott complained to her about taking time off with a "non-serious" complaint.

Parochial School logbook: w/e 20 January 1883

The monitor having returned to school (Fri) the master asked her if she had been to a doctor, the answer being in the negative, she was told she ought not to absent herself on such trivial illness leaving a school of 250 attendances to only 2 teachers, when she replied that her father and mother knew when she was ill and that "if you have anything to say about it, you must go to my father."

It was January 1883 and the scene was set for a dramatic confrontation between powerful forces in the village. The vicar could have had no idea about the consequences of the actions he was about to take. His whole life was to be greatly affected; his curate, Mr Blair, was to be hurled into the turmoil; schooling in the village was to be changed forever; the village community was to be split into opposing camps; and the vicar would end up in court. To make matters worse the Bishop would become involved, and Revd Acraman's living as the vicar of Crich would be in doubt.

What was the action that started the vicar's eventual downfall? In early February 1883 he sacked the popular schoolmaster Mr Scott.

The village was now divided between those that supported Mr Scott and those Revd Acraman. Throw in the Baptists on the side of Mr Scott, and pressure from Nonconformist factory employers, and the scene was set for a battle of wills and ideals. Add to the mix the curate, who started off a supporter of the vicar but then changed sides when he realised the vindictiveness of Revd Acraman. The explosive situation was about to ignite.

Rowdy meeting

A meeting was called in the village clubroom in support of Mr Scott, against his sacking by the vicar and calling for an Inspector's inquiry. It was a very well attended and rowdy meeting. The vicar and curate "gatecrashed" the event and were met with quite a bit of abuse. The vicar accused several prominent Baptists of stirring up trouble. Also, it seemed Revd Acraman had put pressure, amounting to blackmail, on several people not to allow the meeting room to be used.

The meeting ended in uproar, with both vicar and curate jostled out of the room before a "memorial" was signed in support of Mr Scott. Much was made of "memorials" during the times ahead – they were what we would call petitions of support.

The jostling incident with Revd Acraman and his curate, who at this time was still a supporter of the vicar, was to result in a court case. The vicar, however, could find no witnesses to testify about the incident, despite the meeting being so crowded. With no witnesses or anyone willing to support him, one wonders what made him take the matter to court. His court appearance was only the first of many to come.

The conflict between the vicar and his parishioners was very well reported in the press, both in editorial comment and in reporting what happened at the meeting. These reports were certainly critical of the vicar.

On Wednesday 7th February 1883 the *Derby Mercury* reported the onset of the troubles in some detail. In an editorial comment it passed a sad reflection on the conflict.

Derby Mercury: Wed 1 December 1880

𝕷𝖔𝖈𝖆𝖑 𝕿𝖔𝖕𝖎𝖈𝖘.

THE VICAR OF CRICH does not apparently find his parish "a bed of roses" just now, and it is somewhat difficult for an outsider to decide who is most to blame. It may be only a "storm in a teapot," but it appears to be one of those cases in which the harmony of a large parish is broken up, and the clergyman's influence which should be all-pervading, is destroyed over a question which ought never to have been allowed to produce such deplorable results. The Vicar's statement in applying for summonses against two parishioners, reveals a melancholy state of things, for he said he could bring no witnesses, with the exception of a newly-appointed curate, "as the whole of the parishioners were against him". The parishioners on the other hand, complain of "the imperious conduct of the Vicar" and have petitioned the Education Department for a searching inquiry into the state of Crich School. All this unseemly squabbling points, it is to be feared, in the direction of a School Board. At present the parish school is reported to be producing satisfactory results, the only difficulty being an enlargement which is required, but for which funds are not forthcoming, a result due, says a correspondent, to the unpopularity of the Vicar. Should a School Board follow, "they might thank their Vicar for it" says the school master. We are not sufficiently acquainted with the facts to pronounce judgement in the case but it is quite clear that such a strained condition of the relations between pastor and people, as now exists, can only result in evil to both.

The newspaper went on to report, at length, the very rowdy meeting. Although quite long it is worth the read. It goes some way to explain reasons for the dramatic upheaval that was to follow.

Derby Mercury: Wed 7 February 1883

THE VICAR OF CRICH AND HIS PARISHIONERS

EXTRAORDINARY PROCEEDINGS

On Tuesday morning the bellman went round the parish of Crich announcing that in the evening a meeting of the parishioners would be held at the Independent Clubroom, for the purpose of considering the educational arrangements of the parish, and specially inviting all parents to attend. The large clubroom, one of the largest in the district, was densely packed, many remaining by the door unable to get inside. Mr. T. G. Iveson was voted to the chair. Just as the meeting was about to commence the Rev. W. Acraman, vicar of the parish, entered, accompanied by the curate, the Rev. A. Blair. – The Chairman said the primary object of the meeting was to support Mr. Scott, the schoolmaster, and his family (Cheers). Mr. Scott came to Crich about two years ago and came with a very good character from a clergyman. — Rev. W. Acraman: Will you name the clergyman? – The Chairman: You know the name of the clergyman quite well, Mr. Acraman, and that is a very unnecessary interruption on your part (Cheers, and cries of "Turn him out." The Chairman, proceeding, repeated his statement, and again the

Vicar asked "What clergyman?" The Chairman said he thought the interruption unfair, and appealed to the meeting as to whether, seeing that the vicar was present, the schoolmaster, Mr. Scott, should not be sent for that he might give his side of the question. The audience voted unanimously for this, amid great cheering. The Chairman continuing, said Mr. Scott came to Crich a perfect stranger to them, and came recommended by a clergyman. Whether that clergyman was a good man or a bad man he was not prepared to say. Mr. Acraman had come there to say he was not a good man. Mr. Acraman had had correspondence with him of a damaging character, and they would bring that up if Mr. Acraman did not mind (Applause). They were not there to oppose the managers of the school. They believed the managers had been misinformed by one who took the lead in some recent movements (Shame). In all the meetings held about Mr. Scott there had not been a fault found with him, still he had been forced to resign (Shame). Since he had been in the parish he had grown in the respect of the people, and had now the confidence and love of all, save one (Great cheering). Had Mr. Scott been a common criminal he would have been heard in his own defence before the magistrates of the land, but in the treatment he had received he was not heard before one who considers himself a magistrate of the higher majesty. The Chairman went on to show the improvement made in the school, and in its position in the inspector's report, since the appointment of Mr. Scott and added that Mr. Scott had to cease because he could not agree with his vicar. He (the chairman) would like to see a poll of the adults of the parish as to how many could agree with the vicar. He very much questioned whether there were 50 out of the 3000 in the parish who could agree with the vicar (Cheers) – The Curate having here interrupted, considerable disorder ensued. – The Chairman said if Mr. Acraman and Mr. Blair could not keep quiet they had better leave the room (Cheers) – Mr. S. Bower, highway surveyor, said he had never heard a word of complaint against Mr. Scott. The last time the Inspector paid Crich a visit he reported the school as being in the highest state of efficiency. Mr. Scott had been successful in getting the children on so well that a large number had been able to leave school and get work between 11 and 12 years of age. He got more up to the standard at that age than any other master Crich had ever had (Cheers). A letter was here read from Mr. Cowlishaw one of the Guardians of Crich and a large employer of labour in the neighbourhood, who was too ill to attend. The letter expressed sympathy with the work "the Protestation Committee" had undertaken, and the writer said he felt it his duty to enter his protest against one man (Hisses). The writer said he had confidence in the school managers but believed they had been misinformed, and that possibly it had come before them as a question of removing either the vicar or the schoolmaster; and as one was moveable goods, and the other a fixture the moveable goods had to go (Laughter and cheers). – The following resolution was then proposed by Mr. Clarke and seconded by Mr. Boag: "That we parishioners of Crich in public meeting assembled, hereby express our satisfaction with, and perfect confidence in, Mr. Scott as the National Schoolmaster, and in his family as assistants, and our respects for them as resident amongst us." – The Rev. W. Acraman said there was no need for the ferment that was got up. If, after the inspector's next report came, in about six weeks, a deputation of the older inhabitants of the parish chose to visit upon the managers of the school, he would be most willing to take the matter submitted by them into consideration. They might possibly, in place of the school they had, have a Board school, and then he himself should be, as far as his pocket was concerned, a gainer for he subscribed £1 a year to the present school, and was ready to subscribe towards the required enlargement. On proceeding to speak of the progress of Church work in the parish, the audience reminded the speaker that he was not keeping to the subject. He said a managers' meeting was held on the 11th December, there being three clergymen present and four laymen. At that meeting the following resolution was unanimously passed: – "That the managers, deeply regretting that the harmony of the parish was disturbed by the attitude of the master towards the clergy and the assistant mistresses, are willing to consent to Mr. and Mrs. Scott and their family remaining on as teachers for the present, on a distinct promise being made of amendment in these respects." Mr. Scott was not called upon to resign. – Mr. Scott who was received with much cheering, said he had been told that if he did not stop that meeting he should be reported to the inspector and to the Education Department (Shouting and cheers). The inspector had been in the habit of going to the reverend vicar's house to lunch. [Mr. Acraman : Never, never. He came to tea, I think.] Mr. Scott went on to show what difficulty he had had with one assistant whom the vicar was anxious he should keep, and to show the insubordination of assistants and monitors, who were supported and encouraged in this by the vicar, so that he (Mr. Scott) could not rule in his own school. One assistant had been most cruel to the children and Mr. Scott was powerless to prevent it. He thought children, as a rule, would be able to pass the standard when they were eleven years old, if they were properly taught. Then he got into trouble for over-crowding, which he did to oblige the vicar. If they had a School Board they might thank their vicar for it (Cheers). Then as to Sunday work he could not do it. He needed rest on Sunday. The managers at the meeting asked the vicar what fault there was to find and he said nothing only he had spoken disrespectfully of the clergy (Cries of "Oh.") He had not said that three months' notice on either side would settle the matter. – The Rev. A. Blair spoke against School Boards, saying the children of the working people were by that system educated at the expense of the rich. He attempted to read a letter relating to the religious education given, but was so violently opposed by the audience that he had to desist. – The Rev. W. Acraman shouted out, "This is a packed meeting of Messrs. Kirk, Scott, and Co." and then went on to say something else but the uproar was so great that he could not be heard two yards away. – Mr. Abraham Dawes, in response to an appeal from Mr. Kirk said the Rev. W. Acraman implored him not to let them have that room this week. – Mr. W. Curzon said that the vicar told him that if they let that room he should withhold his subscription from that society. – Mr. Kirk spoke at some length on the satisfactory condition of the school and the splendid report of the inspector for the year 1882. He then read an advertisement from the School Guardian for a master for Crich School, application to be made to the vicar. The publication, he said, was dated the 27th; the meeting of managers was held on the 25th. It must, therefore, have been all cooked and arranged beforehand (Great uproar). –Mr. Acraman said the meeting was held on Thursday, and the publication was issued on Saturday. – Rather strong epithets were here freely used on both sides. – Mr. Acraman having used a strong expression said he withdrew that. – The resolution of confidence in Mr. Scott was then passed amid great cheering. – A second resolution was proposed by Mr. Wass of Crich Carr, and seconded by Mr. Vaughan Taylor, to the effect that a copy of the resolution be sent to each of the school managers. – This resolution was supported by the Rev. W. Acraman. It was resolved – "That a memorial be prepared showing the unsatisfactory condition of Crich School, caused by the imperious action of the vicar, and desiring a searching inquiry by the Education Department, and that such memorial be signed by the parishioners, and forwarded without delay to the Education Department." – The meeting then became a scene of confusion, many beginning to " boo" and indulge in cat-calls of every kind. – A vote of thanks having been passed to the Chairman, the audience began to disperse. As the vicar and the curate moved a little towards the door, a great roar was set up, and there was some rough pushing, the curate struggling to get between the vicar and half a dozen men who were trying to push the vicar out. A scuffle ensued, in which the curate was roughly handled, and the vicar was pushed through the doorway. A large number remained in the room to sign the memorial, which was first signed by the chairman. –*Sheffield Independent*

What happened after this meeting was very strange. Given that several hundred villagers had expressed their dissatisfaction with how he had handled the sacking of a popular school master, the vicar went ahead with bringing a case against two of the people whom he alleged had assaulted him. He also stated that he needed police protection as the whole parish was against him.

He decided therefore to bring a summons against Elijah Kirk and Samuel Bennet for common assault. The case was heard at Belper Petty Sessions and, like the rowdy meeting in Crich, was fully reported in the newspapers. However, the vicar could provide no witnesses. He complained that parishioners even hooted at him and his curate in their clerical attire.

Vicar asks for police protection

Derby Mercury: Wed 7 February 1883

Towards the close of the business at the Belper Petty Sessions on Thursday, the Rev. William Acraman, vicar of Crich, made application for two summonses against Elijah Kirk, draper, Crich, and Samuel Bennett, framework-knitter, of the same parish. The applicant said he had come to ask for summonses and police protection. A meeting was held on Tuesday evening at Crich for the purpose of promoting a School Board for the parish. The meeting was held in defiance of the present school committee, which consisted of four laymen and two justices. The meeting alluded to was held in a clubroom at Crich, and was largely attended. The vicar, along with his curate, went to the gathering, and was assaulted by Mr. Kirk and Mr. Bennett, both of whom are well-known in Crich, and took a leading part in the proceedings. These two men got up when the speaking was going on and incited the people to assail him and the curate. He could not bring any witnesses with the exception of the curate, as the whole of the parishioners were against him; and if any of his people were willing to come and support him they dare not. He went on to say that Kirk put his fist into his (Mr. Acraman's) face in a very menacing manner, and threatened him with violence, but he did not touch him. Bennett pushed him out of the room. Had he (the vicar) not been a tall and strong man he would have been knocked down and trampled underfoot. The curate was slightly injured in the room, and had he not given him assistance he would have been, very probably, seriously hurt, as the feeling was so bitter. The applicant said he had to turn back into the room to aid the curate, after he himself had been pushed out. – The Bench: Did either of them strike you ? – No; but they threatened me with violence. Bennett pushed me from behind. Mr. Acraman proceeded to ask if his evidence and that of the curate would be sufficient, as the other side would have ample evidence. – The Bench: It won't be a question of evidence; but we cannot hear the case now. You had better get assistance. – The clerk then wrote out the summons, and whilst this was being done Mr. Acraman went on to say that Bennett told the boys of the village to shout and hoot at him and the curate. The curate could not come down that day very well, as it was not possible for both of them to leave such a large parish at once. He asked the Magistrates to afford him police protection. – The Bench: You can apply to the police in case there is a disturbance. – Mr. Acraman said he feared there would be some disorderly proceedings, as the parishioners were very bitter, and they had even hooted a gentleman who was dressed in clerical attire. He asked if it would be necessary to bring other evidence besides the curate. – The Bench: We think it advisable that you should have a solicitor. – The applicant then left the court.

After the failed court case the village unrest continued and grew more bitter against the vicar. A request was made to the Bishop for the removal of the vicar, for the good of the parish.

Part of the reason for the unrest was the Church's antagonism to Board Schools. The Church had provided education for the children of the poor at its own expense, and it certainly did not wish to give up the control this gave over the education, and some said indoctrination, of the young. There was also some resentment that Nonconformists and dissenters had their children educated at church schools although they did not contribute financially towards them. Board Schools had elected managers. Such a school in Crich would have allowed Nonconformists a say in the running of the school and the appointment of head and staff. In the Parochial School the vicar was the all-powerful controlling voice.

It is highly likely that trouble was stirred up by the Nonconformists in the village. However, the vicar certainly gave them plenty of ammunition to use against him.

So, the vicar now had a battle on two fronts – to keep his job as vicar of Crich, and to block the creation of a Board School in the village.

Crich Stand as it was between 1875 and 1900.

Bishop asked to remove the vicar

The *Derby Mercury* report tried to give a balanced report of what was happening.

Derby Mercury: Wed 14 February 1883

THE RELATIONS BETWEEN THE VICAR OF CRICH AND HIS PARISHIONERS do not improve. The vicar has held a meeting for the purpose of replying to the statements made at the meeting held in support of the schoolmaster, and the disaffected parishioners have had another meeting to reply to the Vicar at which a memorial to the bishop was adopted praying his Lordship to use his influence with Mr. ACRAMAN to get him to resign his living, as his influence for good in the parish was entirely gone. One fact was brought out at the Vicar's meeting which is highly creditable to the Churchmen in the village, and which proves that at Crich, as elsewhere, the Church has been, and continues to be, in the forefront in bearing the burden of educating the children of the poor. The National School, over the management of which all this unseemly squabbling appears to have arisen, was built by Churchmen and is upheld, mainly by subscription amounting to some £50 per annum, all given by Churchmen, with the exception of two small sums given by a couple of Dissenters. Crich has ten Dissenting chapels of one sort or another and in none of these has a collection ever been made for the day schools, where the children of all denominations are educated, the Church alone bearing an annual collection for the purpose, last year's offertory realising about £3, a sum by no means creditable to the parish. It is evident that, if the Bishop has any power to act, the present case is one in which his Lordship's influence is sorely needed, in the interests of all Christian work, in the locality.

If the vicar thought he could ride out the difficulties he was sorely mistaken. His sacking of Mr Scott was not to be a 'storm in a teacup'. Things were not to return to some form of normality for him or the parish. Plans were afoot to form a breakaway school with Mr Scott as its headteacher. A Board School was favoured by some, but not by ratepayers who would have to fund it.

Would the new school be a success? Would there be enough pupils to make it viable? How would it affect the church Parochial School?

Chapter 9
Breakaway school proposed

It was at the annual Parish Meeting in March 1883 that the school grievance was revived and the idea of a breakaway British School suggested.

The meeting was held in the Parochial School to pass the parish accounts and elect officers for the coming year. It was an interesting meeting covering several issues of concern to the parish. Mr Bryan was appointed senior Guardian for the next three years, promising to support the Act which permitted the adoption of workhouse children by respectable and kind foster parents.

Mr E. Kirk, chairman, stated that a bill for £13 2s 0d had been sent to the Clay Cross Company to cover the expense of watching and repairing the road through the landslip, but that this had not been paid. The meeting hoped that the bill would be paid without having to resort to litigation.

Robert Boag and Isaac Pitts were reappointed as Overseers for the parish.

The chairman then brought forward the issue of the educational conflict between the schoolmaster, Mr Scott, and the vicar. The subsequent discussions were covered in the *Derby Mercury*.

Crich workhouse, now called Chapel Row.

Plans for a breakaway school

Derby Mercury: Wed 7 February 1883

PARISH MEETING – THE SCHOOL GRIEVANCE REVIVED

The chairman brought forward the educational position of the parish, which he had said, had been occupying their attention for about two months. They would remember that the parish schoolmaster had been forced to send in his resignation after two minutes consideration. A memorial was forwarded to the school managers, after being passed at a public meeting, signed by 144 parents and ratepayers, asking them to cancel the notice, but not one of the managers had had the courtesy to reply (Shame). A committee was appointed to manage the affairs, and about a fortnight since a deputation was selected to wait upon the managers to know what they intended doing. Three of the managers – Dr Dunn, the Rev. A Blair, and Mr Walker – were in favour of the resignation being withdrawn. – Mr. Wass said he should be led by Mr. Hunt who had since unhesitatingly replied that he was powerless against the vicar. It was well known that Mr. Johnson would go with the vicar, and so the committee had concluded that nothing more could be done. The school had been examined recently, and since that the committee had met, and as the inspector's report was so very favourable they had decided to have a school of their own – a British School, which would be self-supporting when once started. The aid of several influential gentlemen had been promised, and with the school fees and Government grant the school would pay for itself (Hear, hear). The committee did not hesitate to say that no better schoolmaster in the country could be found, and if the meeting approved Mr. Scott would be prepared to stay and educate their children. A board of management would be formed, with a majority of churchmen, to manage the school, and Mr. Scott would act entirely as the board directed (Hear, hear). The parishioners in a body were determined to stand by Mr. Scott as he had given the greatest satisfaction in the past (Hear, hear). – Mr. Scott proceeded to give statistics of the progression of the school during his mastership, from which it appeared that each year during his stay at Crich the school had a better percentage of passes, and this year it was more than self-supporting. He pointed out that the National School would either have to be enlarged or the Educational Department would build another school. The present accommodation was far from sufficient, and at the last examination 86 infants were crammed into a room built for 34. – Mr. Bower said he would like to see a British school, and he felt sure they could raise subscriptions to start one. – The meeting eventually decided to leave the matter in the hands of the committee for the present, and the parishioners would support them. – A vote of thanks to the chairman concluded the proceedings, which lasted over three hours.

Chapter 10
More conflict

The conflict between the warring factions soon spilt over into other church matters as the village meeting in April 1883 proved.

There was a contested church election for a churchwarden with suggestions of ballot rigging. Mr Lee was the vicar's choice, and Mr Iveson the choice of those who supported Mr Scott. Tempers became so riled that police were called upon to empty the church.

To add to the troubles the curate, Mr Blair, and the vicar were in serious disagreement. Mr Blair, once a staunch ally of the vicar, took exception to the measures Revd Acraman took to avenge himself on those who had displeased him.

These acts of revenge included travelling to Derby, to the teacher training college. There he attempted to get them to stop Mr Scott's daughter from becoming qualified. She was a pupil teacher, and Derby College had the authority make her a certificated teacher.

He also had an interview with the local police superintendant to cause trouble for the village policeman, who had also displeased him. On top of this he spread untrue rumours that Mr Scott was trying to obtain the headship at South Wingfield School.

As a result Mr Blair turned against the vicar. The scene was set for the vicar to plot against his curate, and for the whole conflict to blow up in a most spectacular manner with vicar and curate physically attacking each other. Another court case was beckoning.

Two things followed: firstly, the contested election for church warden between Mr Lee and Mr Iveson; secondly, the conflict between vicar and curate, resulting in a well-reported court case.

Derby Mercury: Wed 4 April 1883

𝕷𝖔𝖈𝖆𝖑 𝕿𝖔𝖕𝖎𝖈𝖘.

AFFAIRS AT CRICH GROW WORSE, and the latest development is discreditable both to the vicar and his parishioners, "like priest, like people" is a well-known aphorism; and when we read of a vicar and his curate struggling together on the floor for the possession of a letter, and of the former having to be pulled off the latter by a magistrate who was present, we cannot be surprised that the vestry meeting should have been disgraced by a display of rowdyism and shameful irreverence. If the Vicar of Crich has no more reverence for God's house than to wrangle about possession of the reading-desk, how can it be expected that a meeting chiefly composed of half-educated men labouring under strong excitement will show respect to the sacred edifice! We do not know what power the Bishop has in the matter; but certainly some means should be found for putting an end to the scandal caused by the attitude of the Vicar of Crich and his parishioners towards each other. Religion and morality are alike injured, and the Church is brought into contempt in the eyes of its enemies, so long as such outrages on all decency are allowed to continue unchecked. It will be seen that the result of Saturday's polling was the election of Mr. Lee, the former churchwarden, by a large majority over his opponent, who had been brought forward by the party which opposes the Vicar.

The newspapers clearly disapproved of the goings-on at Crich, especially the unseemly scuffle between the vicar and his curate, in church, in front of what the papers called "half-educated men"!

Before explaining what happened to bring all this about it is necessary to know why there was such great anger between the vicar and his curate, and the importance of "the letter" which is referred to in the reports. The vicar had been to see the Bishop, in Lichfield, to get his curate sacked. The Bishop insisted that the complaints must be put in writing, which Revd Acraman did. The Bishop then forwarded this complaints letter to the Revd Blair for comment. This came out of the blue for the curate. He became incensed, throwing himself even more fully behind the protestors in trying to get the vicar, rather than himself, removed.

Early in April 1883 there was a church meeting to appoint a new warden. In the past these had been straightforward affairs with the vicar's choice being nominated and accepted. This year was certainly very different. For a start the church was packed to overflowing with disgruntled parishioners, and then there was the angry curate. The *Derby Mercury* reported the uproar in full detail.

Derby Mercury: Wed 4 April 1883

Vestry Meeting – The annual vestry meeting in connection with the Crich parish church was held on Thursday, and was characterized throughout by scenes of great disorder. As is well known a disagreement has for some time existed between the vicar, the Rev. W. Acraman, and a section of his parishioners, in consequence of the school managers (of whom he is one) having requested the schoolmaster, Mr. Scott, to resign. It was evident that considerable opposition would be offered to the vicar and his friends at the vestry meeting, bills being placarded in the village urging the parishioners to attend and put down "this rhubarb government." Before 11 o'clock, the time fixed for the holding of the meeting, a large crowd had assembled in the churchyard, and when the vestry door was opened a rush was made to gain admittance. The vestry became so crowded that it was found impossible to hold a meeting there, and it was decided to transact the business in the chancel. The vicar then proceeded to the reading-desk to preside over the meeting, but it had already been taken possession of by the curate, the Rev. A. Blair. The vicar asked the curate to vacate his seat, but this he resolutely refused to do. A good deal of disorder ensued amongst the people, and in the end Mr. Acraman gave way and took his seat near the communion table. He then offered up prayer, in accordance, he said, with his usual custom on such occasions. – The Chair then said that it was important they should remember one or two things in connection with the meeting. That was a meeting of the ratepayers of Crich, and ratepayers alone had a right to speak and vote ("Nonsense"). Well, the books he had seen on the matter said so, they should also remember that they were in God's house, and, therefore, he hoped if anything was to be said and done it would be done kindly and fairly.

The bad-tempered meeting then proceeded with points of order as to who could attend the meeting and whether books had been audited correctly. Some sort of record must have been set as the books were rapidly audited then and there. As usual, Crich ratepayer and farmer George Curzon made his presence felt at a public meeting.

Mr. G. Curzon asked how many were present who did not pay rates. Those, he said, should leave the church (Hisses). – The Chairman said householders who paid rates only had a right to vote at that meeting. He proceeded to read an authority to prove this. – Mr. Scott (the schoolmaster): That refers to church rates. – The Chairman replied that it did not. – This remark was received with considerable uproar. – Mr. J. Lee was about to read the annual accounts, when Mr. E. Kirk proposed that Mr. Robert Green audit them before they were presented. – This was agreed to, and he and Mr. J. T. Lee (who was also chosen) proceeded to the vestry to examine them. They subsequently returned, and Mr. Green declared that the accounts were accurate. – They were then submitted to the meeting and passed. – The Chairman then nominated Mr. Saxton as his warden for the ensuing year – a position he has held for four years. – Mr. Simms proposed, and Mr. B. Taylor seconded, that Mr. Lee be appointed parish warden. – Mr. Bryan then moved as an amendment that Mr Iveson be elected.

Mr Bryan, in proposing Mr Iveson to stand against the vicar's choice of Mr Lee, went on to make a series of minor accusations against Mr Lee. Foremost was that he supported the vicar rightly or wrongly. Reference was also made to a letter Mr Lee had written to the Bishop "against the parish". The Bishop had a meeting with the vicar and warden.

The Chairman said the Bishop asked to see the vicar and churchwarden. The letter he had left at home because he did not think it would be needed. – Mr. Scott: "Oh, have the letter; you can't believe a word he says" (Uproar.) – The Chairman warned the meeting as to the pains and penalties attached to the offence of brawling in church. – The Curate: Is it brawling when you take a fellow clergyman and push him on the floor. – A Voice: He has done you so (Groans).

The Revd J. Mulkerns, vicar at Wessington, once curate at Crich, was a staunch supporter of the vicar. He was at the meeting in support of Mr Lee against Mr Iveson. His contribution to the meeting was not generally welcomed!

The Rev. J. Mulkerns, vicar of Wessington, and late curate of Crich pointed out the necessity of appointing someone they knew, and not a stranger like Mr. Iveson. – A scene of great disorder here took place, in the course of which Mr. Scott endeavoured to speak, but his remarks could not be heard, owing to the fact that a heated controversy was going on amongst those present as to whether he had any right to attend the meeting at all, it being suggested that he was not a ratepayer. – The Rev. W. Mulkerns then attempted to speak but was cried down, several persons advising him to "go back to Wessington, where the geese are fed."

The Chairman then decided to put the choice of Mr Lee or Mr Iveson for warden to a vote. Even this ended up in chaos. Although Mr Iveson won the vote, it was not accepted. A poll was called for. There cannot be many church meetings where the police had to be called upon to clear the meeting.

The Chairman then prevailed upon the meeting to vote, and advised those who were in favour of Mr. Lee to stand on one side of the church, and those who desired to vote for Mr. Iveson to stand on the other. – This was done after some confusion, and in the end Mr. Iveson received 53 votes and Mr. Lee 35. On behalf of the latter Mr. Taylor demanded a poll; and, after some wrangling as to the time it should be held, it was decided that the vote should be recorded on Saturday in the schoolroom. Mr. Scott and others again commenced to speak, but the Chairman said the meeting was at an end and requested the police who were in attendance, to clear the church. After a little time, the company separated, amidst very great disorder.

Having been ejected from church by the police a great many went to the schoolroom for another meeting, to hear what the vicar had tried to silence at the vestry meeting. Elijah Kirk was in the chair.

49

The curate explains

A large number then proceeded to the schoolroom. Mr. E. Kirk was appointed chairman, and there was a numerous attendance. The chairman said that adjourned meeting was held in order that they might hear what Mr. Scott intended saying when the vicar prevented him from speaking. As they were aware, the Vicar of Crich was in a very unfortunate position for himself just now, and he was determined that nothing further should be done at the vestry meeting beyond what he was forced to have done. The vicar, however, did not close the eyes of the ratepayers when he declared the meeting at an end (Cheers).

After Mr Scott had spoken it was time for the curate to explain his bitterness about the vicar's actions and why he had turned against him. He also gave an account of the tussle he and the vicar had at a school managers' meeting.

Rev. A. Blair, the curate, who was received with cheers, having briefly referred to the circumstances which existed in the parish when he came there, said he had not long been in the parish before he began to see through the vicar's peculiarities. On the day he was licensed by the Bishop the vicar got him to accompany him to the master of the Derby Training College. The Rev. Mr. Acraman then spoke most determinedly to that gentleman of Mr. Scott and his daughter with the view of preventing the young lady from becoming a trained schoolmistress in the institution (Cries of "Shame"). On another occasion at Belper the vicar attempted to injure Mr. Thorpe (police officer) in the eyes of his superintendent (renewed cries of Shame) and he (Mr. Blair) left the room as a protest against the course then pursued by the vicar behind the man's back. One of the first things which the vicar desired him (the speaker) to do was to go to Wingfield and ask the schoolmaster to be allowed to see the school. The real object of his visit, however, was to inform the schoolmaster there that Mr. Scott was trying to get his place (Cries of "Shame, shame"). No one had a greater desire to be loyal towards his vicar than he (Mr. Blair) but, he had also to act honestly and fairly (Cheers). For refusing to comply with the wishes of the vicar, as he considered them unjust, he had suffered most keenly (Loud cries of "Shame"). He could make a number of other revelations, but he hardly thought that necessary. He might however, refer to the way in which the vicar, finding that he (the speaker) would not be his henchman in all things, had tried to have him removed from the parish – had, in fact, tried to ruin him (Cries of "Shame"). On Saturday the Rev. Mr. Acraman went to Lichfield, and in a clandestine way tried to get the Bishop's permission to give him (the speaker) notice. The Bishop desired the Rev. Acraman to put his words into writing. He did so, and that communication has been sent by the Bishop to him (the speaker), he took the document with him to the school managers' meeting on Saturday, which was held at the Vicarage. A variety of subjects were discussed and he (the speaker) was about to read a part of the letter of the vicar to the Bishop, which had reference to school matters, when the vicar jumped out of his chair and proceeded to carry out a threat which he had several times repeated as to ejecting him (the speaker) from the house. The Rev. Mr. Acraman first tried to snatch the letter and failing that, got hold of him (the speaker) by the collar and in the struggle they both fell on the floor. Mr. Hurt had to put his arms round the vicar to take him away. The back of the chair was broken. Of course nothing further was done at that meeting. He (the speaker) had sent the Bishop his reply to the Rev. Mr. Acraman's charges. – In the conclusion of his reply he said he could not resign at the request of a man who had himself been asked to resign by the universal voice of his parishioners. (Loud cheers). If he did resign another would come, only to be victimised in the same way, unless his lordship refused to license him (Applause). The meeting, having passed a resolution in favour of the return of Mr. Iveson was brought to a close with a vote of thanks to the Chairman.

The *Derby Mercury* report went on to give an account of the poll that took place for the warden, the vicar having refused to accept the vote in the vestry. The result was reversed with Mr Lee winning over Mr Iveson. If Mr Iveson's supporters were disappointed it would appear the publicans were not.

The poll demanded by Mr. Lee's friends, took place on Saturday, at the National Schoolroom. When the poll closed at three o'clock the numbers were declared to be Lee, 225 Iveson, 117. The Rev. W. Acraman look no active part in the contest. And although both the candidates put in an appearance at the polling booth during the day, neither of them took any part in bringing up voters, nor did the curate, the Rev. A. Blair who is now opposed to the vicar. When the result was announced the crowd which had collected quickly dispersed, and there can be little doubt that the publicans were considerably benefited by the day's proceedings. The friends of Mr. Lee were naturally very pleased at the result, but Mr. Iveson and his supporters were thoroughly convinced that if the voting had been by ballot the result would have been reversed.

Chapter 11
Vicar in court on assault charge

The assault by the vicar on the curate in the vicarage at a school managers' meeting led to a well reported court case. The written detail of the trial is extensive, detailed and fascinating. The verbal battles between the solicitors for the vicar and the curate are wonderfully argumentative. Each party was accusing the other of leaking details to the press. The description of the punch-up in the vicarage, with the local doctor and gentry trying to separate the clergymen is worthy of a soap opera. The malice of the vicar in travelling all the way to Derby Training College to bring pressure to bear on the authorities to prevent the headmaster's daughter qualifying as a teacher is hard to believe. Although the curate won the case it was a nominal victory, with a fine of only one shilling being awarded.

As well as being reported in the local press, where blame was put on both the vicar and his curate, it was also widely reported across the country. Clergy having a punch-up made for good reportage.

Two local dignitaries were to be involved in the court proceedings. They were two of the school managers: Dr Dunn, who was the doctor in Crich and medical officer for the area; and the Hon. F. Hurt J.P., the local 'squire' who lived at Alderwasley Hall. The Hurt family were great benefactors of the village. They paid for the Crich Stand of the time, and supported the church and schools at Crich and Fritchley.

Members of the Strutt family of Belper were amongst the magistrates hearing the case.

Derby Mercury: Wed 18 April 1883

Local Topics.

THE CRICH CLERICAL SCANDAL has assumed greater proportions during the week, as the full report we give elsewhere of the proceedings before the Belper magistrates will show. However strongly we may be inclined to blame the Vicar, the Curate is certainly deserving of equal censure. It cannot be expected that the teachings of either will be received with respect in a parish where both have shown themselves incapable of self-respect. When those who should be examples to the parish demean themselves by indulging in vulgar fracas; when a curate, with evident enjoyment, describes his vicar as a liar and "ferocious" and charges him with having "said the most dastardly and filthy things," and "done dastardly work against him and others," it is quite evident that the influence of both in the parish must be evil, and that, if it is in the power of the Bishop to do so, both should be removed. A portion of the parishioners, too, have apparently given themselves up to rowdy conduct which cannot be too strongly deprecated. It is high time that the peace-loving and devout Church-people bestirred themselves for the sake of religion amongst the people, and made their wishes felt in such a manner as shall bring this scandal to an end.

The paper then went on to report in full.

THE PAROCHIAL DISSENSIONS AT CRICH

THE VICAR CONVICTED OF ASSAULTING THE CURATE

[FROM OUR OWN REPORTER]

Mr.. A. P. Heywood, the Hon. F. Strutt, Sir J. G. N. Alleyne and Mr. Herbert Strutt were engaged for about three hours on Thursday last in hearing a charge of assault brought against the Vicar of Crich the Rev. William Acraman, by his curate, the Rev. Andrew Blair late curate of St. Albans, Leeds. Mr. Jackson, of Belper appeared for the complainant and Mr. Brown, of Stockport, for the defendant. There was a large number of persons in court, including several clergymen, and a good deal of interest was manifested in the case.

Bad-tempered exchanges

From the start there was a combative spirit between Mr Jackson from Belper, speaking for the curate, and Mr Brown, from Stockport, speaking for the vicar.

Mr. Jackson, in opening the proceedings, said the defendant was the Rev. William Acraman, the notorious vicar of Crich.

Mr. Brown here took the first of a long series of objections. He said it was rather early in the case to make statements of that kind. This was a matter to be decided without any personalities on either side.

Mr. Jackson did not see that there could be any objection to the phrase under the circumstances.

Mr. Brown said he should ask the Bench at once to declare that this inquiry must be contained to the circumstances of the assault which was alleged to have been committed and that there should be no irrelevant matter introduced.

The Chairman (Mr. A. P. Heywood) – I think you had better be a little more guarded in your language, Mr. Jackson.

Mr. Jackson – Well, I will simply say the defendant is the well-known vicar of Crich. I don't think he can have any objection to that, for though I can't say whether his fame has reached so far as Stockport or not, it has certainly reached a long way. Proceeding to state the facts of the case Mr. Jackson said the complainant and the defendant were both ex-officio members of the Parochial School Committee of Crich, and the school had until recently been under the mastership of Mr. Scott. His resignation was called for by the managers at the instigation of the vicar, and great dissatisfaction had thereby been created in the parish. Memorials were got up and meetings called in Mr. Scott's favour, and considerable animosity was caused between the vicar and his parishioners. It resulted in a charge of assault which was brought by the vicar against one of the inhabitants in that court six or eight weeks since, but which was dismissed. At that time Mr. Blair was on the most friendly terms with the vicar. He had come from a distance and had only been at Crich since Christmas. From what he heard and saw and what came to his knowledge, a short time since he ceased to be on friendly terms with the vicar. He refused to assist in giving petitions and memorials signed in favour of the vicar and that kind of thing, and since then the vicar had displayed a spirit of vindictiveness towards him and had attempted to get the Bishop to remove him from the parish and that entirely behind the curate's back. On the sixth of March the complainant received a letter from the Bishop enclosing a letter written by the vicar, in which he asked permission to give the curate notice to leave. That letter and the curate's reply having been brought up at the meeting where the assault took place. He proposed to read them to the Bench.

A legal debate took place as to whether the letter sent to the curate by the Bishop, in which the vicar wanted Mr Blair removed from office, was admissible evidence. It was ruled that it could not be read in court. This seemed odd, as it was the contents of the letter which caused the fracas.

The hearing continued with bad-tempered exchanges.

Mr. Jackson – I will go on to the assault. On the 26th March he received this letter. On the same day he replied shortly and on the 27th he replied more fully to the Bishop. On the 28th he received a note from Mr. Saxton who was secretary to the Board of Management of the school calling a meeting at 11 o'clock at the vicarage, though he only received the note at 10.15.

Mr. Brown – What has that got to do with it?

Mr. Jackson – Please don't interrupt.

Mr. Brown – But I shall interrupt if you bring in irrelevant matter.

The Chairman – I think it was a very unjustifiable interruption.

Mr. Brown – But I do object. I say it has nothing to do with the inquiry what Mr. Saxton did.

The Chairman – Well, I think your interruption was quite unjustifiable.

Mr. Brown – Then do I understand that my friend is entitled to go on ad lib to go into anything he thinks proper, without any objection from me as representing the defendant?

Mr. Jackson – Certainly not. Your objection has been overruled, and will you kindly sit down and let me go on with my address.

Mr. Brown – I will if you will go on properly.

Revd Blair began his testimony, but it was not long before he was interrupted and another bad-tempered spat began. The curate also referred to the vicar's previous court appearance (the assault charge against two of his parishioners, which was discharged). This added to Mr Brown's objections.

Bad-tempered exchanges

The Rev. Andrew Blair was then called and sworn. He said – I have been curate of Crich since Christmas, and at first I worked amicably with the vicar, and supported him in his difficulties with the parishioners.

Mr. Jackson – When did you change your opinion with respect to the vicar being the injured man?

Witness – Well I actually saw through him, particularly and found he had a propensity to injure the innocent and –

Mr. Brown – I take exception to this altogether.

The Chairman – I don't think you need interrupt the witness.

Mr. Brown – But I claim my privilege as an advocate to take objection. He is not entitled to go into matter which is irrelevant to the issue before you. The defendant cannot give evidence in reply to accusations made against him and therefore it is necessary that the evidence should be confined to the issue, and if it is not done I can take the opinion of a higher Court on the matter.

Mr. Jackson – It is in the discretion of the Bench, and they have decided.

Mr. Brown – No it is not, the Bench cannot allow anything which is irrelevant when the defendant cannot answer it by his sworn testimony to-day.

Mr. Jackson – It is for the Bench to decide whether it is relevant, and they have done so.

Mr. Brown – It is the first time in my experience that I have heard that an advocate has no right to take an objection. I will submit to your ruling, whatever it may be; but I have my rights as an advocate, and must object to what is not right. Otherwise, I may as well leave the place.

The Chairman – It is usual, when an advocate sees the sense of the Bench is against him, to sit down.

Witness (in a low tone) – Hear, hear.

Mr. Brown – Mr. Blair says " Hear, hear" sir and I shall not allow Mr. Blair's "Hear, hear" (Laughter).

Mr. Jackson – Will you kindly sit down ?

Mr. Brown – I shall not. I object to anything at all being stated with regard to anything precedent to this matter. If the Bench say that they are going into all the –

The Chairman – We are accustomed to have a proper respect paid to the Bench, and the Bench do not see that there is any objection to be taken. You have a perfect right to object to what is irrelevant, but don't let us have any quarrelling (Laughter).

Mr. Brown – Certainly it will not be on my part (Laughter). Mr. Brown then resumed his seat.

Mr. Jackson then repeated his question as to when Mr. Blair changed his opinion with respect to the vicar.

Witness – I loyally supported the vicar when I first came to the parish. I began to see through him before the hearing of the last case at Belper.

Mr. Brown – Now, that is what I object to.

The Chairman – Well, I don't think the remarks need be made. He is not called as a witness to character.

The curate went on give an account of what happened at the start of the managers' meeting before the assault took place. It seemed as though the meeting had been called at a time when other managers could not be present. The vicar objected to Saturday meetings as they tired him out for the following Sunday.

Mr. Jackson – Did you on the 26th March receive a letter from the Bishop, enclosing a letter written to him by Mr. Acraman? – I received a private letter from his Lordship, and also an eight-page letter from Mr. Acraman which the Bishop requested him to write.

Did you ascertain that? – Yes, the last remark in the letter proved that he wanted to do it secretly, and the Bishop made him put it in writing.

On the 28th did you receive a letter from Mr. Saxton, secretary to the Board of Management, calling you to a meeting? – Yes.

Mr. Hurt, Dr. Dunn, and the defendant were there, as well as Mr. Saxton? – Yes.

When the vicar entered the room he shook hands with Mr. Hurt? – Yes, and no one else.

You declined to shake hands with him? – Yes.

Why ? – Because of his going to Lichfield. This was the first time I had seen him after that.

He took his seat at the table? – Yes, Mr. Saxton was on his left and Mr. Hurt, myself and Mr. Dunn on the right.

I believe a long conversation ensued between Mr. Hurt and Mr. Acraman? –

Yes, Mr. Hurt found fault with the way in which the vicar had used his name in the minute-book and Mr. Dunn also.

Was anything said about the meeting having been held on Wednesday instead of Saturday? – Yes, Mr. Hurt wanted it on Saturday so that more managers could attend. The vicar said he could not have it on a Saturday because it upset him for Sunday.

Mr. Jackson – When this was said about the Saturday did you make any remark? – I asked him where he went on the previous Saturday. I said whilst his sister was at my house saying she had come from her brother to try and make happiness, he had gone to Lichfield to try to ruin me with the Bishop.

I believe something further took place and you produced this letter which you had received from the Bishop? – Yes. I had several papers in my hands and I found him very rudely looking over them. He saw the letter which was headed, "The Curate of Crich and his stipend". I asked "Have you seen those words before?" It was the proof that he had been at Lichfield. I wanted to read that part of the letter which referred to school business. The vicar objected, but no one else. I insisted that I had the right to read it. The vicar then said it was not about school matters. He said he had not written to the Bishop about school matters. I said, "You have" and he said he had not.

What did you say then? – I said, "It is a lie, because you have." He then said he would take me by the collar and put me out of the house. I said I was there as a manager and he had no right to put me out. He said he should do as he liked in his own house.

The curate was determined to read the contents of the letter to the managers, and the vicar was equally determined that he would not. The vicar attempted to snatch the letter from Revd Blair and a scuffle took place that resulted in the Hon. F. Hurt being injured as he tried to part them.

Examination continued – I told him he should not put me out when I began reading the letter he carried out his threats. I had only read the heading when he came across passing in front of Mr. Hurt, and made a snap at the letter. That made me turn more towards Mr. Dunn and I continued reading. He took hold of my collar with his right hand and pulled me right over onto the floor. I fell onto my left hip and lay on my back on the floor. The chair was broken. As I lay on the floor I had to keep him back by pushing him with my feet. Mr. Hurt had to pull him from me, he was so ferocious. He fell with me when I went down. My left hip was injured and I could not lie on that side for some days.

The Chairman – Was his object to put you out or to take the letter? – I think it was to put me out.

Mr. Jackson – Then he was taken away and you were assisted up? – Yes.

Cross-examined by Mr. Brown – Whilst you were on the ground were you kicking with your feet? – Witness, after fencing with the question a good deal, denied that he was kicking, though he admitted using his feet. Asked whether he injured Mr. Hurt's finger with his feet he fenced with that question also, and at last said he believed Mr. Hurt's finger was injured, but he did not know how.

Mr. Brown – You know we want the whole truth.

Witness – That is what we want, but you are trying to suppress it.

Mr. Brown – Don't talk like that, sir. You are not in a pulpit, or a vestry, or a drawing-room now.

Witness – Indeed; where are you?

Mr. Brown – Don't be impertinent. You are not here in your clerical capacity.

The Chairman (to witness) – I should

recommend you to answer the questions as shortly as possible.

Mr. Brown – I would recommend you to take that advice.

Witness – It has been given to you but you have not accepted it.

Mr. Brown – Remember you are in the witness-box and you must confine yourself to telling the truth. Now, when you were on your back, yes or no, were you persisting in reading the letter? – No; of course not.

Had you it in your hand? – Yes. – Were you reading? – No, he was afraid to having it read. – Never mind the fear. Were you reading it? – Witness (smiling): No.

Mr. Brown – Don't grin, sir (Laughter).

The Chairman – The Bench must really interfere.

Mr. Brown – The Bench may interfere or not, but I won't be grinned at by a witness, and particularly a witness of this sort, who ought to know better. If he were a dock labourer it might be different.

The Chairman – I should have thought a solicitor in practice would have known better than to treat a gentleman so, to whose cloth alone it is due to show decent respect.

Mr. Brown – I don't respect the cloth – it is the man.

The Chairman (to the witness) – I can only repeat my advice to you to answer "yes" or "no" as shortly as you can.

Mr. Brown – After the vicar got up from his chair and wished you not to read the letter, you persisted in reading it? – Of course; no one objected but himself.

When you were reading it were not you leaning back in your chair? – No, because I turned to Mr. Dunn.

When you fell did you smash the chair? – I didn't fall.

Well, when you reached the ground was the chair smashed? – The top part of the back of the chair was broken off.

Was that in consequence of you leaning back in the chair? – Witness (laughing): Of course not.

What followed was an argument as to whether the vicar was called "a liar" or not. There was much debate as to the difference between telling a lie and being called a liar. It was just not acceptable to call a man "a liar" in his own house. If this happened then he had every right to eject whoever called him that.

Vicar called a "liar"

Now, is it a fact that you called the vicar a liar? – I don't think I used the word "liar." I said what I have already told you. Will you swear that you didn't call him a liar? – I don't remember.

Will you swear you didn't? – It's all the same whether I did or not.

The Chairman – I believe the witness stated that he said, "It's a lie."

Mr. Brown – But did you use the word "liar?" – (No answer).

Surely you, a clergyman of the Church of England, will know whether you called a man a liar or not? – I don't remember.

Are you in the habit of calling men liars? – If I called him a liar it would be perfect truth.

Then you admit that you called him a liar? – I don't admit that I called him one, but he is one (Laughter).

He is a liar, and that you say to-day? – Yes.

Hon. F. Strutt – It is the same when he says he tells lies.

Mr. Brown – But it is a matter of opinion whether the phrase is to be used to a clergyman or not. (To witness) Do you consider it is a proper tone to adopt to a man in his own house? – Far worse conversation has passed in his house from him. He has said the most dastardly and filthy things in his own house.

I ask you, as a clergyman, do you consider that is a proper phrase to use to a person in his own house? – And I tell you, as a man, he has used worse.

Sir John Alleyne – Take the advice of the Bench, and say " yes" or "no".

Mr. Brown – You are showing yourself in your true colours now. You are being photographed as you are at Crich. Now, do you consider that a proper phrase to use to your vicar in his own house? – Under the circumstances, yes.

Apparently the curate had written to the vicar before the trial to see if matters could not be sorted before the hearing.

Well, you have written to the vicar since you took out this summons suggesting that you should withdraw it, have you not? – No; nothing of the kind.

Have you not wished to withdraw it? – No; not the slightest wish.

Is that your letter? –Yes. – Letter read:–
9th April.

My dear Mr. Acraman – As the investigation of the disputes between yourself and me will come out in the Court at Belper on Thursday and I am quite prepared to prove the charge of actual assault on your part against me, nevertheless in order to show you that my conduct does not proceed from vindictiveness or any other uncharitable spirit, but simply to defend myself and maintain the truth, I beg to propose that the investigation take place before impartial arbitrators such as you and I might appoint by consent; and, without shrinking for one moment from defending myself, I am prepared if you are agreeable to come to an amicable arrangement and to continue my services as your curate, provided that you will treat me in a becoming manner and in a way which will tend to the harmony of the parish and the glory of God. I am perfectly willing that the question of stipend should depend upon circumstances. – Yours very truly, ANDREW BLAIR

Mr. Brown – When you wrote that letter, "My dear Mr. Acraman" and so forth, did you feel towards the vicar as you have expressed yourself to-day ? – Yes.

And do you call that an honest letter? – Perfectly consistent and perfectly honest.

May I ask you why you wished this prosecution to be withdrawn to-day? – I had no such wish.

But doesn't it say so ? – The very reverse.

Don't you know it means that the magistraterial proceedings should be put an end to? – No.

Were you going to have impartial arbitrator and a private investigation? – Not private; it does not say so. I wanted something of the nature of an ecclesiastical inquiry. For the sake of Crich I should like to see peace.

"For the sake of Crich," don't talk like that. Your letter was an invitation that these proceedings should be abandoned. – No, I want the whole matter gone into. I am not afraid of the light.

You are very captious. I should not like to be your vicar. – You would not like to be his curate (Laughter).

If he had said, "By all means, I accept your offer," what would you have done? – I should not have believed him (Laughter). Didn't you want to keep this matter out of the papers to-day? – I thought as Christians and brother clergymen –

Don't cant.

Mr. Jackson protested against such a remark.

Mr. Brown – I say it is cant to talk about Christians in an inquiry of this kind.

Mr. Jackson – The witness is a Christian minister.

Mr. Brown – That is a matter of opinion. He is very un-Christianlike.

The Chairman did not think the matter was of much importance.

Mr. Brown – Well it is a test of the spirit in which these proceedings were instituted, and therefore a test of credibility.

Hon. F. Strutt – Well, take it for what it is worth.

There were accusations and counter accusations as to who leaked the story to the press. The vicar blamed the curate and the curate blamed the vicar.

Mr. Brown proceeded to examine the witness with respect to the account of the fracas which appeared in the Sheffield Independent with the object of showing that he supplied it. Witness said he was not editor of a paper, and Mr. Brown said he was not competent to be one.

The Bench requested Mr. Brown not to insult the witness.

Mr. Brown – It is not insulting him any more than telling him he is not competent to be Prime Minister.

Witness admitted that he had answered one or two questions which were put to him by a reporter, but denied that he had furnished any account of the fracas to the newspapers, and suggested that the vicar had done so.

The proceedings went on to repeat what had happened in the vestry meeting and the follow-on meeting in the schoolroom when the curate made his accusations about the vicar's "dastardly" behaviour.

The response to Revd Blair's letter to the vicar, written by Revd Acraman's sister Julia, was then read out, although it was considered ungentlemanly for a lady's letter to be read out in public.

Mr. Brown – It is monstrous and cruel that a letter of a lady should be read in this way. It's very unprofessional on the part of my friend to wish to do so.

Mr. Jackson – I am not going to be interrupted any more, as I have been from time to time. It is very unprofessional of Mr. Brown. Mr. Jackson then read the letter as follows:–

In reply to your note received this afternoon, my brother requests me to say he scarcely sees his way clear to enter into a correspondence at present, especially as through your action he has been obliged to consult a solicitor, and therefore must be guided by him. The many incorrect statements made in the public press present an element of difficulty well-nigh impossible to surmount. – Yours faithfully, JULIA ACRAMAN

Mr. Brown – A very proper letter, too.

Mr Hurt, one of the managers present during the fracas, then gave evidence. He explained how he became injured by the curate lashing out with his feet whilst he was restraining the vicar.

Mr. A. F. Hurt, J.P., said – I am one of the managers of the Crich Parochial School, I attended a meeting of the managers on the 28th March at the vicarage. The notice convening the meeting and the minutes were read, and I said I thought it would have been very much better to have the meeting on Saturday. The vicar said he should prefer not to have it on Saturday, on which day he should like to be quiet. Mr. Blair made a great many remarks, one of which was that the vicar had been to Lichfield about him on the previous Saturday. Mr. Blair proposed to read a letter, but the vicar objected on the ground that the letter did not relate to school matters. Mr. Blair said it did relate to school matters, and proposed to read it to show that it did. On several occasions in the course of the meeting Mr. Blair interrupted the vicar with the remark "That's a lie," or "It's a lie,'" and things of that kind. There had been constant interruptions and very irregular proceedings, I had occasion to interrupt myself sometimes. I think Dr. Dunn also interrupted. I don't mean interrupted with such expressions as "That's a lie" or anything of that kind (Laughter). Mr. Blair said "It's a lie" about something else long before the question of the letter came up. The vicar said if he persisted in reading the letter he would put him out of the house. Mr. Blair insisted on his right, and commenced to read it. Mr. Acraman then went towards him, in front of me, and endeavoured to get possession of the letter. He made a snatch at it, but did not succeed in getting it. I think Mr. Blair rather freed himself at first, and began again to read in a loud voice. Then Mr. Acraman seized him by the collar. I don't know whether his intention was to get possession of the letter or to carry out his threat by putting Mr. Blair out of the house. Mr. Blair then went down on his back on the floor. My impression is that Mr. Blair intentionally threw himself on his back. The vicar continued to attempt to grapple with him, and I put my arms round his middle and after some little struggling got him off. The curate was still on his back on the floor kicking out with his feet at the vicar. Dr. Dunn assisted him up. A chair was broken, but I don't know how it was done.

Mr. Jackson – I believe the meeting then adjourned? – We had agreed to adjourn the meeting some time before the attempt to read the letter. The meeting was practically adjourned then.

Some conversation took place on this point, from which it appeared that though the managers had decided before the assault to adjourn until Saturday the meeting had not been actually concluded. Mr. Hurt further stated that it was very unusual for the meetings to be held at the vicar's house.

Cross-examined – In the course of the proceedings Dr. Dunn several times put his hand on Mr. Blair, who was sitting next to him, and remonstrated with him, reminding him that he was in the vicar's own house. I am not sure that complainant used the word "liar;" very probably he did. When he was on the floor, he used his feet pretty freely and one of them caught my finger and injured it as I had my arms round the vicar. I think in the first instance he was trying to get possession of the letter and then he was trying to put the vicar out of the room.

Mr. Brown – That was your impression was it; but you were best able to form an opinion? – Well, I was rather warmly engaged at that moment (Laughter).

In your opinion was there any intentional assault committed on the defendant by the complainant?'

Mr. Jackson – That is a question for the Bench.

Mr. Brown – No, it is for the witness. Was there an intentional assault or was it merely an endeavour to get hold of the papers? – Unquestionably there was a technical assault, but it was under very great provocation, and I think the main object was to get possession of the papers and also to remove him from the room.

The Chairman – When Mr. Blair first proposed to read the letter was the vicar's first objection made in moderate terms, or was he violent from the first? – He was not violent, I think he said "It has nothing to do with the meeting; it is quite irrelevant." As Mr. Blair continued to insist on reading the letter I suppose the vicar became more urgent that it should not be read? – Yes.

Did he behave otherwise than in a reasonable way during the meeting up to this time? – He did not lose control over his temper in any way until he got up.

Dr Dunn, the village doctor who was the other school manager present at the meeting, gave his opinion as to what happened. The defence were trying to show that the curate behaved in an ungentlemanly manner – calling someone a "liar" in his own home is not acceptable.

Dr. Dunn was then called, and corroborated for the most part the evidence of Mr. Hurt. He thought, however, that Mr. Blair did not throw himself on the floor. When the vicar tried to snatch the letter from him he put his hand, containing the letter, out to the right. The vicar then seized him by the collar on the left side and he fell down on that side. When he was on the floor he kicked out vigorously at the vicar, who was trying to get hold of him. Mr. Hurt took the vicar off and witness picked up the curate.

The Chairman – Did you consider the meeting had legally closed before the scuffle? – No, it had not actually closed. No resolution was submitted to the meeting about the adjournment, but we had decided to adjourn. We were a small meeting and did not transact business in a very formal manner. No resolution was submitted to the meeting after the scuffle. The Chairman – No vote of thanks to the chairman (laughter), or anything of that kind? – Certainly not (Laughter).

Cross-examined by Mr. Brown – You agree with Mr. Hurt that the meeting was practically adjourned before the letter was read ? – If you put in the word "practically" I think that is right.

You say you heard Mr. Blair use the word "liar" twice at least? – I don't distinctly remember whether it was "It's a lie" or "You're a liar." I won't swear.

At all events you protested against Mr. Blair's conduct? – Yes.

Then I take it his conduct was inconsistent with his position, especially in his vicar's house? – Yes, I should say so.

I don't suppose you would have submitted to it if a person had made use of such remarks to you in your own house? – No, I should not.

You would perhaps have used even more forcible measures ? (Laughter.) – Perhaps so.

Then I may take it that in your opinion the vicar was justified in turning him out? – Well, taking it from a broad stand point, I dare say a man is justified.

Re-examined – It was some time before the scuffle that the word "liar" was used. It was clear that that word did not provoke the vicar to commit the assault. It was the curate persisting in reading the letter that did it.

Mr Brown, in summing up for the vicar, attempted to show the curate as an ill-mannered man who had behaved disgracefully and got his just desserts.

Mr. Brown submitted that not even a technical assault had been committed. It was plain from the evidence of the complainant's own witnesses that he was a very ill-behaved and ill-mannered man, and that besides being disloyal to his vicar he was a person who could not conduct himself as a gentleman when he was at the house of the vicar. It was clear that he behaved on that occasion in a manner which was a disgrace to his cloth. He wished to read a letter in the house of the vicar which the vicar did not wish to be read, and it ought to have been conclusive when the vicar made the objection. As he persisted in reading it the vicar, who had behaved in a reasonable and quiet manner throughout, was proceeding to take it from him when he threw himself on the floor, scrawled about; and behaved in a very absurd manner. This was as gross a vindictive prosecution as ever was instituted, and the curate was liable to an action for malicious prosecution.

The verdict

No man had a right to put the criminal law in motion under such circumstances. His letter, which was the most pharisaical composition ever penned, showed the spirit in which he was acting. Mr. Brown quoted from Stone's "Justices' Manual" with the object of showing that an assault is an attempt by force or violence to do a bodily injury to another and that in order to constitute an assault punishable by the criminal law the act must be done with a hostile intention. The vicar was perfectly justified in offering reasonable violence to prevent the reading of the letter in his own house and he was also justified in using violence to turn the complainant out. He was only afraid, after the evidence which had been given by the complainant's own witnesses; that the magistrates would convict the defendant of a technical assault, but he pointed out that they were not bound to convict even if that were proved, and asked them to say that the vicar only acted, under the circumstances, as a reasonable man might be expected to act. He was prepared to call Mr. Saxton, but he would give just the same account as that given by Mr. Hurt and Dr. Dunn, and he did not consider his evidence was necessary.

Mr Jackson, acting for the curate, responded. The Magistrates found the vicar guilty of a "technical assault" and fined him a nominal amount of one shilling. Although a sort of victory for both sides, the curate winning his case but only on a technicality, it was the vicar who was to suffer the backlash from his parishioners in a most dramatic way.

Mr. Jackson replied on the two points of law mentioned by Mr. Brown. He had not given the shadow of an authority for showing that the vicar had the right to run at the curate and attempt to put him out of the house. He had no such right, as Mr. Blair was attending the meeting as one of the managers, and for the purposes of the occasion it was just the same as though the meeting had been held in the schoolroom.. As to the law of assault, he quoted "Stone" to show that the dragging of a man from his chair was an assault, and that "insulting words, however gross, do not justify blows."

The Bench retired for a few minutes to their private room, and on their return the Chairman said – Mr. Acraman, the Bench convict you of a technical assault in this case, and fine you in a nominal sum of 1s and costs.

The costs amounted to 16s 6d, and the money was immediately paid.

Chapter 12
Crich burns its vicar!

The news of the curate's 'victory' over the vicar caused great excitement in Crich. It was not good news for the vicar. Several hundred parishioners paraded an effigy of him through the village before setting fire to it outside the vicarage. The crowd then went through a mock burial service. Eventually the head of the effigy was kicked around like a football. The vicar stayed indoors! This was reported in the local press.

Derby Mercury: Wed 18 April 1883

CRICH

BURNING AN EFFIGY – There was much excitement at Crich on Thursday evening when the result of the police court proceedings became known. The news spread very rapidly, and crowds collected to discuss the best method of showing approval of the result. About eight o'clock an announcement was made that there would be a display of fireworks in the Market-place, in honour of the success of the curate. An hour later a man marched into the square bearing a long pole, and at the top was an effigy supposed to represent the vicar. The effigy was dressed in "top hat" cravat, black coat and vest, with whiskers. An adjournment was made to a field fronting the vicarage. The shouts of the mob in the Market-place caused a large crowd to collect. The noisy element on arriving at a field opposite the vicar's residence lighted the effigy, which being composed of hay and straw, steeped in paraffin and tar, burned for about half an hour. The blaze caused an even greater crowd to assemble. The mob went so far as to read a mock funeral service. Eventually the effigy fell to pieces, and the head was kicked about the field amidst excitement. After the figure had been consumed the disorderly multitude made a tour into the town so as to pass by the vicar's house, which they did, shouting and hooting and hurrahing in a very violent manner.

Chapter 13
New headmaster and new British School

The vicar appointed a new schoolmaster, Mr W. T. Sumner, to replace the sacked Mr Scott. You cannot but feel sorry for the new head walking into a hotbed of unrest and tension. His was certainly a baptism of fire.

Parochial School logbook: 20th April 1883

Vicar introduced Mr. Sumner to the children, but no notice taken of either master or other members of the teaching staff.

Derby Mercury Wed 25 April 1883

CRICH PAROCHIAL SCHOOL – We are informed that the school managers have appointed Mr. and Mrs. Sumner as master and mistress of this school, and they will commence duties early next month. They are natives of Lancashire, and possessed of the highest possible testimonials and parchment entries, having had large and varied experience in important Government schools.

Parochial School logbook: 30th April 1883

I, William Thomas Sumner 2nd class certificate Headmaster (Chester College) took charge of this school. Numbers present during the day - morning 57, afternoon 57. Time-table not adhered to from 2.45 to end of school time. Music taught instead. The children were very orderly - spoke to them respecting the "opposition school" and the many little unprincipled ways that have been used to entice the children that have gone.

At the same time as Mr Sumner was starting the previous schoolmaster, Mr Scott, moved across the road to Mount Tabor Chapel to take charge of the new British School, or Scott's School as it was known. The school opened on the 30th April 1883 with two hundred and forty pupils on its books. There were only about sixty pupils left in the Parochial School. Parents had certainly voted with their children's feet.

The new school was funded by the British and Foreign School Society. This Society was supported by prominent evangelical and nonconformist Christians. Throughout the country the founders of British Schools came into conflict with the National School Society, which founded Church of England Schools. British and National Schools were in direct competition, although the National School Society was by far the larger of the two organisations.

The local committee for the Crich British School – many members of which were local Nonconformist tradesmen and manufacturers – raised subscriptions, to set up the school. The government provided grants to the British Schools as long as the local supporters raised matching funds.

So it was that a British School supported by local Nonconformists, the Baptists in particular, was set up in the Mount Tabor Chapel, nearly opposite the Parochial School. Unbelievably two hundred and forty children were to be taught there. The toilet provision does not bear thinking about, piped water did not arrive in Crich until 1906.

Mount Tabor.

Bad behaviour

The British School was also called: Scott's School; Mount Tabor School; Chapel School; Baptist School; and the Opposition School. In the early days it was more often called "Scott's School."

There was a great deal of conflict between the pupils of Scott's School and the Parochial School. Name-calling and bullying seemed commonplace. Calling "Rhubarb" seemed to be a favourite insult. The misbehaviour became so bad that children from Scott's School even entered the Parochial School and threw stones and swore at the vicar and staff.

Parochial School logbook: 1st May 1883

As the Rev. W. Acraman and master were conversing after school respecting new apparatus the door was pushed open by a number of boys and girls from "Scotts School" who fired a volley of stones into the classroom. At the same time the children shouted "opprobrious epithets" to the vicar - on going out the children used the same epithets to the vicar.

2nd May 1883

At 4.15 this afternoon whilst the Assistant was practising two new songs the door was burst open by a volley of stones. The boys and girls who did this attend "Scotts School". The master went out and remonstrated with them. On the children seeing the master they began to throw at him and called him "opprobrious epithets". When the master went home the children from "Scotts School" threw stones and shouted again.

3rd May 1883

Sarah Ann Harrison informed master that her parents intended taking her away on account of the children attending "Scotts School" calling after her "Rubub" - master went to see the school secretary and on his way back Scotts scholars shouted "Sumner Thunder Rubarb's Schoolmaster".

Chapter 14
Bill posting and intimidation

As the rivalry between the two schools heated up a campaign of posting bills on the walls of the village began.

The managers of the Parochial School began with posters proclaiming that the Education Department had informed them that its architect agreed with School Inspectors in thinking that the 'British' Schoolroom, at the Mount Tabor Chapel, was wholly unsuitable for school purposes. They went on to claim that the Education Department declined to accept the building or make a conditional promise of an Annual Grant. The children would not be examined by the Inspectors and would not, therefore, be able to obtain the certificate of proficiency award required (under the bye-laws of the local Attendance Committee) to be exempted from the obligation to attend school. The 'National' Managers claimed that the acknowledged Government Schools in the parish were the Crich Parochial and the Fritchley 'National' Schools:

> *"at both of which the interests of the parents with regard to the education of their children will always be carefully guarded and considered by:*
>
> *W. T. Sumner - Master of the Crich Parochial School*
> *J. H. Barnes - Master of Fritchley National School".*

The management of Scott's School quickly responded with posters of their own which were liberally posted around the village. The posters denied the claims made by the vicar and tried to reassure parents. As an inducement they were invited to afternoon tea with entertainment.

> The fees will be less than those of the Parochial School. It is placed under the Government for Inspection so that parents need not be afraid of 'summonses' as reported by the Vicar and his party.
>
> The parents can rely on the full support of the British School Committee who will protect them in all things connected with the education of their children.
>
> Parents are invited to consult any of the above gentlemen (The British School Committee) who will be glad to furnish information and who will certainly not mislead them and in whose hands they will be perfectly safe.
>
> Thursday May 1st:
> Public Tea and Entertainment

The antagonism between the National and the British supporters was obviously strong and the Education Department decided to step in. They pointed out that the National School managers' poster included inaccurate and misleading statements and demanded that all the posters, from both sides, be taken down.

Parochial School, after the extension had been built

Even the adults were involved in the dirty tricks that were taking place between the two schools. The following extract refers to the "Logbook" being locked. The original book did indeed have a hinged lock to keep its contents private.

Parochial School logbook: 7th May 1883

Master went at playtime to see Mr. Saxton - whilst away Mr. Dunn a school manager called to see the report. He asked Miss Evans (who was in charge) to let him look at the "Log Book" - she replied that it was locked but if he would wait he could see it as master would be in in a few minutes. He said, "Have you not got the key?" Whereupon Miss Evans unlocked it. Master on his return saw him go out of this school and go straight to Scott's School. He asked Miss Evans for the number of children on the books. When she told him he expressed much surprise having been led to believe it was much less.

Derby Mercury: Wed 9 May 1883

CRICH

THE SCHOOL GRIEVANCE—The persons who have disagreed with the vicar and managers of the Crich parochial school in regard to the educational affairs of the parish held a public tea and entertainment on Tuesday, in aid of the funds of the new British-school which they have opened. The Mount Tabor Chapel has been engaged for teaching purposes, and as it was originally built for a day school, it does not lack the necessary convenience. A committee of managers has been formed with a majority of Churchmen, and the rest are members of various religious bodies. The whole of the parish has been canvassed for subscriptions, and the result seems to have surprised the most sanguine of those interested. The new school has been thoroughly renovated and it is provided with all the newest appliances requisite for teaching purposes. The British-school opened on Monday morning week with 240 scholars, or about four-fifths of the children who have attended the parochial school. The services of Mr. and Mrs. Sumner, of Preston, are engaged. – At Tuesday night's meeting Mr. W. Abel took the chair, and was supported by Mr. Percy Rawson, of Sheffield, Mr. Greenborough, Mr. Dawes (Holloway), Mr. T. G. Iveson, Mr. E. Kirk, Mr. Bower, and other large ratepayers. A capital entertainment was given, and the room was crowded. The Chairman said the school that had been established would belong to the ratepayers, and would not be representative of any party or sect. Mr. Percy Rawson delivered a humorous address. A number of songs were given, Mr. M. M. Day, of Wirksworth, accompanying.

Chapter 15
Villagers want vicar sacked

A week after the new British School opened, taking 80% of the pupils from the Parochial School, the vicar's problems continued. There was an inquiry into his conduct before the Bishop of Lichfield. The meeting was held "in camera" at the Hurt Arms Hotel in Ambergate. The Bishop had to decide whether to agree to Revd Acraman's sacking, as called for in a petition to him by Crich parishioners. The meeting was held on the 11th May 1883.

Hurt Arms Hotel in Ambergate, where the hearing was held, taken from an old postcard. It was built in 1876 by Francis Hurt. The Hurt family were great benefactors in the village and were frequent visitors to the Parochial School. The Toll House was recorded as being at the "Amber Gate of the Cromford and Belper Turnpike Trust."

Derby Mercury: Wed 16 May 1883

EPISCOPAL INQUIRY AT AMBERGATE

(FROM OUR OWN CORRESPONDENT.)

On Friday, the Bishop of Lichfield, accompanied by his secretary, attended at the Hurt's Arms Hotel, Ambergate, for the purpose of holding an inquiry into the charges alleged against the Vicar of Crich. Besides the Bishop there were present the Venerable Archdeacon Balston, Rev. W. Shipton, of Old Brampton, and the Rev. Dr. Potter, of Sheffield (who appeared on behalf of the vicar). It will be remembered that some time ago the following memorial was addressed to the Bishop by a number of the inhabitants of Crich.

We the parishioners of Crich being deeply grieved that after being here 7¹/₂ years, the Rev. William Acraman has in effect lost all spiritual influence in the parish, and that his residence amongst us is wanting in influence for good, very respectfully pray your Lordship to recommend him to resign.

Immediately on receipt of this memorial the Bishop communicated with the vicar, and as a result of the communication the inquiry was opened. The inquiry was a private one and reporters were not admitted. The Bishop stated that the inquiry would be chiefly into the allegation of the memorial as to the vicar's loss of influence in his parish, and the causes which have led to it. No person except the rev. gentlemen above-mentioned were allowed in the room whilst the evidence was being given. There were 21 persons present, in opposition to the vicar, to give evidence as to his general conduct, amongst whom were Mr. T. G. Iveson (who presided at all the meetings in opposition to the vicar), Dr. C. B. N. Dunn, Mrs. and Miss Williams (of Peterborough, who at one time were school-mistresses at Fritchley, near Crich), Mr. H. Sibley, Mr. R. Bryan, Mr. H. S. Scott (the late master of the National School), Mr. J. Burton, Rev. Andrew Blair (curate), and others. Amongst the friends of the vicar who attended were the Rev. T. G. Johnson (Wirksworth) and Rev. J. Mulkerns (Wessington), late curates of Crich, Messrs. Thomas Taylor, Benjamin Taylor, S. Holmes, J. T. Lee (churchwarden), W. Piggin and A. Sims. At the opening of the inquiry a testimonial speaking in eulogistic terms of the vicar, was handed to the Bishop, with close upon 300 signatures attached to it. Mr. T. G. Iveson was the first witness examined. All the witnesses were not called. Although the result of the inquiry has not yet been made known, it is an open secret that the charges which have frequently been made against the vicar were not substantiated at this inquiry, and that the vicar's opponents have failed in their endeavours to bring about his removal.

The Bishop decides

The Bishop went away to consider his response to the plea to have the Vicar removed. On the 16th May 1883, for once, the Revd Acraman had some good news. The Bishop decided against his removal although there was a slight censure over the vicar's actions.

Derby Mercury: Wed 23 May 1883

CRICH

THE BISHOP OF LICHFIELD AND THE CRICH MEMORIAL – The Bishop of Lichfield has replied to the memorial forwarded to him by the parishioners of Crich in February last as follows – "Lichfield 16th May 1883, Dear Sir, – As a result of the inquiry held at Ambergate on Friday last, I have to intimate to you that, although the Commissioners were far from satisfied with the state of the parish, as revealed by the witnesses whom they examined, they could find no sufficient reason to take any further steps with a view to remove the incumbent. I trust therefore that you and your friends will endeavour as far as possible to promote a better feeling than at present exists in the parish, although I am bound to admit that events that have recently occurred were sufficient to have produced a feeling of distrust and uneasiness on the part of the parishioners, and I cannot deem unreasonable the application which you made to me with a view to inquiries being instituted. – I remain, dear sir, yours faithfully, W. D. LICHFIELD. T. G. Iveson, Esq.

At this time the schoolmaster Mr Scott had worries and concerns of his own, but of a nonprofessional kind. The diseases measles and scarlatina were sweeping through the district causing several deaths. Mr Scott's children caught scarlatina and his youngest, Gertrude Margaret Irene Scott died aged about eighteen months.

> **Scarlatina** *(scarlet fever) symptoms – fever, sore throat, headache, vomiting, stomach pains, bright red tongue and a rash. Side effects can be traumatic. Had to be reported as a contagious disease to the medical officer.*

Derby Mercury: Wed 30 May 1883

A death was reported from Crich, through scarlatina, in the house of Mr. Scott schoolmaster. Three children had been attacked by the disease. Mr. Scott has left home for a time. Several other cases of scarlatina were reported from Crich. Measles and scarlatina continue to prevail in the rural parts of Alfreton, and during the present year the medical officer had inquired into no less than 50 cases, and several had ended fatally.

A view of St Mary's Church.

Chapter 16
Mr Sumner's harassment

Mr Sumner and his wife were subject to considerable harassment as the new master and mistress of the Parochial School. It was particularly bad during May and June of 1883 when they, and their pupils, were subjected to quite unpleasant behaviour. It was suggested that the culprits were actively encouraged by Mr Scott. At one time it became so bad that the Parochial School had to close early to protect its staff and pupils from the intimidation.

Parochial School logbook: 29th May 1883

The boys from "Scotts School" started on our own boys in the Lane - the result was a fight. As I was going home I separated them.

Mr Sumner also wrote to the vicar complaining about the harassment and intimidation.

May 1883

"... on our way to and from school, Mrs. Sumner and I are very much intimidated by Mr. Scott and his scholars attending the British School. The children are so rowdy and boisterous to our teachers and scholars that I need hardly tell you it interferes very much with us in teaching good manners as per the Education Code. I have spoken to Mr. Scott regarding it but since then they have been much worse ... at 10 minutes past 4 (on May 1st) the scholars attending the Scott's School rushed into our classroom and commenced ringing the school bell, throwing down the blackboard

and stamping on the floor. I at once went out and the children started to throw stones, etc. On my going home they followed me and I had to hasten my steps or I should have been hurt....Many children complain (on May 14) of Scott's scholars throwing stones and shouting names and (on May 29) many children were crying because Scott's scholars had been hitting their faces with nettles. ... When going to school, the boys stood in a line to oppose us. A stone hit Mrs. Sumner in the face and caused much pain (June 19). ... June 20 Mr. and Mrs. Sumner going home when 50 of Scott's scholars with Mr. Scott stood in the midst of them and shouted opprobrious epithets. Mr. Scott laughed and said: "That's it, boys".

Dr J. G. Dawes - "A History of Crich"

Feelings were certainly high and Mr Sumner ended his letter to the Vicar by commenting rather sadly:

"I rarely go out alone whilst it is light, afraid of intimidation."

Parochial School logbook: 12th June 1883

Rev. W. Acraman visited, informed teachers that "Scotts School" had not been sanctioned by the Education Department.

22nd June 1883

On account of the hooting and intimidation of Scott scholars I have decided to make the registers today at 9.30 and close at 11.45.

Chapter 17
The vicar tries hard

After the Bishop's criticism the vicar seemed to set about improving his standing in the community and raising the profile of the Parochial School against that of the British School. In the June of 1883 he arranged a concert and tea in the school, which was well reported. Good publicity at last.

Derby Mercury: Wed 30 June 1883

CRICH.

CRICH PAROCHIAL SCHOOL – On Tuesday evening the Parochial Schoolroom was the scene of an interesting gathering in connection with the Church Day-schools of the parish, the occasion being a tea and entertainment under the patronage of the Rev. William Acraman, Mr. Albert Hurt J.P., D.L., Mr. E. M. Wass J.P., Mr. Thewlis Johnson, Mr. William Walker and Mr. George Coupe, members of the school committee. The large room had been beautifully decorated. Over the platform were placed, in white letters on a blue ground, the words in bold relief, "Welcome," and other suitable mottoes, such as "Success," "Energy," "Friendship," "Manliness," etc., and an ornamental scroll near the clock, in white letters on a red ground, containing the appropriate motto, "Time and tide wait for no man." A large assembly was present at an excellent and substantial tea provided by Mr. John Stocks, the tables were presided over by parents of the scholars and others. The aged poor of the parish were presented with free tickets by the vicar, and seemed to thoroughly enjoy the good things provided, the numbers present at the tea and entertainment being about 300, the masters and mistresses of Crich and Fritchley working hard to promote it. After tea the vicar presided, and was supported on the platform by the Rev. J. Mulkerns, vicar of Wessington, Mr. E. M. Wass, and Mr. J. Thewlis Johnson, when the following programme was gone through in a most creditable manner, especially the dialogue in character, "Wanted a Wife," which elicited roars of laughter.

Part 1 – Trio instrumental, "Selection by Henry Farmer," Messrs. Glossop, Briggs and Blackham: song "In the Quarries," Children: song "Village Bells," Miss Holmes: recitation "Tom and his Cruelty," Harry Holmes: glee "Absence," Crich and Fritchley Glee Club: recitation "My Doll Rose," Mabel Craven: song "Before all Lands," Children: glee "Comrades in

Arms," Crich and Fritchley Glee Club: piano forte solo "Hill's March," George Haynes: dialogue "Wanted a Wife," Messrs. Sumner and Lee, Misses Lee, Evans, Bates, Holmes, and Mrs. Sumner: song "Them on the Rhine."

Part 2 – Trio instrumental, Messrs. Glossop, Briggs and Blackham: glee "When Evening's Twilight," Crich and Fritchley Glee Club: song "Thy Voice is Near," Miss Stocks: song "Come Soft and Lovely Evening," Children: recitation "The Lark," Annie Parker: song "Cherry

Ripe," Miss Stocks: glee "Come where my love lies dreaming," Crich and Fritchley Glee Club: song "Dream Faces," Mrs. J. J. Parkin: recitation "Going Home," Ellen Stocks: song "Shoulder to Shoulder," Mr. J. T. Lee: recitation "Lost and Found," N. Clarkson: song "Follow me," Children: "National Anthem."

At the conclusion of Part 1 the Chairman delivered an earnest and appropriate address, and the usual votes of thanks terminated the meeting.

Possibly the recitation which caused much mirth.

> WANTED A WIFE
> Of all the girls that ever I knew,
> I never saw one that I thought would do.
> I wanted a wife that was nice and neat,
> That was up to date, and that had small feet;
> I wanted a wife that was loving and kind,
> And that hadn't too much original mind;
> I wanted a wife that could cook and sew,
> And that wasn't eternally on the go;
> I wanted a wife that just loved to keep house,
> And that wasn't too timid to milk the cows;
> I wanted a wife that was strikingly beautiful,
> Intelligent, rich and exceedingly dutiful.
> That isn't so much to demand in a wife
> But still she's not found, although I've looked all my life.

In newspaper reports much mention was made of "glees" taking place in Crich. A glee is a part song, usually scored for at least three solo voices, and normally sung unaccompanied. Glee singing societies became wildly popular in the 18th century, and remained so throughout the 19th century.

Quieter times

The *Derby Mercury* liked to spice up its paper with amusing little oddities, such as the following. The first was a ditty about Crich church bells and scurrilous comments about the characteristics of neighbouring villages and towns. The second, a humorous anecdote about the Crich postman.

Derby Mercury: Wed 11 July 1883

CURIOUS RHYMES – At Alfreton we noted the following lines on church bells:-

    Alfreton kettles,
    Pentrich pans,
    Crich great rollers,
    Wingfield ting-tangs.

We have obtained from another part of the county a more extended version as follows:-

    Crich two roller boulders,
    Wingfield ting-tangs,
    Alfreton kettles, And Pentrich pans,
    Kirk Hallam candlesticks,
    Cossall cow-bells,
    Denby cracked pancheons,
    And Horsley merry bells.

The next rhyme is certainly not flattering to the places named:-

    Ripley ruffians
    Butterley blacks,
    Swanwick bulldogs,
    Alfreton shacks.

Some fifty years ago Ripley was noted for its rough characters, but at the present times the people do not lack polish. We are told that blacking-pots did the duty of drinking glasses during the fairs at Ripley half a century ago. Butterley blacks cannot be accounted for charitably on any theory but the close proximity of the Butterley Ironworks. As for Swanwick bull-dogs, it must be a libel, for until recently it was one of the quietest hamlets in England. Alfreton shacks is easily accounted for. For generations past Alfreton always had, down to twenty years ago, a notorious set of idlers in it, ready for anything except working for an honest living – easily earning the cognomen of Alfreton shacks. There has happily been since then a marked improvement, with the drawback of rowdyism, characteristic of a mining population. The date of the origin of the rhyme is probably about 1800.

These lighter pieces were in stark contrast to the serious issues that filled most of the paper. Large page sizes, no photographs of course, small print size and very full and flowing text made for heavy reading.

Derby Mercury: Wed 25 July 1883

𝕺𝖉𝖉𝖘 𝖆𝖓𝖉 𝕰𝖓𝖉𝖘 𝕬𝖇𝖔𝖚𝖙 𝕯𝖊𝖗𝖇𝖞𝖘𝖍𝖎𝖗𝖊

A DERBYSHIRE POSTMAN – In his book on The Peak and the Plain the Venerable Dr. Spencer T. Hall thus wrote:- I leaned over a wall on the hill between Crich Cliff and Holloway, to contemplate the prospect, and presently became aware of the approach of a village postman or foot-carrier with his load, sliding along so slowly that one would wonder how he could expect ever to reach his destination. He had a bundle on his head, a basket in one hand, a parcel in the other, a bag slung over his shoulder, and a letter case strapped under his arm. His shoes were white with dust, his face the colour of a piece of broiled ham, and would, one might think, have been scorched, but for the basting of perspiration that dripped over it from his brow. On reaching the place where I stood – as he probably calculated on a gossip as well as a rest – down went the parcel and basket from his hands, next followed the bundle off his head, sling went the bag with a bang from his shoulder, and now he was leaning too, with folded arms upon the wall by my side. To my remark that it was a hot day, he answered only with a sound between a grunt and a humph, and the same when I said, "but the scenery is very beautiful." When I tried again to draw him out by a word about fine hills he seemed to think, like a girl to whom I had once made the same observation, that "they are that, fine and hard to get up." Certainly there could scarcely be a more beautiful landscape any where. Up behind us arose a craggy and wooded hill, how high it was impossible to see. Down below us went a steep slope to the shining river; away again beyond which rose rock above rock, wood above wood, and peak above peak, to the very heavens. "Can you tell me," said I, "the name of yon beautiful knoll just opposite." "What, yonder?" he replied, pointing to the very spot. "Yes, yonder," was my hopeful answer. "Why, that," said he, "is t'Cowms." "Cowms, Cowms,' I enquired, "why do they call it Cowms?" – "Why!" shouted he in reply, "becoss it is t'Cowms, I s'pose." "Exactly so," I said, "but why should it have this name in preference to any other?" "Why?" he retorted, "because that name's t'right 'un." Despairing of a solution by any other method, I now thought of getting the etymology of the word through its orthography, but here I fell into a worse fix than ever. "Can you tell me," I asked, in the most civil tone, "how the name of Cowms is spelt?" Upon which be turned his hot face upon me, and, opening wide his eyes and mouth with a loud "Ugh!" exclaimed, "The idea o' spelling Cowms, why I should think anybody knows what Cowms is about spellin' it. It niver is spelt, mon; it doesna' neyd spellin'. This was a poser, and I gave up all hope. It now came his turn to question me. It was on my quietly remarking this was from that I lived in. " Why," asked he with eagerness, "where dun yo' come from? "Nottinghamshire," was my answer. "Nottinghamshire!" he cried out, "then dun yo' know anybody there as I know?" "It is impossible for me to tell that," I said, "before you have told me whom you know yourself." "Well, then," he rejoined, "dun yo' know Paul Duffield?" "What," I asked, "do you mean Paul Duffield who keeps the Robin Hood at Sutton-in-Ashfield?" "Aye" he shouted, in evident delight. "Well, then, said I, "as it happens, I do know him." "Then gi'e us yer hand," again cried the postman, "for hey's my brother-in-law."

However, it was not long before Crich was back in the news on a more serious note.

Chapter 18
British School problems

The new breakaway British School quickly hit problems because of the quality of its accommodation. Obviously this was to the delight of the vicar and the new schoolmaster of the Parochial School, Mr Sumner.

Derby Mercury: Wed 22 August 1883

THE CRICH SCHOOL DIFFICULTIES – On the 9th of August a letter was received by the secretary of the Crich British School, stating that the Education Department refused to pass the plans submitted of the British School, which was opened about four months ago by the parishioners, who were opposed to the vicar and the Parochial School. The building is not satisfactory in many points, and the Department now intimate their proposal to at once issue a final notice. Accordingly, a meeting of the ratepayers was called on Wednesday night, and it took place in the independent Club-room. There were present – Mr. T. G. Iveson in the chair, and Messrs. Sibley, Burton, Cowlishaw, Taylor, Bower, Boag, and other rate-payers. – The Chairman stated, in accordance with the letter which the managers of the British School had received, that they felt bound to consult the ratepayers on the steps they would now take in regard to the educational affairs of the parish. The department in London would not accept the school they had opened, and the question was whether the ratepayers would undertake to provide accommodation for 200 children, or let the department issue a notice for a School Board. The managers of the British School had done all they could to get their building passed but they had failed and now must leave the matter with the ratepayers to decide which of the two alternatives they would accept. – The correspondence with the Education Department respecting the new schools was read, and the Chairman said it was open for the meeting to express an opinion on future action. – The Chairman, as an individual, said he would like to see a good British School. He knew there were very great objections by the large property owners against a School Board. – A ratepayer asked if it was beyond possibility for funds to be raised to erect a new British School? – The Chairman said he did not see why the people should not build a free school, and prevent a Board being established. They did not want a fine school – Mr. Bower said he had had an interview with the Rev. W. Acraman, and suggested to him that the parish should select five ratepayers and the church select five also, and work things out the same as if they were a School Board, but the vicar rejected the proposal. – Mr. B. Taylor said that if they could get 20 people to guarantee so much money, he would give an average of what these 20 contributed, and then a British School could be erected. He should oppose a School Board, and at the same time he felt sure a Board could not be established for the parish. – Several of those present spoke against a Board being forced on the parish, and hoped money would be found to build a British School. – Mr. Kirk said if they had a School Board the cost would not be above 2d. in the pound to provide for about 200 children. – After a good deal of discussion, Mr. James Leate moved the following resolution, which was seconded and carried without dissent:- "That this meeting having heard the statements of the managers of the Crich British School, and the correspondence with the Education Department, desires to place the educational affairs of the parish in the hands of the department for a speedy settlement." – The meeting concluded with votes of thanks to the chairman, and also to the managers of the British School for their endeavours to carry on the school successfully.

All the odds were on a School Board being formed in Crich – at a cost to ratepayers. However, the vicar had other ideas.

Derby Mercury: Wed 29 August 1883

THE SCHOOL GRIEVANCE – A correspondent says the promoters of an opposition school at Crich have had their plans upset by the Education Department. The unhappy state of affairs in the parish gave rise to a resolution on the part of the vicar's opponents to establish a British School, mainly for the purpose of finding a place for Mr. Scott, the ex-master of the National School. The resolve was so far carried out that a building was secured and a fair number of scholars placed under the tuition of Mr. Scott. All appeared to be smooth sailing, but now the Department says the building is not suitable for an elementary school. After such notice, coupled with the knowledge that the Government grant would be withheld, The managers decided to consult the ratepayers, and they have considered it advisable to leave themselves in the hands of the Education Department, So it appears a School Board is very likely to be formed.

Chapter 19
Threat of a School Board looms

Although the managers of the Parochial School were delighted with the accommodation difficulties of the rival British School, they also had problems of their own. Because of the overcrowding in their school they themselves were in danger of being taken over by a School Board.

Derby Mercury: Wed 12 September 1883

District News

CRICH

EDUCATIONAL AFFAIRS – A final notice has been issued by the Education Department respecting the school accommodation of this parish. On Saturday morning Mr. George Dawes, parish clerk, received the order stating that 145 children required school room – 75 for Crich and 70 for Crich Carr. The orders were posted on the church and chapel doors on Sunday. The notice sets forth that the accommodation must be provided in three months, or a School Board will be formed. No steps have at present been taken in regard to the order, but it is expected the ratepayers will hold a meeting shortly.

Parents took advantage of the conflict between the two schools.

Parochial School logbook: 20th September 1883

Because master informed Mr. Sellors that his wife kept children at home she removed them this day and sent them to "Scotts School". This master did at the request of Mr. Sellors. Master finds much difficulty in getting regular attendance - the people making a "loophole"' of "Scotts School" the attendance at which is a direct evasion of the Education Acts of 1870 and 1876.

86

Some five weeks later neither the Parochial School nor the British School had taken steps to solve their accommodation problems and the spectre of a Board School for Crich loomed large. It was at this time that Mr Scott resigned from the British School to take up a new appointment elsewhere – Mr Rowbotham replaced him as head teacher.

Derby Mercury: Wed 10 October 1883

SCHOOL AFFAIRS – No steps have yet been taken by either contending parties in Crich to comply with the final notice issued by the Education Department five weeks since, ordering that accommodation is to be found for 145 children. It is considered that the notice will be allowed to lapse, and a school board be formed. The managers of the British School have issued a notice stating "that Mr. Scott has been offered and has accepted a better appointment: but the school will be carried on as heretofore by a thoroughly efficient certified master, with wife as assistant." The notice proceeds:- "The committee feel sure that as this school is working under the control of persons who have been appointed by the parishioners, parents will not remove their children to place them under an irresponsible clerical director whose aim in the past has been to retard education." Mr. Rowbotham of Hasland, near Chesterfield, has been appointed Mr. Scott's successor. At a recent public meeting and concert held in the British School, the chair was occupied by Mr. J. Ward, of Crich Carr, and there was a large attendance. Votes of thanks were accorded to the school managers for the way in which they had carried on the school – Mr. Iveson, Mr. Kirk, and others addressed the meeting; and said that if there should be an election they hoped the people would support the friends of the British school, and then put them in a majority on the School Board.

Vicar fights idea of School Board

The vicar came out fighting against the threat of having a School Board in Crich. He had powerful allies in the Duke of Devonshire, the Hurt family of Alderwasley, and the manager of Johnson's wire works. He made a forceful speech in the interval of a school concert for unity in working against having a School Board and for funds to build extensions that would remove the need to have one. Interestingly it was thought that one large classroom was adequate for 70 infants. It must have made a pleasant change for the vicar to receive more positive press coverage.

Derby Mercury: Wed 21 November 1883

During the interval the Rev. William Acraman gave an address. The rev. gentleman said the Education Department had determined that accommodation for 145 more children was required in the parish, so that the school in which they were assembled would need a classroom to accommodate 70 infants added to it, and a new school would have to be built at Crich Carr for 75 children. They all knew that their school had not as many children in it as it once had, but they were a united body, teachers and scholars working in harmony. Although their numbers were not large, yet "progress" had been their motto, and upwards of 100 scholars had for some time been attending the school, though he feared a good number of children did not at present go anywhere, or only attended school irregularly. Their master had been much criticised; yet he had held on, and was getting more appreciated and understood. By several parents opinion had been expressed that their children had made progress, and in his own visits to the school he had noticed a decided improvement in manners and behaviour. Mr. Acraman then spoke on the evils and expense that a School Board would bring by contested elections and much higher rates, and proved his statements by quoting the rates of the neighbouring parishes of Belper, Heage and South Wingfield. He advocated voluntary schools and religious education and objected to the people being compelled to pay rates to erect schools when they had one large school which had been maintained since 1848 and another school at Fritchley. A School Board could easily be averted by "a long pull and a string pull and a pull altogether." He then read a subscription list amounting upwards of £370, including £100 from the Duke of Devonshire (conditional on there being no School Board), £60 from himself and some relations, £40 from the Misses and Mr. Albert F. Hurt

& co, and stated that the plans had been approved by the Education Department. In conclusion, he exhorted all with public spirit and true Christian feeling to work together for public good. – Mr. Crozier, manager of the wireworks of Messrs. Johnson and Co., proposed that the best thanks of the meeting should be given to Mr. Acraman for the arduous efforts he had made to avert a School Board, stating the vicar had gone into the matter fully and worked heart and soul so that he richly deserved a hearty vote of thanks in appreciation of his valuable services and to prove their perfect confidence in one who had so quickly raised nearly £400. – Dr. Gaylor, in a thoughtful and able address gave his experience of a School Board at Belper, and also in other parishes, and considered that they would do well to show their high appreciation of their vicar's labour amongst them. He himself had the honour of knowing Mr.. Acraman for a considerable time, and had often been asked to come over to their entertainments. He was highly pleased with what he had heard and seen both of the vicar's work and of the first-class entertainment they had had that night, and considered that thanks were also due to the teachers and children who had so ably sustained their parts. He then seconded the resolution, which was put to the meeting by the Rev. J. Mulkerns, vicar of Wessington and was carried with acclamation and with much enthusiasm.

Much praise is due to the headmaster Mr. Sumner and to the assistant mistress in getting up the entertainment by which it is expected that a good sum will be raised for the building fund.

The local papers of the time often mentioned the hymns and religious songs composed by the vicar – often concerned with temperance.

Derby Mercury: Wed 19 December 1883

CHURCH OF ENGLAND TEMPERANCE SOCIETY. – The annual tea and meeting in connection with the Crich Band of Hope was held in the National Schoolroom on Tuesday evening. The vicar presided and presented medals to those members who had joined the society a year ago. Mr. Gentles, of Derby, and the Rev. C. Baker, vicar of Matlock Bath, gave thoughtful and interesting addresses on temperance, and a cantata, especially written and composed for the Crich Band of Hope by the vicar (the Rev. Wm. Acraman) entitled "The Temperance Army and the Blue Ribbon Boy" was rendered by some of the members and was very heartily received by the audience.

Chapter 20
Vicar fights off School Board

At the turn of the year things started looking better for the vicar. His attempts at stopping a School Board were bearing fruit, and the tone of the articles about him in the newspapers was certainly more supportive.

Derby Mercury: Wed 2 January 1884

CRICH.

PARISH CHURCH – On Christmas Day the parish church presented a very attractive appearance being most tastefully decorated, as in former years, with evergreens, mottoes, &c – the reading desk by Miss L. Acraman, the pulpit and lectern by Miss Lee (Wheatcroft) and Mrs. Wagstaffe and the font by Miss Shaw. The Misses Hurt's (Chase Cliff) head and under gardeners undertook the decorating of the pillars, and other members of the congregation took active part in the work generally.

CHURCH SUNDAY-SCHOOLS – The Sunday School at Crich is in a prosperous condition, upwards of 200 being connected with it, while a small Sunday-school is still carried on at Fritchley. The scholars of both schools, with their teachers, met at the Parochial Schoolroom yesterday (being New Year's Day) for the annual prize distribution with Christmas trees, the latter kindly presented by Mr. Hurt, of Alderwasley.

CHARITY DOLES – The annual gifts to the poor of the parish were distributed on St. Thomas's day, in the Parochial Schoolroom, by the vicar and churchwardens. The gifts were in the shape of warm clothing.

THE EDUCATION DIFFICULTY – A communication has been received from the Education Department with reference to the Crich Parochial School. The document is to the effect that no order for a School Board will be issued if the enlargement of Crich Parochial School and the building of the new school at Crich Carr is completed within a reasonable time. The vicar (the Rev. W. Acraman) has already commenced the work of providing additional accommodation.

Derby Mercury: Wed 2 January 1884

District News

CRICH

EDUCATIONAL AFFAIRS AT CRICH are looking more hopeful. The much-abused vicar, Mr. ACRAMAN, has succeeded in saving the parish from the incubus of a School Board. This success may, perhaps, be very unpalatable to the little knot of busybodies who would have liked to air their importance at the School Board; but the more sensible portion of the inhabitants cannot fail to be thankful that what might have been, and in all probability would have been, an intolerable burden, has been averted, and we hope that they will remember that for this they are indebted to the energy of the Vicar. The estimated cost of building a new school and enlarging the existing one so as to meet the requirements of the Education Department is about £700. Of this sum £600 and two sites, one by the Duke of DEVONSHIRE for the new school and one by Mr. A HURT for the proposed enlargement – have already been promised. The church-workers in Crich should find little difficulty in obtaining the money still required.

Chase Cliffe House, home of Elizabeth, Emma and Selina Hurt who were great benefactors to the village.

British School needs help

Whilst the vicar was promoting the new Crich Carr School and enlarged Parochial School the managers of the British School were not sitting idly by. They had over 250 pupils on roll and alleged the numbers were growing. Because it was a private school and the building at Mount Tabor had been deemed unsatisfactory they were not entitled to Government grants. They decided to rectify this. Representation was made to the Education Department to say – if they could provide suitable accommodation, would they be treated in the same way as "the other school in the village"?

In January 1884 the British School had a parade through the village followed by a "double-sitting" tea. The newspaper report showed that the Misses Hurt of Chase Cliffe did not restrict their support just to the Parochial School. It also confirmed a close relationship with the management at Lea Mills. On the 7th January 1884 the Parochial School logbook complained of intimidation of workers by an overseer who was "a dissenter". It was alleged he insisted workers should send their children to the British School, not to the Parochial School.

> *Parochial School logbook: 7th January 1884*
>
> Charles Stocks took away his children from the school because he was afraid if they remained he would lose his work - as he works for the Lea Mills and their overlooker being a dissenter is using all the intimidation he can in favour of the so called "British School" - Sarah and Emma Hyde likewise removed for the same reason.

Derby Mercury: Wed 16 January 1884

CRICH

SCHOOL AFFAIRS – On Saturday afternoon the children attending the recently established British School at Crich had their first treat. After parading the village they assembled at their schoolroom, where they were provided with tea, 258 in number. About 300 adults then had tea the room being twice filled. Two large Christmas trees had been presented by the Misses Hurt, of Chase Cliff, near Whatstandwell. A public meeting was held in the evening at which Mr. Broom, of Lea Mills, presided. Mr. Broom distributed a few prizes. Mr. Bush having urged the people to be energetic in their support of the schools, the Chairman briefly addressed the meeting, and then called upon Mr. Kirk, the treasurer. – Mr. Kirk said they had 250 children, and the number increased week by week. If they were under Government they would be entitled to about £150 grant. Not having that the money had to be found in some other way. They had that week asked the Education Department whether, if the committee erected a suitable building, the school would be put on a level with the other school in the village. To that communication no reply had yet been received. If an affirmative reply came they would soon begin to build. Let them, however, not be afraid of the cry that had gone forth that they would have to succumb (Laughter). Their private school could not be put down if they had efficient teaching. Mr. Brown had asked the vicar some months ago to have a larger number of managers appointed for the parochial schools, but he would not. He had absolute control there and could appoint or dismiss managers as he chose. – Votes of thanks were passed to Mr. Wildgoose, of Lea Mills, Mr. and Mrs. Brown, and the Misses Hurt and others.

Obviously the competition and rivalry between the two schools was taken advantage of – not only by parents, but also by the pupils themselves. There were several occasions when pupils would switch between schools to their advantage, especially when it helped them avoid a caning!

Taking advantage

> **Parochial School logbook: 30th January 1884**
>
> At 9.50 this morning I counted 62 children going to the Mount Tabor Chapel School. On calling the registers this morning I find that Thomas Austin who was admitted on Monday from the Mount Tabor Chapel School has returned, telling his companions that he only came here until the master had forgotten to cane him as he had been promised punishment by the Mount Tabor schoolmaster.

In the first part of 1884 the hard work the Vicar had put into improving the Parochial Schools was paying off. He was receiving some positive publicity, and church services were increasing in congregation.

Derby Mercury: Wed 30 January 1884

CRICH.

NATIONAL SCHOOL – The annual examination in religious knowledge has recently taken place, the examiner being the Rev. Egbert Hacking, Diocesan Inspector. The following is a copy of his report written on the school masters parchment; – "The school has greatly improved in general order and religious knowledge in the short time Mr. Sumner has had charge of it." About 100 scholars successfully passed the exam. Fritchley National School was also examined on the same day, the inspector being much pleased with his visit to the two public schools of the parish.

PAROCHIAL TEA. – One of the many successful gatherings in connection with the parish church took place on Monday evening in last week in the national schoolroom, the choir and bell ringers having a strong wish to hold an annual gathering of their friends. After tea a miscellaneous entertainment was given, the Rev. William Acraman, the vicar, presiding. Glees by the choir and songs by Mr. John Dawes, Mr. J. T. Lee, Miss M. Stocks and others, and a cornet solo and some good readings, were well received. A most pleasant evening was wound up by some games for the younger people, when the National Anthem heartily sung brought the proceedings to a close. The services at the fine old parish church continue to be well attended.

As well as the Parochial School doing well, the British School had its plans for a new school passed by the Education Department.

Interestingly the papers make reference to a private school in Crich Carr run by Miss Griffiths, and to the British Night School.

Derby Mercury: Wed 26 March 1884

CRICH

EDUCATIONAL AFFAIRS – Some progress has been made in dealing with the educational difficulties at Crich. The parochial schools are being enlarged, a branch school is being built at Crich Carr and the British School Committee have had the plans for a new set of buildings to be erected at Crich generally approved by the Education Department. It has also been decided that the private school conducted by Miss Griffiths at Crich Carr can be continued. Towards the close of last week Mr. Briggs assistant inspector, examined the scholars attending the British Night School, and also 12 day scholars who applied for labour certificates. All passed in reading, with the exception of one. The result of the examination in writing and arithmetic has not yet been reported. The average attendance at the British day school now exceeds 200.

Derby Mercury: Wed 23 April 1884

CRICH.

CRICH NATIONAL SCHOOL– One of the largest and most successful gatherings held in the parish for some time took place in the Crich Parochial School on Tuesday April 15th, the large and spacious room being filled with an enthusiastic audience. The object of the meeting was to commemorate the completion of an infant school enlargement at Crich and a new public school at Crich Carr, which (with the chief school at Crich and that at Fritchley) provides three National Schools for this large and scattered parish of 3,000 souls and saves the place from the incubus of a School Board. The proceedings commenced with a substantial tea at 5.30pm provided by Mr. J. Stocks, and presided over by those connected with the church and schools, and was followed by an entertainment at 6.30 o'clock some 300 to 400 persons being present and the room presenting a most elegant appearance. The large platform was elegantly decorated

New British School planned

with choice hot house plants and shrubs (and flowers for the scholars) through the kindness of Messrs. A Hurt of Alderwasley, William Walker of Lea Wood, Holloway and George Coupe of Crich, some of the managers at Crich Schools. The vicar, as chairman, announced that upwards of £600 had been raised and two valuable sites of land given for the schools worth more than £100, taking the total upward of £700, which was sufficient to meet the actual cost of building, while from £59 to £100 was needed for school material and working expenses. There was, therefore, great cause for thankfulness that so much had been done in a limited time. His remarks were well received and were followed by a most interesting distribution of prizes to those who had been successful in the Government examination, the examination on Holy Scripture and in drawing, while hearty praise was awarded to Mr. and Mrs. Sumner, the head teachers, and to the assistant mistresses for the success that attended their efforts and the progress made by the scholars. An able and appropriate address was given by Mr. J. G. Wilson, solicitor, of Alfreton, who as a school manager of many years experience heartily congratulated all present on the success that had attended the vicar's efforts and those of his friends, to avert a School Board and to promote good Church schools.

In May 1884 the British School bought a plot of land just off the Market Place on which to build their new school.

Derby Mercury: Wed 28 May 1884

District News

CRICH

THE BRITISH SCHOOLS – The British School Committee in Crich have purchased a site, half an acre in extent, situate near the Market Place, Crich, on which to erect new school buildings.

A new building was certainly needed. Mount Tabor Chapel was most unsuitable as a school, having only two adult toilets for over 200 children. The Medical Officer of Health visited the school and reported on the "nuisance arising from the closets." He also reported that it was so unhygienic that it might produce an epidemic.

Also at this time there was an attendance problem with all the schools in the Crich area. The Belper Schools Attendance Committee stated they would look into this.

Derby Mercury: Wed 4 June 1884

District News

CRICH

SCHOOL ATTENDANCE – It is stated that the Belper School Attendance Committee have decided to investigate all cases of non-attendance at school in the Crich district instead of deputing the work to a sub-school attendance committee. The attendance of children has been irregular and a good number of cases are down for investigation at the next meeting of the Belper committee.

THE BRITISH SCHOOL – We hear the medical officer of health for the district has recently visited this school, and reported that "there were only two filthy closets, one of which opened close to the schoolroom. They were not adapted for the purpose. The school was over-crowded, and the nuisance arising from the closets ought to be rectified, or with such a large number of people, and the heat of the summer, it was enough to produce an epidemic." The clerk was ordered to send a copy of the report to the trustees of the school.

Chapter 21
Stormy meetings; quarry problems

Reports of public meetings at Crich often showed them to be rowdy and uncontrolled! It wasn't just the issue of the new schools that caused ructions. The villagers had a reputation for awkwardness, especially, it seems, farmer and ratepayer Mr George Curzon. George Curzon was known to be a village "character". Some years earlier he attacked the village tax inspector, his daughter, Sarah, joining in the assault. Apparently George paid the inspector, Mr R. W. Smith (publican of Crich) the amount owing, then thought better of it, and demanded part of his money back. When this was refused the assaults took place. He was fined £5 13s 6d or one month's hard labour in Derby gaol. The fine was paid.

The reported rowdy meeting of April 1884 concerned ongoing problems with the Clay Cross Company who owned the quarries at Town End. Also covered were the rate to be set and road repairs near the Wesleyan chapel. During the meeting whistles were blown, impolite exchanges made and there were frequent interruptions. This made for a lively meeting.

Derby Mercury: Wed April 1884

PARISH AFFAIRS AT CRICH.
NOISY MEETING.
On Tuesday evening a vestry meeting was held at Crich for the purpose of nominating overseers of the poor, appointing a surveyor of highways, and passing the highway accounts. The proceedings commenced in the vestry of the church at five o'clock. Mr. Robert Boag was appointed chairman. – Mr. CURZON wanted to know at whose instance the meeting had been called for five o'clock, when it was well-known that the time was usually fixed for six o'clock. – The Assistant-Overseer said it was his own doing. It was thereupon resolved to adjourn to the parochial school room, the meeting to commence at six o'clock. At the time named the school-room was crowded, some three hundred parishioners being present. – The CHAIRMAN, in calling upon Mr. Dawes, the assistant

overseer, to read the highway accounts, observed that each gentleman in the meeting would be at liberty to speak in due course, but it would greatly facilitate the business if after having spoken once, he would sit down and not interrupt other speakers. – The parish accounts were then read, showing total receipts, £441. 6s. 5d. The expenditure had been £383. 13s. 1d. The balance against the surveyor was £57. 13s. 4d. – Mr. CURZON complained that nothing had been said about the expenses of coming to Alfreton in connection with the Crich-landslip (Interruption, and cries of "Give the man a fair hearing"). He did not like a thing dropped in that way ("Oh, oh"). It was nothing but right (A voice: "All right, George, I'll back you'll see that it'll be all right," and interruption). He thought the Clay Cross Company were going to huddle this matter up. Was this going to Alfreton to be smothered up in this kind of way? (Laughter, and a shout, "Why, you'd ha' done better if you'd stopped at whaom.") The speaker was going on to allude to the lawyers when there was a fresh outbreak of interruption. – Mr. KIRK hoped the meeting would allow Mr. Curzon to proceed. – Mr. CURZON said the Clay Cross Company want 100 yards through their parish, and only paid 10s. a year. The company ought to be ashamed of themselves for refusing to pay 13/- which was asked of them on account of the "slip." – The Assistant Overseer said that of the total amount of law expenses Mr. Jackson's

bill amounted to £27 9s. 4d., and the Clay Cross Company paid towards that sum £11 3s. 2d., reducing the bill to £16 16s. 2d. Mr. Bower's (the surveyor's) expenses for witnesses, &c, amounted to £12. 1s. The amount had been approved by the auditors. – Mr. CURZON: Let's have things fair and honest (Disorder). – Mr. BOWER (the surveyor) explained what had been done respecting the Clay Cross Company and further stated with regard to the case that he was advised by the first three lawyers he saw to sue the Clay Cross Company by indictment. If he had done that the expense would have been enormous, but by taking action in the County Court, they had kept the expenses down. He was very pleased that Crich was not "growling" like Bonsall, which had had to pay hundreds of pounds in law expenses. – Mr. KIRK, as a member of the committee, confirmed what Mr. Bower had stated. – Mr. CURZON again essayed to speak, but his utterances could not be distinctly heard because of the shouts and derisive laughter which his rising created. He was understood to say that there had been very great complaints about some of the parish work. A good deal of parish money had been spent. Addressing the surveyor he asked: Is not that so? (Great laughter, and considerable interruption). – Mr. BOWER: You see Mr. Curzon has unfortunately been on my track (laughter), for a long time. Well; I excuse him (Renewed laughter). I know it is part of his nature. About three weeks ago he thought he had a case, for he went to Mr. Wm. Yeomans, and asked if a certain road was indictable (Loud laughter). – Mr. CURZON (excitedly, and going close to the table at which the chairman was sitting): What? – Mr. BOWER: You asked him if it was indictable (Laughter). – Mr. CURZON: When? Mr. BOWER: Three weeks ago (More laughter). – A man in the meeting here called out to Mr. Curzon, "You know what I told you yesterday, George" (Re-newed laughter). – On the motion of Mr. DAY, seconded by Mr. KIRK, the accounts were passed. – Mr. LEE suggested that the parish labourers should have a higher rate of pay. – Mr. CURZON next wanted to know who had given Mr. Bower instructions to put a footpath near the Wesleyan Chapel in repair? Was it a lawful road? This was followed by great interruption, which lasted for two or three minutes, there being calls from all parts of the room. One parishioner was heard to say "I'll tell you what, George; there is no common sense or reason about you" (Much laughter). – Mr. BOWER: Hallo! are they at the old game again? (Interruption). – A man who was stated to be named Stocks shouted "There's no man in this parish ta'en in more ground than you, George" (Laughter). – During this disorder Mr. Curzon was excitedly addressing those near him, but it was very doubtful if his remarks were heard. – One individual in the meeting blew a shrill whistle, a proceeding which was several times repeated. – Mr. BOWER justified his action with regard to the footpath near the Wesleyan Chapel, by causing a letter from the residents in the locality to be read. – A PARISHIONER: George doesn't understand chapels (Disorder). Mr. Bower was about to speak when Mr. Curzon again interrupted. After some time the latter was heard to remark, referring to the former, "they said if the footpath was mended they would vote for him (the surveyor) again" (Great laughter). Subsequently Mr. Curzon produced a book, and, waving it aloft, amidst cries of "Sit down," he shouted, "We want an Act of Parliament to make laws, and not Samuel Bower." (Continued merriment and a voice: "Now then, read out your Parliamentary news.") The CHAIRMAN appealed for order, and after some time the business was proceeded with. – Mr. S. Bower was re-appointed surveyor. – Mr. CURZON asked what had become of the market toll? – There were, however, cries of "Sit thee down" and ultimately the speaker resumed his seat. – Messrs. R. Boag and Isaac Petts were nominated overseers. – Then followed a discussion as to the surveyor's salary. – The SURVEYOR explained that he had had much additional labour in connection with the "landslip," but he did not ask them to remunerate him for that. They could not do so; all they could do was to add to his salary. – After various opinions had been expressed, and after Mr. Curzon had several times risen to speak, the meeting increased the surveyor's salary by 6/-, making the amount (which includes the collecting of the rates) £37. – Mr. BOWER stated that a 6d. rate would cover the expenses of the year; thereupon a proposition was made that a 6d. rate be collected. There was a counter-motion for a 5d. rate but this was withdrawn, and the original proposition was agreed to. – Mr. Curzon did not remain altogether quiescent during these latter proceedings, for he often tried to gain a hearing, but he was generally induced to sit down by a gentleman near him, who more than once pulled him by the coat. The meeting concluded with the customary vote of thanks to the chairman.

Reference was made to the Clay Cross Company not paying up for landslip damage. They were often in the local papers for non-payment of any damages caused by their operations. The reports often contained harrowing reports of injuries caused to men in Crich quarry caused by falling stone, explosions and faulty equipment. At one time they cut what was already a poor wage. Sadly it seemed from the reports that they were not "good employers" or supportive of the community in which they operated.

Derby Mercury: 18th July 1883

RECENT LANDSLIP AT CRICH – Samuel Bower v the Clay Cross Company. The plaintiff is the surveyor of highways at Crich and claimed £13 for expenses incurred in guarding and repairing a road damaged by a recent landslip at Crich Stand. It was alleged that the defendants were responsible for the expense. – Mr. Jackson, solicitor, of Belper, appeared for the plaintiff, and the defendants were represented by Mr. Etherington-Smith, barrister of the Midland Circuit. – Mr. Jackson, in opening the case, said the action was bought to recover an amount which was expended by the plaintiff in repairing and lighting and watching a highway at Crich. The highway was near to an immense hill of limestone, which was a very interesting instance of volcanic action. It was originally formed in regular patches, which was forced upwards from the mass of sandstone, and now resembled an umbrella, or the upper part of an onion in shape. The Clay Cross Colliery Company quarried this limestone. A landslip occurred and a road, of which Mr. Bowers was surveyor, was removed twelve or thirteen yards down the hill, along with several houses. For some time the Company looked after the

Landslip

road and then, on 30th October, several months afterwards, they renounced all responsibility. Mr. Bower, then on seeing that the place was dangerous, took charge of the road and had it repaired. It was contended, however, that the defendants were responsible, owing to the fact that the slip was caused by their quarrying. – Plaintiff and other witnesses were called and Dr. Dunn of Crich explained the geological formation of the rock – Mr. Smith in defence, submitted that the slip was not caused by reason of the negligence of the defendants, but he contended that it was due to natural agencies. – A number of witnesses were called in support of this view, after which his Honour summed up. – After a long consultation the jury were unable to agree and they were discharged.

Courtesy Rosemary Hall

This photograph shows evidence of the 1882 landslip which demolished several cottages and pushed sideways the Crich to Holloway road. The central figure is believed to be George Curzon with wife and daughter.

Chapter 22
New schools

In August 1884 Crich Carr School was opened along with the new extension at Crich Parochial School.

Derby Mercury: Wed 20 August 1884

District News

CRICH

PARISH CHURCH – The anniversary sermons in aid of the large Sunday-school connected with this church were preached by the vicar to large congregations. The collection amounted to nearly £11.

CRICH CARR – The new national-school built through the exertions of the vicar and completing (with the new infant school in Crich) the necessary accommodation required by the Education Department to save the parish from a school board, was opened on Monday (August 18th). We understand that the event will be publicly commemorated at a later date.

Also at this time the foundation stone for the new British School was being laid. This was in spite of the fact that the new accommodation that had been provided at the Parochial School and at Crich Carr meant there was no shortage of space for all the children in the parish. Feelings were still running high and the Nonconformists were adamant they wanted their own school.

All this meant that instead of a single Board School for the village there were to be three schools – Crich Parochial, Crich Carr National and the British School. There was also Fritchley School. The church and influential ratepayers had won the day.

New Schools

Derby Mercury: Wed 17 September 1884

CRICH
THE SCHOOL DIFFICULTY.

The memorial stones of the new British School now in course of erection at Crich were formally laid on Tuesday. The accommodation at the parochial school some time ago was found to be insufficient and the Education Department required further provision to be made. With regard to the parochial school the requirements of the Education Department were completed with important additions being made to the building. The British School Committee, although there was apparently now no lack of accommodation at the parochial schools, persisted in carrying on their venture. A notable feature in connection with the difficulty was a munificent gift of money by the Duke of Devonshire for the enlargement of the parochial schools as required by the Education Department. This donation was made in order to avert the formation of a School board, which at that time seemed imminent. The new British School is being erected on a site half an acre in extent, situated near the Market-place. The land was purchased from Mr. Henry Young for £100. The new building will be of stone, having a total length of 92ft 6ins, and a height of 15ft to the collar beam. There will be four principal rooms – a main room in the centre room for mixed children, 51ft by 20ft; two classrooms at the one end 18ft by 15ft each; and an infant's room at the other 28ft 6in by 18ft. The total accommodation to be provided is for 213 children. The estimated cost of the whole scheme is £1000, including the cost of land. Mr. A. Cowlishaw, of Crich, is the architect, and his plans have been approved by the Education Department. Mr. Wharmby of Whatstandwell is the builder. The schools are expected to be completed by the 1st of November. It is understood that fully a fourth of the sum required for the erection of the school has been obtained. Shortly after three o'clock the scholars attending the British School walked in procession from the Mount Tabor Chapel to the site. They were headed by the banners belonging to the Baptist, Primitive Methodist, and Wesleyan Sunday-schools. The following gentlemen had been invited to lay the stones – Mr. Robert Wildgoose of Holloway, President of the British School Committee; Mr. T. C. Iveson, Crich; Mr. E. Kirk, treasurer to the fund; Mr. E. Greenhough, the secretary; Mr. R. Bryan, Crich Carr; Mr. R. Boag, Crich; Mr. F. Cowlishaw, Crich and Mr. T. Dawes, Crich. There was a large attendance, including Mr. W. B. Bembridge of Ripley; Mr. T. Tomlinson, of Belper; Mr. S. Bower and Mr. H. Boag. Mr. Wildgoose, who was to have laid the principal stone, was not present, and his place was taken by Mr. Bembridge, Mr. E. Kirk also laid a stone. The other stones were then laid. A collection was afterwards made on behalf of the building fund. A public tea meeting was afterwards held in Mount Tabor School, followed by a public meeting in the Baptist Chapel.

The commemoration of the opening of Crich Carr School and the new infant extension at Crich was held in October 1884. At the ceremony the vicar was proud that their schools were built and paid for whilst the British School had only its foundation stones laid. He accepted that the other school had more scholars but thought his school had the better education. In fact the British School was nearing completion.

Derby Mercury: Wed 8 October 1884

CRICH.

THE SCHOOL DIFFICULTY – On Tuesday evening a tea meeting and concert was held in the Parochial Schools, Crich, for the purpose of commemorating the opening of the Crich Infants' School and the new Crich Carr National School, by which the necessary public school accommodation is provided and the parish saved from the expense of a School Board. The Vicar (the Rev. Wm. Acraman) presided and supporting him were the Rev. H. M. Mosse, the Rev. J. Mulkerns (Wessington), Rev. J. C. Gregory (curate of Crich), Dr. Gaylor (Belper), and Mr. J. Saxton. In opening the proceedings, the Chairman said the meeting was held one week earlier than at first intended, as Lord Edward Cavendish, M.P. had kindly intimated in a letter that possibly he would be able to attend if they took that date, but he much regretted that Lord Edward had not found it possible to be with them. An interesting letter from Archdeacon Balston, of Bakewell, was read in which the writer said:-

Had it been possible for him to be present, he should have been glad to have borne his testimony to the good work the vicar had accomplished in bringing about the building of the church schools. He considered all were indebted to the vicar for the strong persevering energy with which, in the face of much difficulty and opposition, he had carried his point, and set an example to others worthy of their following.

– The Rev. H. M. Mosse expressed his sympathy with, and good wishes for, the success of the work they were engaged in. – The Chairman said they were commemorating the opening of the new school at Crich Carr, and of the new infant schoolroom adjoining that building, which they had already found be a great convenience. It was said that they had now in the parish more school accommodation than was necessary. He was heartily glad that this was the case, because it put a School Board further off (Applause). If they had not built at the time they would have had a School Board, for they must remember that it was their duty as citizens simply to do what the Government of

New Schools

the land told them to do. The authorities demanded a school at Fritchley, and it was built. In the course of time they said they must have a school at Crich Carr, and that had been built, and what was better still, they had paid for it (Cheers). The time to commemorate was when a place was bought built and paid for, not when the foundation stone was being laid (Hear, hear). There had been raised out of the £700 needed, some £620 at least, thus leaving them with a deficiency of about £80. Considering the greatness of the amount and estimating the sites at £150 they had raised £850 (Hear hear). It had been remarked that competition was good and of course no one present was a stranger to the fact that other schools had arisen in the parish. All he could add was that if they were rightly conducted he said nothing about them. But a school must be a school (Hear hear). They believed that in their schools they gave the best article (Hear hear). They were quite content with their number and with their progress.

They did not consider that the strength of a school by any means depended upon the number of scholars attending it, but the proficiency of those scholars – in the way they passed the Government examinations, and the way in which they learned to fulfil the duties of this life, and to prepare for the life which was to come. This was the whole basis of the national schools, which were the glory of England, and for which the clergy of the Church of England had worked hard in order that every family might have the advantage of its village school. The concert which took place afterwards included the performance of an original cantata, entitled "A Day in the Harvest Field" specially written by the vicar. The characters were admirably represented by school children. Mr. W. T. Sumner, the schoolmaster, conducted and Mr. Walter Glossop accompanied on the piano. The newly-formed brass band was also in attendance and played a selection of music. The concert was repeated on Wednesday evening.

Crich Carr School.

In December 1884 the British School opened. During the address at the opening there was a call for harmony between the church schools and the British School. Each had got what it wanted, and the fear of having a Board School was removed.

Derby Mercury: Wed 17 December 1884

OPENING OF THE CRICH BRITISH SCHOOL.

On Tuesday evening the new British School at Crich was formally opened. The building was designed by Mr. A. C. Cowlishaw, Crich and will accommodate 230 children. The contractor was Mr. Wharmby of Whatstandwell. The total cost has been about £1,100 nearly the whole of which has already been subscribed. The opening proceedings commenced with a free tea given to 268 children. Afterwards there was a public tea in the schoolroom, at which about 300 persons were present. Mr. R. Wildgoose, of Lea Mills, presided, and amongst those present were the Hon. F. Strutt, of Belper; Mr. W. B. Bembridge, Ripley; Mr. F. Percy Rawson, Sheffield; Mr. W. Randall, Crich and Derby; Mr. R. Bryan, Mr. E. Kirk, Mr. J. Iveson, Mr. R. Boag, Mr. S. Bower, Mr. J. Burton, Mr. H. Sibley, Mr. J. Hopkinson, Mr. F. Cowlishaw, Mr. T. Gill, &c. Letters of apology for non-attendance were read from Mr. T. Roe. M.P.; Alderman H. H. Bemrose, Derby and Alderman Higginbottom, Chesterfield.

The CHAIRMAN said he hoped that any strong feelings which had existed during the last two or three years might now subside, and that there might be harmonious working on the part of the school authorities in the parish.

The Hon. F. STRUTT who was cordially received, said he rather hesitated to take any part in dissensions concerning school matters in Crich. But now that this school was built all dissensions would be at an end, and therefore it gave him great pleasure not only as a magistrate but as a member of the Belper School Attendance Committee to assist in a small way in this work, which had been so well carried out by such an influential committee in this parish. He did not wish to allude to the past but desired that bygones should be bygones, for everybody should now be satisfied, for each party had a school to which they could send their children (Applause). There was not, now the Conscience Clause was in force, a great deal of difference between a National School and a British School but there was this important difference, that in the former religious instruction was given according to the tenets of the Church of England, but in the British school there was no dogmatic teaching of any kind (Applause), he was perfectly sure that no one in Crich wished that their children should receive no religious instruction at all and so far as this school was concerned the children would be taught as much religion as at a national school (applause), though people would doubtless say that it was a Godless school. Continuing, the speaker congratulated the promoters upon the excellent school buildings and upon having prevented the necessity for a School Board. Alluding to the private adventure schools which he had heard were being started in the district, he pointed out the importance of poor people especially sending their children to an efficient public elementary school, in order that they might obtain the certificates of exemption to allow them to work full time or half-time, which could only be obtained from a school under Government inspection. If a child went regularly to school from an early age there ought not, and would not, be any difficulty in its passing the standard by the time it reached the age at which by the Factory Act it could be employed. We were just now undergoing in England a kind of revolution, and all the householders in the country had had given to them the franchise (applause) – which they had never possessed before. It seemed to him especially important in view of this fact that the rising generation should be educated so that they would make the best use of the rights and privileges granted to them as citizens. It was equally important that this should be done whether they were Liberals or Conservatives;

Nonconformists or Churchmen. It might seem a little thing to make a cross upon a paper and put it into the ballot box but these crosses elected the Government of the country. Each individual was a power in the State, and it was of the utmost importance that he should be educated to enable him to exercise that power rightly, and in addition, it might fairly be said that education was a means of making life brighter and happier. The speaker dwelt upon the advantages which were now offered for acquiring knowledge, and said that if scholarships were only given from the elementary schools to our grammar schools, clever and persevering boys could obtain exhibitions to the universities, and the poor could then obtain as good an education as the sons of noblemen. We had now at the head of the Education Department a gentleman who began life in as low a position as any boy in this parish to-day. The present Vice-President of the Council, Mr. Mundella (loud applause), who represented a great neighbouring constituency, began life by sweeping out an office in Leicester, and by self-education and his industry, coupled with his great ability, he succeeded not only in business but, taking up politics comparatively later in life, had obtained one of the most honourable offices under Her Majesty's Government (Applause). Mr. Mundella had always taken a great interest in the working classes and he (the Hon. F. Strutt) could remember once, twenty or thirty years ago, on Mr.

Mundella finding on visiting the factories in Germany that the workmen could read and write well, and that at his factory in England but few could do so, how anxious he was that the poorest classes in England should be better educated than they then were. It was to him a cause for congratulation that the educational affairs of this county were in the hands of one who had the education of the people so much at heart and who so thoroughly understood the work he had been called upon to perform, as Mr. Mundella did (Applause). He must again congratulate them upon the completion of the school, which he had great pleasure in declaring formally opened (Loud applause).

Mr. F. Percy Rawson, Mr. E. Kirk, Mr. Bembridge and others also addressed the meeting, which closed with the usual votes of thanks.

The new British School, now Crich Junior School or the "Bottom School".

Crich Carr School

Then as now, Crich Carr had a reputation for its musical talent.

Derby Mercury: Wed 7 January 1885

WHATSTANDWELL. SCHOOL GATHERING.– On Tuesday evening 30th ult the first annual gathering of managers, children, and friends took place at the Crich Carr National School. After a good tea had been partaken of by the children and friends, which had been catered for by Mrs Peacock, and ably presided over by Mrs Hawkes, Misses Acraman, and Shaw &c., the chair was taken by the Rev. Wm. Acraman, Vicar of Crich. The room was crowded, and the programme, which was well arranged, was rendered with the highest credit to all who took part in it; especially the children, who had been so well trained in their songs and recitations by Mrs. Hawkes, who accompanied them on the piano. Mr Glossop's Septet Band also performed some excellent music. The entertainment was brought to a close with the vote of thanks to the chairman and performers, proposed by Mr W. T. Sumner, of Crich, and seconded by Mr G. Shaw. Mr Nathaniel I. Hawkes proposed that thanks be given to the Rev. J. S. Gregory for the great interest he had taken in that night's proceedings, and for the very valuable help that he had rendered. Mr W. T. Sumner seconded the resolution. The school, which is a new one, and built at the order of the Education Department, was only opened in August last. Considering the time the school has been open, and the peculiar circumstances under which the teachers of the National Schools labour in the parish, the highest praise is due to Mrs Hawkes for the very great pains she must have bestowed on her pupils to bring them up to their present state of proficiency. At the close of the meeting Mr N. I. Hawkes spoke of the great need of a harmonium for this school, especially as the children are so very much interested in the musical part of their education. In response to these remarks, a lady handed 6s. to Mrs Hawkes as a first contribution towards supplying this want. The piano was kindly lent by Mrs J. Merchant.

In May 1885 it was all change at both the British School and the Parochial School.

Mr Sumner left for a new school in Chester. It would appear that he did remarkably well during a most difficult and challenging period. He was replaced by Mr C. J. B. Ellis.

Derby Mercury: Wed 6 May 1885

CRICH.

DISTRIBUTION OF PRIZES AT THE PAROCHIAL SCHOOLS – The second annual prize distribution took place on Tuesday evening, when there was a large attendance. The Rev. W. Acraman vicar, presided, and was supported by Mr H.H. Bemrose of Derby (who delivered an address on religious education), and Mr. Binns of Manchester. The Vicar congratulated the parish upon now having ample school accommodation, and being safe from a School Board. A feature of the entertainment was a floral cantata, "Spring Flowers" written by the vicar.

APPOINTMENT – Mr and Mrs Sumner are leaving Crich where they have laboured so long and successfully amongst the little ones. Mr. Sumner has been appointed head master of Barrow Schools, Chester.

In May 1885 there was some confusion in the British School logbook. Mr Dyson was a respected head for many years. The entry for 12th May must refer to a previous master.

British School logbook 11 May 1885

H. Dyson commenced duties as head.

12 May 1885

Her Majesty's Inspector's Report - The master who is not competent to conduct a school like this has sent in his resignation and the managers are prepared at once to appoint a certified competent master.

Chapter 23
More scandal for the vicar

In the October of 1885 yet more scandal was to surround the vicar. He was accused of a serious offence by his domestic servants. The Belper magistrates heard the case "in camera" so that the details were not fully covered.

Because the case was a serious one bail was not granted, and he had to await his trial at Leicester imprisoned in Derby gaol. As he was to find out, this was not to be his only stay in that place. The vicar was acquitted of the offence.

Derby Mercury: Wed 21 October 1885

DERBY BOROUGH POLICE NEWS

SERIOUS CHARGE AGAINST THE VICAR OF CRICH.

On Wednesday Mr. E.G. Jackson, solicitor of Belper took out a warrant against the Rev. W. Acraman vicar of Crich, charging him with a serious offence. The warrant was executed by Police-sergeant O'Neil when the accused was walking along Bridge Street, Belper. Mr. Acraman was brought up on Thursday before Mr. G.H. Strutt, charged with an unnatural offence, which he is alleged to have committed in his house a short time ago. – Mr. Jackson appeared for the prosecution, and Mr. Walker for the defence. – The accusation appears to have arisen through information given by Mr. Acraman's domestic servants. A statement was afterwards made by the boy. – Prisoner was remanded to Derby gaol until the Petty Session the 22nd inst. Mr. Walker applied for bail, but the application was opposed by Mr. Jackson, and refused. – Mr. Acraman, who was ordained deacon in 1865 and priest in 1866, by the Bishop of Peterborough, has been vicar of Crich since 1875.

The Belper police authorities have received a letter from the Public Prosecutor stating that he will take up the case against the Rev. W. Acraman.

On Sunday, at the request of the Bishop of Southwell, the Rev. Canon Wade, of Nottingham, preached at the Crich Parish Church both morning and afternoon. The evening service was dispensed with. The congregations were large.

In the *Derby Mercury* there were several references to the sex-scandal case.

Derby Mercury: Wed 4 November 1885

𝕯𝖊𝖗𝖇𝖞𝖘𝖍𝖎𝖗𝖊 𝕿𝖔𝖕𝖎𝖈𝖘

Derbyshire cases tried at the Autumn Assizes at Leicester before Mr. Justice DENMAN were more than usually numerous, forty-two persons being sent there to be dealt with in connection with sixteen charges. The case which no doubt excited the most attention was the charge against the Vicar of Crich. Of its merits the public can say nothing, as it was very properly investigated by the magistrates *in camera*, but notwithstanding the opinion of the judge that there was evidence upon which there must be a trial unless the principal witness was shown to be unworthy of belief, the case broke down before the Grand Jury and Mr. ACRAMAN was discharged. It is right to say that the rev. gentleman warmly declares his entire innocence, and asserts that the evidence was a simple concoction from beginning to end.

DERBYSHIRE ASSIZES.

Mr. Justice Denman, in opening the assizes at Leicester on Friday. As to the very serious charge against the Vicar of Crich, there was evidence upon which there must necessarily be a trial, and they could not take upon themselves to throw out the bill unless the principal witness was shown to be unworthy of belief.

[Before Mr. Justice DENMAN.]

THE CRICH CASE. – The Grand Jury threw out the bill against the Rev. W. Acraman, vicar of Crich, and he was discharged.

THE CHARGE AGAINST THE VICAR OF CRICH

There were very large congregations at Crich Church on Sunday to welcome the vicar on his return and he received quite an ovation from the Sunday School. We are requested to say that the report that the charge against Mr. Acraman arose out of statements made by a member of his household is incorrect; and to supplement what has already appeared in our columns with regard to the case by saying that immediately on hearing that the charge was laid against him, he went to Belper and gave himself up.

Chapter 24
Village life continues

After the scandal of 1885 things settled down somewhat. The newspapers covered the happenings of village life – reporting the serious and the mundane.

Derby Mercury: Wed 6 January 1886

CRICH

THE NATIONAL SCHOOLS – The three National Schools which furnish sufficient accommodation for the wants of this large parish, of which the vicar is chairman, and has worked hard to promote their welfare, have been recently visited by the Diocesan Inspector, the Rev. Wm. Brooke. B.A., and we append beneath the satisfactory report that he gives:– Crich Parochial School: The character of the religious education in this school is much better than it formerly was, but still higher standard should be aimed at, and this will no doubt be done by the present master, who evidently takes great pains. A fair proportion answered on both subjects, but did not show very great intelligence. The repetition needs a little care to ensure accuracy. The infant's class is in good hands. Fritchley National School: Religious instruction is carefully given in this school; all the children had a fair knowledge of their work, and some, especially among the elders, showed very fair intelligence. The repetition was accurately and well said, and a good tone is apparent throughout the school. The infants' division is satisfactory, and in another year's time will, with the rest of the school, undoubtedly make great progress, judging from the result of Mr. and Mrs. Cousin's work already visible. Crich Carr National School: Good progress has been made with the religious instruction of this school, and great pains taken with satisfactory results. The children are intelligent and in good order, and two-thirds answered well; the repetition was exceedingly well said. A few Scripture prints for the infants will be of great value.

Derby Mercury: Wed 5 May 1886

CRICH

BAPTIST BAZAAR – Mr. J. A. Jacoby M.P. opened a bazaar in the British School, Crich, on Easter Monday in aid of the Baptist Chapel at that place. The stalls were well supplied with a variety of goods, including electro-plated ware from Mr Mark Wallis, Sheffield, and general cutlery from Rawson Brothers, Sheffield. Mr W. Walker's string band gave their services. Among those taking part in the opening ceremony were the Rev. W. H. Tetley, Derby; Mr W.B. Bembridge, Ripley; Mr W. Abel and Mr. T. H. Bennett, Derby. About £200 was the sum required for clearing off a debt, and towards this the greater portion was realised.

Derby Mercury: Wed 2 June 1886

CRICH

PAROCHIAL SCHOOL – On Tuesday night the annual entertainment and distribution of prizes in connection with the Crich Parochial School were held under most favourable auspices. The children attending this school are examined yearly in Scriptural knowledge, the successful competitors are awarded prizes obtained by the proceeds of what is known as Simms's charity. The school is in a highly satisfactory state, under the mastership of Mr. C. J. B. Ellis – After several musical selections the vicar (the Rev. W. Acraman), who presided, called upon Mr. J. G. Wilson of Alfreton, to distribute the prizes. – Mr. Wilson in course of an interesting address, said there were many people who preferred the Board-school system to voluntary schools. He was pleased, however, that a School Board had been found to be unnecessary in Crich, and he had no doubt that the ratepayers were glad of the fact. Rewards were then distributed to about 50 scholars. – A successful vocal and instrumental entertainment was then given, the performers including Miss Holmes, Miss M. Stocks, Mr. Walker (Ripley), and Master Mountney. Mr. Granville Norton, of Derby, presided at the piano. After this there was presented a new and original cantata entitled "Lucy Hamilton" from the pen of the vicar. Several of the hymns in the cantata have also been composed by the rev. gentleman. The characters were sustained as follows: Mr. Hamilton, Mr. Joseph Smith; his daughter, Miss Minnie Mee; nurse, Miss M. Wetton; waitresses, Misses M. H. Ellis and A. Shipley; uncle, Mr. Ellis; merchants, Messrs. Ellis, Norton, Cossens, and Smith. There was a good attendance.

Derby Mercury: Wed 23 June 1886

CRICH

WHITSUNTIDE FESTIVITIES – On Whitsun Monday the members of the Black Swan Friendly Society attended divine service at the parish church at noon. The sermon was preached by the curate, the Rev. T. F. Schmid. In the evening a number of friends met at the Church School by invitation to congratulate Miss Saxton, of Crich, on her attaining her majority. On Wednesday the members of the Women's Sick and Burial Society attended church, when the vicar preached. On Thursday the children and adult members, with the teachers of the Crich Sunday Schools, numbering 200, had their annual demonstration.

PARISH CHURCH – Sunday last being the anniversary of the accession of Queen Victoria to the throne, a special service was held in the church in the evening, suitable hymns and special psalms being sung. There was a large attendance. The vicar was the preacher. The organist, Mr. Ellis, played "God Save the Queen" at the commencement of the service and the "Hallelujah Chorus" at the conclusion.

Bits and bobs of village life

Derby Mercury: Wed 11 August 1886

CRICH

MAGISTERIAL ORDER – An order has been made that all dogs must be kept under control for a period of two months in the parishes of Heage and Crich from August 5th. This is in consequence of a dog supposed to be mad having been found at Bull Bridge.

Derby Mercury: Wed 17 November 1886

CRICH

PAROCHIAL SCHOOL – On Tuesday an entertainment was given in the above named building in aid of the funds. A general concert formed the first part, in which there was some good vocal and instrumental music, and the second part consisted of a cantata, specially written and composed for harvest gatherings and schools by the vicar, the Rev. W. Acraman and which was well received by a large audience, assembled not only from Crich but from the adjacent parishes of Wingfield, Heage, Ripley &c. The cantata opens with the "Star song", beautifully sung by Miss Mary Stocks, one of the Sunday School teachers, and leads up to another beautiful melody welcoming morn, which was very tastefully rendered by Miss Holmes, one of the assistant mistresses, whilst the scholars joined her in a jubilant reapers chorus. There is a charming song for little girls; a pleasing melody about the four seasons for infants; a most taking schoolboy's song, very well rendered by Arthur Shaw (of St Peter's National School, Belper) and William Wright and Caleb Martin (of the Crich Carr and Crich National Schools): appropriate words descriptive of school life, introducing the song to the audience, which was further carried out later in the cantata by recitations expressive of the blessings of religious education, extremely well given by Miss Mary Haynes and Miss Maggie Ellis. A trio ("The Bells") suggests evening, and this, with a full chorus, ("Hail Welcome Night"), brings all to a close. The platform was suitably ornamented with sheaves of corn, and Messrs. William Walker (violin), Enoch Shore (viola), Blackham (violincello), and Mr Grenville Norton, of Derby (piano), rendered very material assistance. The following programme gives the general concert that preceded the cantata, an asterisk marking the encores:– School song, "Harvest," the scholars; overture for violin and piano, "Le chant du pont" Messrs. William Walker and Granville Norton; *song, "The Steam Arm," Mr John Wildgoose; *cornet solo, Mr Matthew Platts, with piano forte accompaniment, Mr C. B. Ellis; duet for violin and viola, Messrs William Walker and Enoch Shore; song, "Moonlight and Starlight," Mr Amos Shaw; *song, "Some Day," Mr William Walker; song, "Wouldn't you like to know," Miss Mary Stocks; cornet solo, "The lost chord," Mr M. Platts; *new patriotic song, "The Primrose Knight" (Rev Wm. Acraman) Master Arthur Shaw.

> *The encored song called "The Steam Arm" was very popular at this time. It concerns a soldier who lost an arm at the Battle of Waterloo and had a scolding wife. He had made and fixed a steam arm which proceeds to run amok in spite of the soldier.*

The Whitsun parades, marches and "demonstrations" were an important part of village celebrations that continued for over 100 years.

Courtesy Beryl Calladine

Whitsun march down the Common.

Courtesy Beryl Calladine

Whitsun march down Bowns Hill.

Chapter 25
Drama of the frantic cow

Then, as now, amusing newspaper articles appeared about animals. This item about a cow getting loose on its way to Mr Higton, a Crich butcher, obviously offered a bit of light relief from the rest of the more serious articles. You cannot help but feel sorry for the cow.

Derby Mercury: Wed 9 February 1887
A "FRANTIC COW" – A few days since a cow was bought in Derby by Mr Higton, butcher, Crich. The animal was very quiet, and had to be removed to Ambergate Station by rail. On arrival there she seemed distracted with the noise, and, when once loosed from the barriers that prevented her escape, she took across country and gave her owner an inconvenient chase. She got in a wood near Crich and, darkness coming on, had to be left for the night. Next morning the cow had disappeared from the wood, having crossed the canal, railway, road and river Derwent, and entered the Ambergate Wire Works, and taken refuge in the fitting shop. By great exertion and diligence the cow was removed, but again made off and got to the farm of Mr. Smith at Alderwasley. There she seemed to settle down, and after allowing her time to reflect she was killed. Every effort had been made to get the animal to Mr. Higton's but without avail. The way in which she cleared walls and fences was marvellous. It is supposed the noise on the railway drove the animal frantic.

River, Road, Rail, & Canal, WHATSTANDWELL, Nr. Matlock

An early sketch of Ambergate Wireworks c1850.

Richard Johnson and Nephew's Wireworks at Ambergate, where the frantic cow took refuge, was one of the largest employers of Crich men at the time. The Wireworks, opened in 1876 by Richard Johnson, was run by his nephew John Thewlis Johnson. Mr Thewlis, as he was known, was a great benefactor to the whole area. He had Ambergate church and school built, and supported both the Crich Reading Rooms and the Parochial School.

John Thewlis Johnson.

It is interesting to note that in 1877 they obtained the licence from America to produce barbed wire. The machine they installed to make the wire was known as "Billy-up-tup" by the workforce, so-called because of the noise it made.

Chapter 26
Queen Victoria's Golden Jubilee 1887

The celebrations for Queen Victoria's Golden Jubilee were the main event in 1887. The beacon at Crich Stand was lit. The High Sheriff, Frederic Arkwright of Willersley, Cromford, was in charge of organising the beacon lighting.

Derby Mercury: Wed 18 May 1887

TO THE EDITOR OF THE DERBY MERCURY.

Sir – I have been requested by the County Jubilee Committee in Worcestershire to give publicity to the fact that in that county a scheme has been organised for lighting beacon fires on the hill tops on the night of the 21st June and I am requested to promote a similar scheme in this county.

I have very willingly promised to do all I can to get the idea carried out throughout the county, and shall be glad to have the assistance and co-operation of all those who approve of it.

The difficulties seem to be in making the proposal known in every part of the county, and in arranging for the fires to be lighted in all the most conspicuous places. The former I hope to get over by asking you to insert this letter in your widely-read journal; the latter by asking that one person in every country parish where any high point is situated will kindly communicate with me so that an organised "Plan of Campaign" may be universally adopted.

In those parishes (and they are not a few) where a Jubilee Committee had been formed the secretary would, I hope, take this preliminary step; in other places some loyal inhabitant might take the initiative in the matter upon himself.

The idea, of course, is to light fires simultaneously on all the highest points so that they may be visible one from another, and so form one continuous succession throughout all those parts of the country where the scheme is adopted.

In this neighbourhood for instance, we should illuminate Crich, Riber, Masson, Barrell Edge &c. and the succession would be carried on northwards by Darley Flash, Longstone Edge &c. to Axe Edge and Kinder Scout; southwards by Alport, the Chevin, &c. to the boundaries of Stafford and Leicestershire, and to the east and west in a similar way.

The fires need cost nothing, as a barrel of tar would probably be readily given for the purpose, and willing hands would easily be found to light it.

If (as I hope) the scheme is taken up, I shall be very pleased to receive communications from anyone whose eyes this letter may meet, and who is willing to co-operate in this matter.

I am, yours faithfully,

FREDERIC C. ARKWRIGHT, Willersley, Cromford. High Sheriff.

Advice was given on how to build and light the bonfires.

Derby Mercury: Wed 8 June 1887

Derbyshire Topics

JUBILEE BONFIRES
TO THE EDITOR OF THE DERBY MERCURY

Sir – As you kindly inserted a letter from me on the above subject a few weeks ago, I venture to ask you to publish this, as I see by a letter from a correspondent in your issue of last week that some people still think that Derbyshire is doing nothing in the matter. My previous letter has elicited so many private replies from various parts of the county promising cooperation in carrying out the scheme, that I am in hopes the Derbyshire hills will give a good account of themselves on the night of the 2lst. I append a list of the heights where I have received intimation that fires are to be lighted, and I have no doubt arrangements have been made for many others about which I know nothing. My object in writing again is to give further publicity to the scheme, and if possible to stimulate the laggard places to lose no time in making arrangements for carrying out the idea on any high point in their own neighbourhood. To prevent misunderstanding and to ensure uniformity and simultaneousness let me add that 10 o'clock (railway time) on the night of the 21st is the time appointed and generally agreed upon for lighting the fires, and that in many cases a flight of rockets will be sent up at 10 punctually, to be followed at 10.10, 10.20 and 10.30 by other successive flights. I have had many queries as to the best way of building and lighting a fire, but I am not attempting to lay down any particular law in this matter. Let every fire be built with such material and of such a size that circumstances of the locality suggest, only let there be plenty of space for oxygen (air) to get in to create a draft and to mix with the other gases so as to cause a maximum of flame with a minimum of smoke; given a good stout pole, well let into the ground, to form a nucleus, plenty of dry faggots, furze, old tar and petroleum casks, with a few gallons in each, some soft bright coal, with shavings stuffed in to fill up crevices (but so as to leave plenty of air holes), light at the top, and, given a fine night, success is assured. For these who want more accurate information as to building the pile, let me commend the letter from Canon Glover, which appeared in the *Times* of June 3rd. – I am, yours faithfully,

FREDERIC C. ARKWRIGHT, Sheriff.

Derby Mercury: Wed 29 June 1887
CRICH

On Tuesday the scholars of the Crich, Fritchley and Crich Carr schools marched to church where a service was conducted by the Rev. W. Acraman. The scholars subsequently marched to the Market-place, where a Jubilee hymn was sung. At the Parochial School over 500 persons sat down to an excellent tea, afterwards adjourning to the vicarage grounds where the remainder of the day was enjoyably spent.

The village built a stone circle containing a stone inscribed *VR 1887* on common ground at the top of Sandy Lane. This area was for common use of the village, as decreed by the 1786 Enclosures Commissioners. Trees were planted in the circle to celebrate Victoria's long reign. This area became known as the *Jubilee*. A second circle was built to celebrate Queen Victoria's Diamond Jubilee in 1897.

The 1887 circle.

Chapter 27
Happiness and tragedy for the vicar

In 1888 the Revd Acraman married Esther Taylor, the daughter of the curate of Twyford, Leicestershire. He was fifty and she only twenty. The marriage took place in Derby on the 8th February 1888 and was conducted by the Revd William Jellicorse Ledward, vicar of Pentrich.

They had one daughter, Laura Ada Essie Acraman, known as Essie, born on 17th January 1889. Tragically his wife, Esther, died a few days later.

The vicar had a marked preference for younger women, as subsequent events would prove.

Courtesy Beryl Calladine

Crich Church and Crich Stand.

Chapter 28
Village news, shows and fairs

Between 1889 and 1892 the local newspapers continued to report what they considered to be of interest to their local readers. The heady excitement of the annual celery show, lively parish meetings, school reports, the start-up of Crich Brass Band and new Reading Rooms were some of the events covered. Mr A. W. Moody replaced Mr C. J. B. Ellis as head at the Parochial School.

Derby Mercury: Wed 27 November 1889

CRICH
FRITCHLEY NATIONAL SCHOOL – The annual examination of this school took place October last. The following is a brief summary of the report – "Mixed School: The school is in good order, and has passed a creditable examination; reading, writing, spelling and composition are good and arithmetic fairly good; mental arithmetic and the style of the work generally are good; recitation and grammar have been carefully prepared; and the boys answered well in geography; singing by note is good. Infant class: The infants show good results in reading and writing, and careful instruction has been given in object lessons and occupations; needlework is good, and discipline, marching and musical drill are all satisfactory; this is a good infants class." The percentage of passes is 92.4 which is the highest in the town of Crich. The scripture examination for the Sims Charity was equally satisfactory, and reflects great credit on the master (Mr Cousins) and assistants. The children passed at the rate of 99 percent.

Derby Mercury: Wed 4 December 1889

CRICH
CONCERT – Miss Dawes having at considerable trouble collected a variety of talent to give a concert on behalf of the funds of the new Reading-room, there was a large attendance at the British School on the occasion of the performance which took place on Wednesday night. The vocalists were Miss Jacques (soprano), Mrs Welsh (contralto), Mr Robinson (tenor), Mr Dawes (baritone), and Mr Sanderson (humorous). Miss Dawes and Master Moreton were the solo violinist performers. Mr J. Sanderson pianist, and Mr E Swift of Long Eaton, accompanied. Nearly £7 was realised on behalf of the Reading-room, which was opened a few weeks since. Several encores were given. Mr Sanderson being recalled twice, whilst Mrs Welsh, Mr Robinson, Master Moreton and Miss Jacques had to also respond to cordial encores. It is probable there has never been such a capital concert in Crich previously.

Derby Mercury: Wed 2 April 1890

CRICH

The annual vestry meeting was held in the National School, Crich, on Tuesday night, when the proceedings were very animated. Mr Robert Boag presided, and there was a large attendance. Directly after the meeting commenced Mr Young entered the room, and was told by Mr Curzon to go about his business or he would put him out. – Mr Young: Shut up. – Mr Curzon: You must go; chuck him out (Laughter). – Mr Young: Set somebody else on that George; you can't do it. – At the request of the chairman Mr Young withdrew, remarking that if Mr Curzon had been a woman he would have taken a parting kiss (Loud laughter). – From the accounts it appeared there was a balance in the hands of the surveyor amounting to £84 16s 1d. – Mr R Boag and Mr Joseph Radford were voted overseers. – A discussion took place about the fixing of public lamps, and the meeting became very excited. Mr Curzon constantly interrupted, and beat the floor with a stick. – It was decided to have a rate for the parish highways of 4d in the £ against 7d last year, as 4½ miles of main road would be taken over by County Council. – Mr Samuel Bower was re-elected surveyor at a salary of £25.

Derby Mercury: Wed 25 June 1890

CRICH

DERBY AND DISTRICT TEACHERS' ASSOCIATION On Saturday last the members of this association visited Crich at the invitation of the president, Mr. Dyson, of the British School. For a short time on arrival they considered some points in the Education Code and passed resolutions – (a) disapproving of the distinction drawn between trained and untrained teachers; (b) protesting against drawing being made a compulsory subject; and (c) claiming the teacher's certificate should entitle the holder to obtain payments in all compulsory subjects. An appeal was made by Mr Hesketh on behalf of the orphans awaiting election to allowances on Saturday next. Tea was then partaken of, after which a vote of thanks was accorded to Mr and Mrs Dyson for the excellent provision made for the comfort of the visitors. A start was then made for the noted limestone quarry, where arrangements had been made with the manager to have some shots fired, which interested the party considerably. An ascent was next made to the famous Crich Stand to view the extensive scenery. The return journey was made by the village of Crich to Ambergate station for Derby where the party arrived about ten o'clock having spent a very pleasant time.

News, shows and fairs

Derby Mercury: Wed 8 October 1890

CRICH

CELERY SHOW – A celery club having been established at the Black Swan Hotel, the first annual exhibition took place on the 27th September, when the prizes were awarded as follows: 1. S Amat 8½ lb, 2. E Leafe 8 lb, 3. B.J. Bullington 6lb, 4. J. Lee 5½ lb, 5. C. Stocks, 6. A Dawes, 7. L. Wragg, 8. G. Lynam, 9. H. Cheetham, 10. H. Brumwell; the best plate of kidney beans, J. Kneebone, collection of vegetables, 1. A Dawes, 2. C. Stocks

Derby Mercury: Wed 15 October 1890

CRICH CATTLE FAIR

This fair was held on Saturday, when there was a large attendance of buyers, and a fair amount of business transacted. The supply of cattle sheep and pigs was unusually large, and trade was brisk. Horned stock of the better class was not numerous. Best milch beasts fetched £21 to £28, and newly calved cows went up to £25, barren beasts made £14 to £16, stirks £10 to £12, heifers £18 to £20, bulls £8 to £10; ewes 45s to 50s, sheaves 40s to 45s, and tup lambs 40s to 50s. Rams made £7 to £8 for very good animals. There were not many calves on offer but they made 30s to 50s. Pigs sold well, small ones realising 16s to 18s, and large 30s to 50s. Only a few horses were shown, and none of them were of the best kind. The day was beautifully fine, and in the afternoon the village was visited by hundreds of people. The pleasure fair was held in the latter part of the day.

Courtesy Rosemary Bower

The cattle market was held between the Cross and the Church.

Crich Fair was the second week in October, behind the Jovial Dutchman.

Derby Mercury: Wed 25 March 1891

CRICH

SOIREE – The first annual soiree in connection with Crich United Brass Band was held in the British Schoolroom on Friday evening. The committee have adopted this course in the hopes of augmenting their funds. The attendance was only fair, and it is to be regretted that the committee's efforts did not meet with more support.

Derby Mercury: Wed 19 November 1891

OBSTRUCTING THE LIGHT TO A CHAPEL IN CRICH – The Rev. J. Shepherd of Sheffield, formerly of the Ripley Primitive Methodist Circuit, and a number of others, as trustees of the Primitive Methodist Chapel at Crich sued John Wildgoose, landlord of the Rising Sun Inn, Crich, for £50 damages sustained through his having obstructed the free access of light to the chapel through the erection of a building close by. Mr Kershaw, solicitor, Ripley, appeared for the plaintiffs, and the defendant was represented by Mr James Potter of Matlock. – His honour held that in regard of the east window of the chapel the light had been appreciably obscured, after it had been enjoyed without interruption since 1853. But as no evidence had been given to show the amount of damage done to the property, he was obliged to assess it at only a nominal sum. He therefore gave a verdict for the plaintiffs for 40s, with costs.

News, shows and fairs

Crich Brass Band has seen many changes since its formation in the 1880s.
However, it is still very active and can be found at village events to this day.
The photograph shows the band in the early 1930s, leading a procession through
the village to Town End.

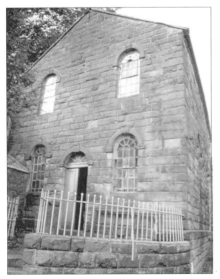

Primitive Methodist Chapel, on Sun
Lane, Crich.

128

It was in April 1892 that the death was announced of the highly respected Dr Dunn, of Crich, aged fifty-five. Florence Nightingale sent her condolences.

Derby Mercury: Wed 27 April 1892

CRICH

DEATH OF DR DUNN – A large circle of friends in Derbyshire will lament the death of Dr C. B. N. Dunn who for upwards of 30 years has practised at Crich. The deceased gentleman has been ailing for several months, but last week his condition considerably improved. On Saturday, however, unfavourable symptoms supervened, and death took place on Monday. The late Dr Dunn was born in West Riding of Yorkshire and was apprenticed to the late Dr Charles Trotter of Holmfirth, until the latter's death, after which he finished his apprenticeship with the late Dr Dunn of Belper. He studied at St Bartholomew's Hospital, receiving his diploma in 1860. The deceased was medical officer and public vaccinator for the parish of Crich, but a letter resigning this position was read from him at the Belper Board of Guardians last Saturday. He was the first chairman of the Bull Bridge, Crich, and Ambergate Gas Company, which position he filled up to the time of his death. He took a keen interest in antiquarian matters. The funeral took place on Thursday in the parish churchyard at Crich. The deceased was 55 years of age. Many beautiful wreaths and floral designs were placed on the coffin from friends including a cross sent by Miss Florence Nightingale, who was a former resident of the district, having been born at Lea Hurst. The wreath bore the following inscription:– "This cross, in sacred memory and hope everlasting, is offered to the bereaved wife of C. B. N. Dunn, with the deepest sympathy of Florence Nightingale. London, Easter, 1892

Courtesy Beryl Calladine

Home and surgery of Crich village doctors for over 100 years.

129

Chapter 29
Vicar sued

The vicar's brushes with the law continued. In November 1893 he was sued for non-payment of a bill for breaking in a colt that he owned. Once again he lost his case. This would not be his last visit to the courtrooms.

Derby Mercury: Wed 1 November 1893

A HORSEBREAKER'S CLAIM – The Rev. W. Acraman, vicar of Crich, was sued by John Jackson, horse breaker of Swanwick, for £6 6s, for breaking a colt, keep of the animal and shoes supplied. – Mr. Nelson, solicitor, Alfreton, represented the plaintiff. – The colt was left with plaintiff in order to be broken in, but the defendant said when the animal returned it was in a wretched condition, and had serious injuries upon its body. Defendant had paid £8 into court in settlement of the claim. – His honour gave judgement for the plaintiff for £6 6s.

Vicarage, Coast Hill, home of Revd Acraman.
This was the second vicarage; the first was just above the church
on Cromford Road.

Chapter 30
Quarry troubles

The Clay Cross Company owned the limestone Cliff Quarry at Crich. There was a catalogue of disputes and accidents with the parish and workers. The following are newspaper reports from 1893 and 1894.

Derby Mercury: 19 July 1893

KILLED THROUGH HIS OWN FOLLY.

A singular fatality reported from Crich. During the course of his everyday labours a lad employed at the quarries had had occasion to remove some stone through a narrow tunnel leading out of the quarry. The stone was loaded in trucks which were drawn along by a couple of ponies, of which the lad had charge. A man saw the lad about to lead the ponies into the tunnel, and, evidently meaning mischief ran up to him, seized the whip off him, and began to crack it. The pony took fright, and the lad, being unable to retain his hold of the reins, was for the moment in imminent danger of losing his life, but he jumped out of the way in the nick of time, and instead of being hurt himself, the man was knocked down, run over, and killed. – Mr. W. Harvey Whiston, coroner, held an inquest at Crich on Wednesday afternoon on the body of Eli Barnes, the man who was run over. It appears that a boy employed at the quarries had charge of a couple of ponies attached to a truck laden with stone, and had to remove the stone through a tunnel out of the quarry. The deceased saw the lad about to lead the animal into the tunnel, and evidently intending to make mischief, rushed up to him, took the whip off him, and began to crack it. The ponies became frightened and ran away, and the boy seeing his danger jumped out of the way, but Barnes was knocked down and killed. A verdict of "Accidental death" was returned.

Derby Mercury: 21 February 1894

CRICH

DISPUTE – The quarry men at the Cliff Limestone Quarry have received notification that a reduction in their wages of 1d per waggon would be made.

Quarry troubles

Derby Mercury: Wed 28 February 1894

CRICH

THE QUARRYMEN'S DISPUTE – The men met Mr Jackson, the manager of Clay Cross Company, on Wednesday morning, to try to come to a friendly decision with regard to the notice that the men would be reduced by 1d per waggon. Mr Jackson declined, however, to entertain their views, and the result is that the men are still out of work.

Derby Mercury: Wed 18 April 1894

CRICH

SERIOUS ACCIDENT – A serious accident occurred on Friday at the Bull Bridge limekilns belonging to the Clay Cross Company. As a workman named Alfred Vallence was working in company with another, by the name Charles Ludlam, breaking the kiln with large hammers, his foot slipped and he fell, and by some means or other the whole force of the hammer from Ludlam came on to his head and severely fractured his skull. Dr Macdonald is in attendance.

Courtesy Beryl Calladine

Clay Cross Company limestone quarry, with the Stand in view.

Chapter 31
Village events 1893 – 1896

As usual the local papers continued to print the mundane, informative and whimsical.

Derby Mercury: Wed 20 December 1893

CRICH

CONSIDERABLE changes in the Postal service in Matlock and the surrounding towns and villages will be made shortly after the advent of the New Year.

Instead of the mails reaching Matlock Bath per road from Derby, the whole of the bags will be set down by the 12 o'clock (midnight) mail train, which arrives at the Bath at 3.53 every morning. Mail carts will take mails to the town of Bakewell, and to Rowsley, Winster and Wirksworth, and there will be a horse post to Crich. Crich will receive its letters by seven o'clock in the morning, over an hour and a half earlier than at present, and will post much later in the evening.

Derby Mercury: Wed 27 December 1893

CRICH

A RATHER remarkable case of longevity is recorded at Crich. Three years ago eleven people died, and their total ages amounted to 900, or nearly an average of 82. In the present year ten persons have died reaching an average age of 79, in all 790 years.

Derby Mercury: Wed 28th February 1894

CRICH

GRAND CONCERT – A splendid concert was given on Friday evening in the British School at Crich in aid of the Crich United Brass Band. The band is now in a very prosperous state, this concert probably the finest given by them. The vocalists were Mrs J Worthy, Miss Stocks, Miss Jackson, Mr B Elliot, Mr White, Mr S Burton, who were accompanied by a very able pianist, Mr H Price. Altogether the concert was a grand success.

Village events

Derby Mercury: Wed 7 March 1894

CRICH

READING ROOM – On Wednesday evening the annual meeting of the Crich Reading Room took place in the billiard room of the institute. Mr Boag was in the chair, and read the balance sheet, which was adopted. The receipts had unfortunately decreased slightly. This was very much regretted, and the people were stirred to more energy, all the members unanimously agreeing to endeavour to get more members. Mr A. F. Hurst was re-elected president; vice-presidents, Messrs Jacoby, Jackson, Thewlis Johnson, J. B. Smedley, A. S. Smedley, G .J. McDonald, H. D. Boag; treasurer; Mr G. Connell; secretary, Mr H. Dyson, and a committee of twelve.

Dr J. G. Dawes records in his book 'A History of Crich' that the Reading Room was built at a cost of £300 raised in 1887. The foundation stone states that it was built in 1889. On the stone are the names: H. Dyson, R. Wildgoose J.P., J. A. Jacoby M.P., E. Kirk, J. Dawes. It followed in the tradition of the Lending Library which was attached to the Church Sunday School in 1833, and the one in the small building opposite Victoria House. The Quakers also established Fritchley Lending Library in the middle of the 19th century.

Derby Mercury: Wed 4 April 1894

CRICH
SALE OF WORK – A sale of work was opened in the British Schoolroom on Monday, in aid of the same school, by Mrs Broome of Holloway. The stallholders were Mrs F Cowlishaw, Mrs W Dawes, the Misses Cowlishaw, Dawes and Allin, Mrs Dawes, Mrs Peach, and Mrs Wood. The Crich United Brass Band played sections at intervals during the evening.

CRICH CARR
NATIONAL SCHOOLS – A good meat tea was on Friday evening last given to the school children by the directors of the above school. Ladies of the district presided over the different tables, and the tea was very heartily enjoyed by the children. In the evening the incumbent of Ambergate Church supplied a magic lantern entertainment. The late schoolmaster, Mr J. L. Whitehouse, who has been over to America was very heartily welcomed back to the school.

Derby Mercury: Wed 18 April 1894

DEATH OF MR KNIGHTON – Mr J. Knighton, one of the most respected tradesmen in Crich, died on Wednesday. Deceased, who was a prominent Baptist, had attained the age of 70 years.

TENNIS CLUB – The third annual meeting of the Crich Tennis Club was held in the Parochial School, on Thursday evening. The balance sheet of the past year was read by Mr Moody, and adopted, and showed a small balance in favour of the club. On Saturday, the 21st, the first match is to be held. The following officers were elected: The Rev. J. P. Neville, B.A., president; Mrs J. I. Lee, treasurer; Miss Dawes, secretary; and a committee of three.

Derby Mercury: Wed 2 May 1894

PROPERTY IN THE MARKET – At the King's Arms Inn on Monday a freehold dwelling house, with a workshop attached was offered for sale. The house, substantially built of stone, is situate near the Market-place of Crich. The bidding started at £200, but the lot was withdrawn at £255. Mr Cheetham was the auctioneer, and Messrs E. G. and T. Jackson of Belper.

Derby Mercury: Wed 17 October 1894

AN OLD FRIENDLY SOCIETY – On Saturday the centenary of the Independent Friendly Society, Crich, was celebrated, having been started in the year 1794. There are now members in the club who have been in for 65 years. The Crich United Brass Band was in attendance and preceded the members up to the parish Church, where the Rev. W. Acraman, the vicar, held a service. They then marched down to the Independent Clubroom, where a splendid repast awaited them. They had catered for the dinner entirely in their own party. After dinner the vicar addressed the members. – Dr Macdonald read the statement of accounts, which showed that they had now a capital of nearly £1,400, which was invested in property &c.

Exemption certificate

Whilst parish life was continuing its unpredictable way some of its children were trying to obtain an exemption certificate. This certificate was awarded once a pupil had reached a certain standard of education. It meant they could leave school early and start working. They were not elaborate documents, as the example below shows.

Courtesy Rosemary Hall

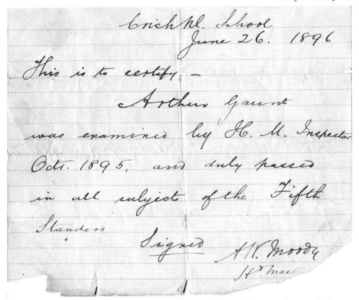

Thirteen-year-old Arthur Gaunt's exemption certificate – he could leave school.

Here is what reaching the Fifth Standard meant:

STANDARD V	
Reading	A short ordinary paragraph in a newspaper, or other modern narrative.
Writing	Another short ordinary paragraph in a newspaper, or other modern narrative, slowly dictated once by a few words at a time.
Arithmetic	Practice and bills of parcels.

Chapter 32
Drunkenness in the Jovial Dutchman

Drunkenness and some Crich residents were not strangers! The papers often contained reports about alcohol-induced behaviour in the village. This article about the Jovial Dutchman is particularly amusing. There was much laughter in court.

Derby Mercury: Wed 24 June 1896

Quarter Sessions

A CRICH PUBLICAN'S COMPANY – Joseph Dronfield, landlord of the Jovial Dutchman Inn, Crich, was summoned for permitting drunkenness on his licensed premises on May 28. – Mr Clifford (Derby) appeared on behalf of the police to prosecute, and Mr. Stone (Derby) was for the defence. – Mr. Clifford stated the facts, and called Police-constable Cosgrove, who said he visited the house and saw two men named George Frost and Charles Walker there. They were covered with blood and dirt, and appeared to have been fighting. The landlord was present, and witness asked him what he was about to allow the men to be there in that condition. Frost was in a chair all of a heap from the effects of drink – beastly drunk. The man had blood on his hands, face, and clothes. The landlord said the men had been having a dust, and he had taken Frost out of the way. Going home with Frost for safety, witness afterwards returned to the house, and saw Walker and five other men. This was about one o'clock. Walker staggered away and was very drunk. Answering Mr. Clifford, the officer said he could not tell whether beer or whiskey had been in the glass in front of Frost. It was drained quite dry (Laughter). – Elizabeth Wolley, Crich, said she saw Walker and Frost fighting "just on the end of the sign." Walker was drunk and used a lot of disgusting language to her. – Joseph Radford, a carter, of Crich, said a "man with a slop on" went into the Jovial Dutchman. They called him "Doctor Frost." Witness said he and Walker had something to drink. He could not say whether they were glasses or quarts (Laughter). "They had none to mean owt" (Renewed laughter). – Mr. Stone alleged that the fight took place while the landlord was absent, and it became a question to what extent he was liable. All the men went into the house together, yet it was sworn that two of the party were drunk. – The landlord said four men had three quarts of beer in two hours. They were quiet, until Frost arrived, and then the tussle occurred. Frost went out of the house as sharp as lightning. Frost had two two's of whisky, and he believed one was knocked over. – Joseph Smith, a blacksmith's striker, gave some amusing evidence, and said he was having an idle morning, which he filled up with drinking (Laughter). – The Bench convicted in a penalty of £2, and £2 3s and costs. – George Frost and Charles Walker, the two men mentioned in the case, were then brought up and charged with being drunk on the premises. They were each fined 5s each and costs.

The Jovial Dutchman as it would have looked at this time.

Chapter 33
Murder in the barn

The big excitement in Crich during 1896 would have been the infamous murder which took place at a farm on nearby Lindway Lane on the 9th May. The lane is just over the fields from Wheatcroft and Plaistow, although in 1896 it was technically in the parish of Brackenfield. The Brackenfield barn murder of Lizzie Boot by Billy Pugh really hit the national headlines. Train and charabanc trips were organised to the site. Crich and surrounding villages were full to capacity with visitors wanting to see where the deed took place and to return home with some "bloody souvenir." Accommodation in the neighbourhood was very difficult to find. Pugh was caught, literally red handed, and was tried and hung in Derby Gaol, the first to be executed in the newly built chamber. Many of the witnesses were Crich folk.

Elizabeth (Lizzie) Boot was a 20 year old housekeeper at Lindway Lane Farm, Brackenfield. She was with her niece, Beatrice Boot, when William (Billy) Pugh called. What he wanted is somewhat unclear (although robbery was eventually given as his motive). For reasons unknown, they both went into the barn, where a disagreement occurred. The result of this was Lizzie being "done to death" with a billhook. Pugh, realising that Beatrice would be a witness, went off to find her and to silence her. Fortunately, a neighbouring farmer, George Hitchcock, came into the yard just as Pugh was heading for the house. He saw Pugh who changed direction and went off (covered with some blood and evidence of a struggle).

Hitchcock went to find the farm hands – William Bryan and Harry Towndrow – who had been working in the field whist the murder had been committed. Bryan went into the barn to fetch a fork and discovered the body. Hitchcock went to fetch neighbours Mary Saunders and Ann Greenhough to help. Mary Saunders' daughter (Sarah) was courting William Pugh at the time. Police were contacted at South Wingfield.

Murder in the barn

The investigation began (initially through rumour, then the police were involved).

Shortly after the murder Pugh went to his girlfriend Sarah Saunders' house and whilst there contrived to cut himself on her father's razor, this in order to account for blood on his clothing. Strangely, her father, John Saunders, then shaved Pugh! Rumour was already spreading, through Beatrice saying she had seen her auntie go into the barn with Pugh, that he might be involved.

Pugh returned to his nearby lodging house, the home of Luke Wilson and his wife Hannah, who just happened to be the sister of his girlfriend Sarah. There he changed his blood-stained shirt for a clean one, leaving the bloody one in his room. He then returned to the Saunders' house. When the shirt was found by Hannah Wilson shortly afterwards she washed it. Guilt overcame both Luke and Hannah, who then burnt the shirt.

Two of the brothers of the murdered girl, John and Henry Boot, went to see Pugh to ask him what he knew of the murder. They noticed blood still on Pugh's wrists. John Boot then cycled to South Wingfield police house to fetch P.C. Wilson. Wilson, in the company of the Boot brothers, questioned Pugh (and others). Pugh was arrested on suspicion of murder and taken to the Alfreton lock-up. Lizzie's body was removed from the barn and taken to her mother's house (Ellen Boot – a widow). This removal was owing to the fear of rats attacking the body. The police surgeon later examined the body and conducted the post mortem at the house.

On the following Monday morning, the 11th May, the inquest was carried out at the Plough Inn, Brackenfield. After hearing all the evidence the jury were unanimous that William Pugh was the culprit and should stand trial. On his way from the inquest to the Alfreton lock-up a major cock-up occurred. His conveyance went past the funeral procession for Lizzie Boot. Obviously strong emotions were aroused and there was a bit of a fracas.

The hearing was held in Alfreton. After hearing the evidence Pugh was ordered to be tried for murder in Derby at the Summer Assizes. Crowds waited to see him transported down to Alfreton railway station on his way to Derby Gaol.

Great interest, or morbid curiosity, followed the case and Mr Limb was besieged in his farm by thousands of sightseers. They nearly stripped his farm for 'mementoes'. A little late in the day Mr Limb decided to charge the sightseers for a tour – the money raised was to go for a suitable tombstone for the murdered girl. Just over £11 was raised which provided for her gravestone in Brackenfield churchyard.

After a two-day trial Pugh was found guilty and sentenced to hang. Whilst he was awaiting his fate he 'found religion.' Eventually, on the eve of his hanging, he confessed that indeed he was guilty. His motive, he said, was robbery. He had promised to take his girlfriend to Alfreton for the afternoon and to 'treat her' – but had no money. So, Lizzie Boot died because Pugh wanted to take his girlfriend out on a date to Alfreton.

A new execution chamber had been built in Derby Gaol, complete with new gallows. Pugh was the first to be executed on them. The hangman, Billington, and his assistant, Wilkinson, carried out the execution on 5th August 1896, just three months after the murder. Press were present at the hanging and wrote about it in fine detail. He was buried in the precincts of the gaol, as was the custom. The new execution chamber spared him the extra ordeal of having to pass by his newly dug grave – a situation previous condemned felons had to suffer.

Extracted from *The Brackenfield Barn Murder* by Peter Patilla

Billy Pugh – murderer

Lizzy Boot – victim

Chapter 34
Landslip, footbridge and turnpike

In March 1897 alarm was raised about the landslips which were occurring in the Crich area. These were causing significant changes to the geography of the region. The slippage that was happening in Whatstandwell was causing the River Derwent to slightly change its course, and the Midland Railway was considering changing its railway line to the opposite side of the valley. The canal was closed, as was Robin Hood Road – which had been raised six inches.

Derby Mercury: Wed 10 March 1897

THE landslip which is at present in progress in the neighbourhood of the Midland Railway at Whatstandwell, though it has not at present assumed very alarming proportions, may, nevertheless, become very serious unless the movement of the land is arrested. The spot where the landslip has manifested itself is between the new and old stations at Whatstandwell and towards the base of the hill which rises up to Crich Stand, a hill which has during recent years been the scene of at least two landslips of considerable magnitude. The summit of the hill, in the neighbourhood of the quarry, has, however, been the only portion previously affected, and although considerable damage was wrought on these occasions, the present landslip, should it assume the gravity which is quite within the bounds of possibility, would probably eclipse them in extent of damage. It is, of course, impossible to say to what extent the movement is likely to alter the configuration of the land without better knowledge of the extent to which the hillside is affected than can at present be obtained. It is a fact, however, that the hills in the neighbourhood referred to are by reason of their peculiar formation, rendered particularly treacherous, and it is even hinted at that the railway company may yet find it necessary to lay a new permanent way on the opposite side of the valley, and out of the reach of the hills, the vagaries of which have always occasioned more or less anxiety. We hear it stated that the company have endeavoured to arrest the movement of the land by means of a judicious distribution of heavy masonry, but those who understand the nature of these landslides in the Peak district will be probably inclined to believe that should the present movement be due to the dislocation of any considerable portion of land, the efforts of man to cope with the position must inevitably prove futile. It is conjectured that the recent earthquake is probably the cause of the slide, and the symptoms at present noticed are certainly in favour of the assumption that the occurrence is something more than superficial. The railway company have been watching the phenomena for over a fortnight and it is stated that in addition to the canal – which runs between the railway and the base of the hill being rendered impassable, the metals of the permanent way have been raised almost six inches, and a movement of the river bank has already been perceptible. The opening of cracks in the land up the hillside is anything but reassuring – in fact, they seem to point to the hypothesis that the slide is occurring over a considerable area.

Derby Mercury: Wed 7 April 1897

PARISH MEETING – A large meeting of the ratepayers of Crich took place on Wednesday evening in the Parochial School, Mr. H. B. Boag presiding. Mr. Leafe read out a list of the recipients of charities of Cooper, Gisborne, Cornthwaites and Kirkland, and the Rev. Acraman also read accounts connected with the charities. They were passed. The Parish Council accounts were then presented and showed a balance in hand of £15 8s 6d. The question of a footbridge over the canal to Whatstandwell station was then fully gone into, and a petition to the Midland Railway Company having been drawn up, the ratepayers were asked to sign the same.

Mr Shaw brought forward an important matter, that of repairing the turnpike road leading from Bull Bridge to Holloway, stating that he thought, with many others, that the road ought to be taken over by the Derbyshire County Council. It was, however, clearly proved by Mr Dawes and other gentlemen that the County Council had been repeatedly requested to take over this road, but would not do so, their excuse being that there was sufficient through traffic. Votes of confidence in the Council and thanks to the chairman concluded a good meeting.

143

Chapter 35
Police crackdown on gambling

During March 1897 the police went undercover, and in disguise, to trap illegal domino players and other gamblers in the village. The reports of the police raids make interesting reading.

Derby Mercury: Wed 17 March 1897

A MYSTERIOUS RAILWAY PORTER AMONGST THE PUBLICANS – Albert E. Slack of the Black Swan Inn, Crich, was charged with permitting gaming to take place on his licensed premises, contrary to section 17 of the Licensing Act 1872, on the 19th February, at Crich. Mr. R. S. Clifford, Derby, appeared for the police, and Mr. J. Potter, Matlock and Derby, defended. In opening the case, Mr. Clifford said that in consequence of complaints Superintendent McDonald sent an officer in private dress, in the attire of a railway porter. Police-constable Wallis stated that he entered the house about seven o'clock. The landlord was present, with five or six others. In the presence of the landlord remarks were made that games had been played, and a quart had come in. Joseph Slack asked for dominoes, and a game was played, the loser paying. Witness had a drink of the beer. He paid for beer for men from whom he received information. Police-constable Cosgrove deposed to visiting the house and saw

dominoes, but they were not in use, and Mr. Potter asked the Bench to say the evidence was not sufficient to commit a man of good character. The only witness he suggested had told falsehoods by the bushel to ingratiate himself in the graces of the men he associated with at the house. The defendant was called and said he allowed the dominoes to be taken into the room on condition that money or beer were not played for. Luke Wragg, quarryman, Crich, stated that the officer, Wallis, wore a railway porter's cap. In conversation Wallis talked glibly, and had got a very good story prepared. There was no liquor paid for by men who lost at dominoes. John Wragg, Crich, deposed that he was at the house and had a game of dominoes. It was a friendly game for amusement. The landlord did not stand by and see a game played, over which the bargain was for the loser to pay. – The Bench convicted in a penalty of £2 and costs. – Thomas B. Hallsworth, of the Bull's Head, Crich, was charged with a like offence by permitting the playing of bagatelle. Mr. Clifford prosecuted and Mr. Potter defended. Police-constable Wallis stated that he went to the Bull's Head and saw a French bagatelle board. Four men were playing, and one of them told him they were having a game of 140 up, and the two losers paid, Walter Sellors and Kneebone. The landlord told the men to be quiet and keep the door shut. A second game was arranged, but he did not stay to see it played. Police-constable Cosgrove gave evidence, and then the defendant was examined and denied that anything took place at the bagatelle board to arouse suspicion. John Heapy said he had played many times on the board, but never gambled. John Greenhough was examined and said he was at the house, but saw no gambling over the bagatelle. The Bench imposed a penalty of £2 and costs. – Samuel Stocks, Royal Oak, Crich, was charged with a like offence by allowing dominoes to be played on February 10th. Mr. Clifford again prosecuted and Mr. Potter defended. — Police-constable Wallis spoke to seeing a game of five chalks up. The landlord seemed a bit fly, but he was not quite fly enough. There was cheating detected. On the table was a cloth, and everything was done brazen enough. – Mary Ann Lambert, daughter of the landlord, denied that beer was played for, and there was no suggestion that money was at issue. – Mrs. Stocks, wife of the defendant, said it was untrue that a bargain was made to play points up for beer. – Henry Cowlishaw and Thomas Sellors were called, and the latter said they had a game, but there was no end to it because it was all friendly. Other witnesses said the game was merely played for pastime. In this case the Bench convicted in a penalty of £2 and costs.

Just above the church, the *Bull's Head* – scene of illegal gambling.
The original old vicarage is the large house at right angles and Crich Stand
is in the distance.

Chapter 36
Measles epidemic

There were many epidemics which hit the community during these years. In July 1887 it was a particularly bad measles epidemic. It caused several deaths and closed both Crich and Fritchley Schools for a month.

Derby Mercury: Wed 7 July 1897

CRICH

EPIDEMIC OF MEASLES – A serious epidemic of measles has broken out in the villages of Crich and Fritchley. Dr Edward Gaylor, the medical officer of Belper Rural District Council, has visited the locality, and finds there are about 120 cases, some of the children being attacked in somewhat severe form. Three deaths have occurred at Fritchley, with pneumonic complications. All the schools have been peremptorily closed for a month, acting on the instructions of the medical officer. Only a few months ago the disease was prevalent in the district.

Fritchley School.

Chapter 37
Another head sacked

On 21st May 1897 Mr Alfred W. Moody resigned as master of the Parochial School to take up a new appointment at Bonsall. The new headteacher, Mr George Henry Kent, quickly clashed with the vicar. He began his headship on the 4th October 1897 and was fired three days later. There were accusations, counter-accusations, scuffles, court cases, intemperate letters, threats and many suggestions of wrong-doings. All this came to a head with the curate, Revd Neville, being accused in court of assaulting the head. The vicar also made yet another of his court appearances.

By any measure all this must have been a situation that the vicar could have done without. Whilst there is no evidence of Revd Acraman's state of mind at this time, his behaviour in relation to the conflict that occurred (and others that followed over the next couple of years) does not appear to be that of a wholly rational mind. Here, in 1897, he was sixty-two, widowed with a young daughter, and ravaged by religious and educational infighting in the parish.

Parochial School logbook: 21st May 1897

Mr. A. W. Moody resigned being master for 7¹/₄ years during which 428 children have been admitted and average increased from 100 to 168. Governt grants have gone from £50 to treble that.
Vicar visited, presentation of cheque from managers and a handsome Duplex lamp subscribed from teachers and pupils.

Mr J. H. Barnes cert. teacher took charge.

Headmaster asks for a blackboard

In July 1897 Revd Acraman advertised for a headmaster for Crich National School, and later interviewed and appointed George Henry Kent, an assistant teacher from Gainsborough. Mr Kent arrived in Crich on the 24th September 1897. His first day as head was on 4th October 1897. He was sacked by the vicar on the 6th October.

Parochial School logbook: 4th October 1897

George Hy Kent take charge.
   George Hy Kent Master
   Mrs. Inez Scarff Infant Mistress
   Miss M Brumwell Assist
   Nellie Moodie PT
   Mary Radford Monitress

6th October 1897

The vicar sent the Rev. P. Neville for a boy to go out with him at 11.00am. This has been going on for a length of time. Some boys even going as soon as school begins and then being marked present. [not true JHBarnes]

{Assume this added later by J. H.Barnes who took over temporarily when Mr Kent was sacked}

After 3 days in the school the vicar gave me 3 mnths notice for no reason whatsoever. When I went to the vicarage to see him the curate told me he was at Whatstandwell, when he was in the whole time. As I persisted in seeing him the vicar went out at the back and told a policeman to order me off. I called at the vicarage and gave Mr. Neville a list of the materials necessary for the working of the school, including blackboard and copy books.

8th October 1897

As attendance has fallen off I have decided to close the school at 12 o'clock till Oct 18th it also being the Wakes.

On the day of Mr. Kent's sacking, 7th October, letters flew between the two men.

Below is the wonderfully irate letter from Mr Kent to the vicar, threatening to send for the School Inspector.

This came with letter from Mr Kent to H. Mr. 9.
Oct 7/97
Dimple Villa
Crich

Sir,

I want to see you and you I am going to see I want to know reasons for what you have done You can't meet me like a man but I shall see you X. If you are not at my house by 5.30 to-night I send the letter for an Inspector to come I have plenty of witnesses & proofs of your dishonesty in filling Form $\overline{IX}$. I am not afraid. I can substantiate my statements & also find legal advice if necessary. Geo Hy Kent.

X Mr. Kent was in his notice is he ? & I ? from Mr. Kent at the school :—
? ? the letter

149

Vicar replies to head

This was the vicar's reply with counter-threats to Mr Kent warning him against making accusations to the Her Majesty's Inspector (HMI). All further letters from Mr Kent were to be sent to the secretary of the school managers, Mr Wheatcroft.

What seems apparent is that the curate, Revd Neville, went to the school, on the instruction of the vicar, to remove Mr Kent. Mr Kent was accused of working against the Parochial School and in the interest of the rival British School. The ensuing scuffle resulted in yet another court case. There were now two court cases pending over the summary sacking of Mr Kent. The first was against Mr Neville for assault, and the second against Mr Acraman for wrongful dismissal.

The curate went to the school to remove Mr Kent, who refused to leave – a policeman was present. Mr Neville then took Mr Kent by the collar to forcibly remove him, and a scuffle occurred. This resulted in a summons for assault against Mr Neville, who was found guilty of a technical assault at the subsequent court hearing. A fuller account of the event came out at the later inquiry into the dismissal of Mr Kent.

Derby Mercury: Wed 10 November 1897

A CRICH CLERICAL CASE – James Percy Neville, of Crich, described as a curate, was summoned for assaulting George Henry Kent, headmaster of the Crich Parochial School on the 13th October. Mr. J Potter, Matlock and Derby, appeared for the complainant, and Mr. W. Mortimer Wilson, Alfreton, for the defence. – Mr. Potter, in opening the case pointed out that his client had occupied a similar position at Gainsborough. He came to Crich on October 4th, and after three days in school was given three month's notice. This very much upset him and he declined to leave the school grounds when asked by Mr. Neville. The result was that Mr. Kent was ejected, and considerable force was used in doing it. Mr. Potter contended the complainant was there in the discharge of his duties. – Evidence was given by the complainant, Mr. Dawes, the Rev. E. Walters, and Police-constable Cosgrove. – The latter maintained that no more force than necessary was used to eject the complainant, who had returned to the premises a second time after consulting his friends. – The defence was that no more violence was used than was required. The defendant was a manager, was in a position to judge what was good for the school, and therefore, as a point of law, was perfectly justified in his actions. – The Bench convicted, and said a technical assault was committed. It had not been shown Mr. Neville had any authority to interfere; it was not shown he was a legally constituted manager. – A fine of 10s. and costs was imposed.

Chapter 38
Indignation Meeting

Such was the feeling in the village against the sacking of Mr Kent that an "Indignation Meeting" was called. Posters were displayed around the village, and the meeting was well attended with about four hundred villagers present. The vicar thought it a plot by the Nonconformists and considered it none of their business.

Derbyshire Times: 6 November 1897

INDIGNATION MEETING AT CRICH
THE VICAR AND HIS PARISHIONERS

On Tuesday night, a meeting of the ratepayers and inhabitants of Crich was held in the Independent Club Room, to express sympathy with Mr Kent and protest against his arbitrary dismissal from the position of headmaster at the Parochial School. There was a good attendance, probably 400 persons being present, and including church people. The chair was taken by the Rev. L. Latchley, Congregational minister at Fritchley, which is a part of the parish of Crich. The meeting, according to the posters, was called as an indignation meeting, and occasionally there was strong vitriolic language which expressed very great indignation. The speakers were moderate in their expressions, taken on the whole, but an occasional outburst of epithets caused one to wonder how far the disapproval of the people would go.

The chairman said he had been asked to preside at that important and to him very painful meeting. As he was there at their request, he must ask them to give him and all who might follow him a patient hearing. He did not think, as far as he was personally concerned, he should have chosen that office for himself. If he were to ask all persons separately whether they would prefer to have had such a meeting as that, or the reverse, they would have preferred the reverse. They called it an indignation meeting, and the very word indignation implied something about which they were to be very indignant. They were also asked to express sympathy with Mr Kent and to protest against his arbitrary dismissal as headmaster of the Parochial School. Putting the two things together a feeling of injustice prevailed, or was implied to prevail, throughout the meeting. They had gathered there to receive more light on what he termed a very painful subject. He called on Mr Kent to give his statement.

Mr Kent explained how he came to be appointed. It seems the vicar promised him a villa in its own grounds as part of the terms of employment. The dirty house the family came to seems to be at the heart of the dispute which resulted in the sacking.

Mr Kent, who it appears came from Gainsborough, and was at Crich only a few days when he received notice to leave the school, made his statement from notes and memoranda, which were read. He was deliberate and calm in all he said. He began by reference to the way in which he was brought to Crich, and said he informed the Rev. W. Acraman, he was willing to be guided by him as to the Sunday School. In the course of the first letter or two Mr Acraman wrote that he was not an interfering man with his teachers (Laughter). To this a reply was sent that he should be willing to do all he could to further the interests of the parish and consider the welfare of the children. The position was accepted and arrangements made about the house in which he was to reside. He was told it was a villa, and stood in its own grounds, and that it was in fairly good condition. His wife came over with him to Crich, and they found the house not in a very nice state. She went to the vicar and he declined to see her. When he saw the vicar all he could get out of him was about the Sunday School; he could get nothing about the day school, although he kept asking. There was an interview about the house as to the necessary cleaning etc. Mr Neville, the curate, went to the house and proposed that they should wash the walls with soap and water (Laughter). Then a letter was received from the vicar. It stated that as Mr Kent seemed so unsettled and disappointed with the house, the place and the people, and the people with him, that it would be best to terminate the agreement as soon as possible, although it was a sad disappointment to the writer (Laughter). There were the interests of the school to consider, went on the letter, and suggests he would be more happy in another county. Three months notice was given from October 6th. There was an offer to set him free at once. The notice was received at nine o'clock at night. He was at supper, but could not finish.

Mr Kent, on receiving his notice from the vicar, attempted to see Revd Acraman for an explanation. The vicar was having none of it and refused to discuss the matter. The newspaper account went on to describe Mr Kent's description of what happened next. This included how the vicar attempted to stop him obtaining another appointment in the county, and how the curate threw him physically out of school.

He went to the vicarage and Mr Neville answered the door and said Mr Acraman was out. He would add that he began work on the Monday and got his notice on the Wednesday night! Mention was then made of a visit to the police station for the officer to come and order him away (Laughter). However the decision was irrevocable according to a further letter, and it was added in a communication that if there was any more annoyance the matter would be placed in the hands of the proper authorities. Still the vicar declined to see him or to offer any other explanation. He declined to see Mrs Kent and said he never had dealings with master's wives (Laughter) The reasons for dismissal were required and it was stated that they had been given in a previous letter. A proposal was made by him (Mr Kent) that he should receive £50 to go out. This could not be considered. He was told the nurse and daughter had had to go away because of being upset. A letter was, however, received saying the matter had been placed in the hands of Mr Wheatcroft, solicitor, Belper, and anything he had

to say could be to him. A full quarters salary was offered in discharge of all claims. There was no answer to this letter. Another post was applied for and a gentleman went over to see Mr Acraman and asked for the reasons of dismissal. He told that gentleman that he (Mr Kent) had been unmercifully beating the children. (Laughter) He would say that the children had been running around wild. Some of the teachers had smoked cigarettes in the school. Mr Kent then alleged the vicar had been to Hazlewood to prevent him getting another school. He was told this by the vicar of Hazlewood. An explanation was next given of the manner in which he was got from school. He went to the school daily and Mr Neville came, as also a policeman. He alleged Mr Neville asked the policeman to order him off the premises. Mr Kent asked the policeman to obtain from Mr Neville the reason why he was dismissed. The reply was that the reasons were contained in the letter. Mr Neville, he alleged, got hold of him and put him out of the yard by force, throwing him down eight steps.

The meeting continued with several people speaking in favour of Mr Kent and against the vicar. These included the head of the British School, Mr Dyson, and other prominent Nonconformists. The vicar was dismissive of their views as he considered it was nothing to do with them what he did in a parochial church school.

Mr Dyson, master of the Crich British School, moved the following resolution:- "That the ratepayers and inhabitants of Crich in this meeting assembled hereby express their dissatisfaction with the action of the Rev. Wm. Acraman, manager of the Crich Parochial School, as to the dismissal of Mr Kent, and deeply sympathise with Mr Kent in the trying position in which he has been placed." In the course of a few words, Mr Dyson said he had been asked what business it was of his to interfere in the matter. His only business for interfering was that he did not like to see a fellow teacher unfairly and unjustly treated. It was his duty as well as his right to interfere. Wherever they saw tyranny and oppression, it was their duty to interfere, and to do their utmost to uphold the principles of right and justice. Crich Parochial School was mostly supported out of public money. The managers were simply the trustees for the people and spent the money as such. That money ought not to be spent to gratify private animosity. He was pleased to be able to tell them a lot of the church people were downright ashamed of what the Vicar had done. (Applause). The reason, or reasons, for dismissal of Mr Kent were ridiculous. Mr Kent had been a successful teacher elsewhere, and so long as a teacher in a public school did his duty he ought not to be under Mr Acraman or any other manager for dismissal. That power ought to be in the hands of a committee. It appeared to him that Mr Acraman knew he was in the wrong when he dare not face Mr Kent. There had been five teachers in the Crich Infant School the last year. They were under Mr Acraman. Not only had this wrong been done to Mr Kent, but there had been an attempt to ruin him by preventing him from getting another place.

Mr Seeds seconded the resolution, and maintained there had not been time to know what Mr Kent could do. Was three days sufficient to test any man at any kind of work, much more in a school? He was sorry for Mr Kent, and was sorry they had not a better shepherd in Crich.

The Rev. E Walters supported the resolution. He took up that position because he was a man and only a man. These two young people went to Crich, without friends, and were cut adrift. He claimed that any man acting as Mr Acraman had done was not fit to have charge of a mother's son. One of the reasons why Mr Kent was so summarily dismissed was because he was a man with spirit.

The resolution was then put to the meeting and carried unanimously and with great cheering. – After thanks to the chairman the gathering separated.

Despite the resolution of four hundred parishioners at the indignation meeting, the vicar ignored the opinions expressed. Another court case loomed.

Chapter 39
Court case

The case against the vicar for damages contained much more detail as to what had happened between him and Mr Kent.

Below are two copy letters from solicitors used by Revd Acraman in connection with his defence. The first is from Mr Wheatcroft, who was also the Secretary to the Managers of Crich National School. In this letter Mr Wheatcroft resigns his position as Acraman's solicitor for the case. Whilst he does not give specific reasons for his withdrawal from the case, it is fairly clear that Mr Wheatcroft did not agree with the decision that a claim of assault against the curate Mr Neville, brought by Mr Kent, should go undefended.

It also appears that Mr Wheatcroft was not over pleased by the views of lay persons regarding the law. This suggests that he had had enough of his expertise being questioned by the vicar.

Early photograph of Crich Parochial School. Date unknown.

J WHEATCROFT
SOLICITOR

29th October 1897

Rev. W Acraman
Dear Sir
With reference to our late conference yesterday, and
having fully considered the matter I have finally decided
to withdraw from the business. I have no wish to add
to your difficulties or cause you any pain by assigning
my reasons & I therefore refrain from doing so. The
course I have decided to adopt will leave you ample
time to entrust the business to other hands and leave
you free to allow the charge against Mr Neville to go
undefended.
I send you copy of Mr Potter's letter received yesterday
which will put you in possession of the position of the
business up to date. I am returning to Mr Neville by this
post the summons served upon him.
I shall be pleased to reply to any letter from you, but
you must excuse me in declining to lose any more of my
time in useless discussions of worthless lay opinions
and gossip upon legal matters.
Yours faithfully
Jno. Wheatcroft

See Appendix 2 for a copy of the original letter.

The vicar's new solicitor, Mortimer Wilson of Alfreton, spelt out the
options. He was suggesting that because of the vicar's unpopularity
in Crich a settlement might be preferable before the trial, as there
would be a great deal of publicity. He went on to say that as Mr Kent
had a new position he was suggesting making an offer of a month's
salary of £7 10s 0d with between £10 and £12 for "expenses".
Already on offer was a quarter's salary "without prejudice". He also

expressed regret that Mr Kent was successful in the assault case against the curate Mr Neville.

The vicar had a choice to make: settle before trial and avoid publicity, or go for trail with all the attendant press attention. The worst scenario would be to start the trial, get the publicity and then settle out of court.

FIRM
WILSON & SON

PARTNERS
JOS^H GEO. WILSON
W. MORTIMER WILSON

TELEGRAMS
"WILSONS, SOL^RS, ALFRETON"

Alfreton

11th Nov: 1897

Dear Sir

Yourself: Kent

Herewith we send you copy of a letter received by us this morning from Mr Potter of Matlock Mr Kent's Solicitor which we enclose for your consideration. As things now stand no action can be commenced before the January Court so that you have a little time to consider the matter. From what you have informed us Mr Kent gave great provocation to the Managers and you would have a reasonable ground upon which to convince the Judge that you had just cause for summarily dismissing him and should this be established he could not recover anything. On the other hand there is no doubt that if the matter comes to trial there will be a great deal of publicity given to it and the ill-feeling which already exists in the Parish will be much increased.

You have already offered a quarter's salary "without prejudice" and considering that Mr Kent has now got another berth a months salary of £2:10:0 with something for his expenses say £10 or £12 altogether would be a fair thing to offer should you be disposed to settle at all. Kindly let us know your views at an early date. We regret very much that the Belper Bench took the view they did of the assault case.

Yours faithfully
Wilson & Son

Rev. Wm Acraman

See Appendix 2 for a copy of the original letter.

So, the vicar decided to take the case to trial with all the publicity which would follow. The following is a transcript of the vicar's defence to the court.

"The Revd. WILLIAM ACRAMAN says:-

I am Vicar of Crich and Manager of the National Schools. In the month of July last on behalf of the Managers of the National Schools I advertised in "The School Guardian" for a headmaster of the National School and in consequence of an application from Plaintiff I went to Gainsboro' where the Plaintiff then held the post of Assistant Master at St. John's National Schools and had an interview with Plaintiff. On my return to Crich I wrote to Plaintiff offering him the post of Master at the salary of £90 per year & house rent and rates. On Friday Sept. 24th Plaintiff's wife arrived at Crich with the furniture but she did not unpack the whole of it & complained about the house. On Saturday Septr. 25th Plaintiff arrived himself. I afterwards saw Mr. Haynes (the landlord of the house) about something being done to the house but he informed me Mr. Kent had said he did not intend to settle. He commenced sole charge of the school on 4th October. In consequence of what my Curate (the Revd. J. P. Neville) reported to me and also in consequence of other things on my return home on Oct 6th I wrote to Plaintiff the letter of that day giving him 3 months notice to quit. The same day he made some improper remarks in the Log Book. (Copy hereto) I received a letter from the plaintiff on the 7th Octr with a copy of a letter he intended writing to the Inspector on October 8th. The statements therein are absolutely false.

On October 8th the School broke up for a week's holiday and during the holidays I heard on good authority that Kent had said that if he went into school again he should not teach the children but recommend the children to go to the British School. In consequence of Plaintiff's conduct generally on the Saturday following (16th Octr) I asked Mr Wheatcroft the Secretary of the Managers to write at once requesting the plaintiff not to enter the School again and summarily dismissing him. Mr Wheatcroft had personally offered plaintiff £22-10-0 to go without prejudice but it was not accepted.

Rev W Acraman

The curate's transcript

What follows is the statement from the curate the Revd J. P. Neville who had already been found guilty, and fined, for a technical assault on the head Mr Kent.

In his statement he paints a wonderful picture of Mr and Mrs Kent banging and ringing the vicarage door for over an hour demanding that the vicar see them.

The Revd. J. Percy Neville says:- *I am Curate to the Defendant and am a Manager of Crich Schools.*

Friday Septr. 24th Mrs Kent with a girl called at Vicarage to see the Vicar (without having sent any notice that she was coming) about 3.00 – 3.30 pm. I told her that he was very tired and at rest and could be seen later in the evening she went away very displeased. The same evening about 7.00 – 7.30 the Vicar & I called on her at her house in Dimple Lane and as she complained much about the house being dirty, I went over the rooms, which I found in fair order. I left thinking her all right. Afterwards I heard she was abusing the Vicar about not attending to her wants. On Saturday Septr 25th Mr Kent arrived at the house. Tuesday Sept 28th I called on Kent to ask him to visit the School and the Temporary Master Mr Barnes he spoke most abusively of me and the Vicar, telling me I was no gentleman and asking me impudently "why did you go over the rooms of my house". Wednesday Octr 6th Kent called at Vicarage about 4pm and gave me a list of materials wanted for the School. Mr and Mrs Kent came to the Vicarage about 8pm. I told them that the Vicar was at Whatstandwell. He abused me saying that he told me before that I was no gentleman, that I was lying in saying the Vicar was not in, and both he and his wife were most rude to me and abusive of the Vicar. They tried to force their way into the house but I induced them to go. About 10 pm they returned to the Vicarage and began to ring the bell violently. I had gone to my bedroom and did not come down again. He continued ringing and calling until 11 pm. Meanwhile the Vicar returned and called a Policeman to remove him. About this Kent made a false entry in the Log Book. Mon Octr 18th I came with Mr Barnes at 8.00 – 8.50 a.m. to open the School – found Mr Kent in the yard – I asked him to go – he refused – a crowd gathering – including Mr. Dawes, Dyson, Walters &c who were urging the parents to fetch out their children. I went for the Policeman and came back with him. Dawes entered premises and said to me "Kent has as much right to be here as you". On the advice of Mr Barnes I asked Dawes to go as a trespasser. He went out. I then begged Kent to go. He refused again saying in the presence of the Policeman that he would not go except he be put out by force. I then asked the Policeman to put him out. He was unwilling but said if I put my hand on his shoulder he would stand by me and see that he would not strike me. I then put my hand on the collar of Kent's coat, to lead him, the Policeman accompanying us to the top of the steps leading to the street and as we reached the top he resisted and pushed back. I had to push him gently down the steps. I was quite calm.

Revd. J. P. Neville

There was an explanatory footnote by W. Acraman to Revd Neville's statement:

** Mr Dawes is Treasurer. Mr Dyson Master of the British School. Mr Dyson was at the Crich National School it is stated till about half past nine, instead of teaching at his own School ?? advising Kent. Walters is a Baptist minister newly come to Crich and sends his children to the British (I believe) and seems to promote it".

One of the teachers at the school, Inez Scarffe, also gave a written statement.

Mrs INEZ SCARFFE says:-

I am a mistress at the National Schools at Crich. I remember the plaintiff coming to Crich as headmaster of the National Schools. It was in October. It was just prior to the Wakes week. On Friday before the Wakes Week (8th October) I was at Kent's house the Plaintiff had a discussion. He also had a discussion with me at the school earlier in the day. The Plaintiff said he was upset at having received Notice – it had taken the heart out of him – if he could not teach them they might as well go to the British.

Mrs I Scarffe

Mrs Scarffe's statement to the Managers was stronger than this. It was "that he would recommend them to go to the British School." This was why the Managers were asked not to allow Kent to continue teaching.

Housekeeper and pupil statements

The vicar's housekeeper, Mrs Wetton, and two pupils at the school also made written statements.

Mary Wetton says:-

I am Housekeeper at the vicarage at Crich. I remember Wednesday October 6th. About 7 o'clock Plaintiff came to the Vicarage. He asked to see the Vicar. I told him he was out. He went away saying he would call again. About 10 o'clock at night the front door bell rang violently. No one opened the door. The bell kept ringing until after 11. I heard someone speaking outside and saying it was 11 o'clock. From the voice I heard I should say it was Kent. He rang so violently that he woke Mr Acraman's little daughter. The Plaintiff came to the Vicarage before this day. The Vicar was never in when he called this day.

Mary Wetton

James Poyzer says:-

I am nine years of age and a scholar at the National Schools at Crich. I remember the Plaintiff coming to the Schools on the first day. He caned me, but I had done nothing to warrant the punishment. He hurt my thumb. At the time he caned me he said I was the first boy he caned and he should always remember me. I have never seen the vicar fetch boys out of the School and then send them back to get marked.

Jaz Poyzer

**One of the best Scholars in Crich National Schools.   W. A.

Walter Perry says:-

I am nine years of age and attend the Crich National Schools. I remember Mr Kent coming to the Schools at Crich on the first day. In the morning before School time I was standing against my mother's door and Kent came to me. He asked me if I went to the Baptist. I said No. He then asked my mother who was standing near if I could take a note to Mr Dyson at the Baptist School. I took the note and then went direct to the School.

Walter Perry

Note: Thus the first morning Mr Kent took charge he began by sending our Scholar to the British School with correspondence.

PATRICK COSGROVE says:-

I am a Police Constable and stationed at Crich. On 6th October last about 11 o'clock at night the Revd. W Acraman fetched me to order the Plaintiff away from his house. I went to the Vicarage and when I got there I found the Plaintiff and his wife standing in the road against the front door of the Vicarage. The Plaintiff told me he had been there an hour and had been ringing the bell. I told him to go away. I passed the Vicarage about 10.15 the same evening and met the Vicar going home.

P. C. Cosgrove

(Note the Vicar was out & in fact was a mile away seeing his Church warden)

Also in the records was the folowing note:

The Rev. W. H. Turner Vicar of Hazlewood will be called upon subpoena to give evidence as to the commencement of Plaintiff's engagement there and the terms upon which he is engaged.

Mr Alfred Moody Headmaster of Bonsall School will state that he had been headmaster of the Crich School for $7\frac{1}{4}$ years till July/97 W. A. & will speak to its efficiency & will deny the allegations of the plaintiff which amount to fraud against himself & defendant.

Mr J. H. Barnes of Matlock will state that he is a certificated teacher and that he took temporary charge of the Crich School after the dismissal of Plaintiff, he witnessed the struggle between Plaintiff & the Rev J. P. Neville & will speak generally as to the efficiency of the School.

So here were the statements made by the vicar and those he called upon as witnesses to confirm and support his version of events. It is not certain whether Mr Kent went to the same trouble.

Notwithstanding all this preparation for trial, a settlement was made out of court. The affair did find itself in the public realm due to the late acceptance by Mr Kent of the managers' offer of pay in lieu of three months' notice. This is referred to in the following press cutting, dated 25th January 1898.

Press Cutting: 25 January 1898; unknown newspaper

The Vicar of Crich
And his schoolmaster
– Action for Damages
Settled out of Court

Before his honour Judge Smyly Q.C. at the Alfreton County Court, on Monday, a case was down for settlement in which George Henry Kent, a schoolmaster, of Hazlewood, was the plaintiff, and William Acraman, clerk in holy orders at Crich, was the defendant. The present proceedings were a sequel to those heard at the Belper Police Court some two months since, when, our readers will remember, the curate of the present defendant was fined in a comparatively small sum and costs for assaulting the present plaintiff, Mr Kent, by forcibly ejecting him from the premises of the Crich National School, where he had been engaged as schoolmaster by the present defendant. In the county court action the plaintiff claimed as damages the sum of £30 9s comprising the following items: One quarter's salary in lieu of notice. £22 10s; one week's salary £1 4s; expenses of removal £5. The defendant paid into court the sum of £12 10s at the same time.

DENYING LIABILITY

The plaintiff accepted this sum, and thus it happened that the action was practically settled out of court. However, on Monday, at the Alfreton County Court, Mr W.B. Hextall (instructed by Mr W.M. Wilson) brought the matter forward informing his Honour that it only came before him on account of the question of costs. He now asked his Honour to allow the defendant costs according to what the Registrar (Mr Hubbersty) thought fair or would allow. The action was brought on the 5th January, and the defendant forthwith paid into court through his solicitors, Messrs Wilson & Son, the sum of £12 10s. His preparations for defending the action were completed, and the sum paid into court was allowed to remain until Thursday last. When, at almost the last moment, on the evening of Friday, January 21st, a telegram was received from the plaintiff's solicitor, Mr J. Potter of Derby and Matlock, which was to the effect that plaintiff would accept the sum.

PAID INTO COURT

Messrs Wilson & Son at once communicated with Mr Potter,

who replied that delay was caused because his client was a schoolmaster who lived right away at Hazlewood. He emphasised the fact that the money was paid into court on the Monday, and Mr Potter would have had notice concerning it on Tuesday morning, and that, with all the time at the disposal of the plaintiff and his solicitor, the money was not accepted until five o'clock on Friday evening. Under the circumstances he thought it was justified in applying for such costs as the Registrar thought fair and right. – His Honour said he thought the defendant was entitled to such costs as the Registrar would be of the opinion were fairly incurred. Judgement was delivered accordingly.

The report of the unfair dismissal case and letters courtesy of Alan Howe

Whilst the vicar was having his troubles, life and work continued as usual back in Crich.

Courtesy Hugh Potter

Canal at Bullbridge crossing road and rail. Crich had several boatmen listed as living there, even though it is over 900feet above sea level.

Chapter 40
Vicar on remand

If the vicar thought that his appearance in court over the sacking of Mr Kent was to be his last, he was sadly mistaken.

There had been rumours circulating Crich about the vicar's attachment to a young girl. Eventually the rumour and innuendo surfaced, and the matter was brought to court. The vicar was to stand trial, be found guilty, and be sentenced to two years' hard labour in Derby Gaol.

In September 1899 he was arrested on two serious charges against a young girl and a young boy. Amazingly, at the initial hearing in Belper his solicitor was not in attendance. Some of the details of the hearing were not allowed to be reported.

The summons for the offence against the girl stated that she was thirteen years old. The vicar was adamant that this was incorrect as she was nearer fifteen; he wanted the summons changed – even though the age of consent was sixteen. He wanted the summons for the offences against the boy dismissed, on the grounds that the boy was a known liar.

A case was found to be answered and the vicar was not allowed bail before the next hearing, despite a passionate plea that he had money for whatever bail was set. His plea to be allowed some anonymity for transportation to Derby Gaol was allowed and he went in a private carriage in the company of the superintendant.

His request for a press blackout so as not to prejudice his case could not be granted from a public court. The following newspaper reports are quite extensive as the case drew a great deal of attention, not only in Derbyshire but across the country. "Disgraced vicar in sex scandal" always made for good headlines.

Derbyshire Times: 2 September 1899

SENSATIONAL ARREST OF A DERBYSHIRE VICAR
Two Serious Charges

A few weeks ago The Derbyshire Times made an announcement that it was not improbable an arrest would be effected in a Derbyshire village which would cause a sensation. It is now an accomplished fact. During the last month, or rather more, inquiries have been proceeding at Crich regarding certain accusations against the Rev. William Acraman, for many years vicar of this ancient parish. The police have had the matter in hand, the local constable P.c. Cosgrove, reporting to his superintendent at Belper, Mr. McDonald. In turn the facts were laid before the Chief Constable, Captain Holland. A day or two since he applied at Belper for warrants, and these were granted.

On Thursday morning the police paid an early visit to Crich, and proceeded to the Vicarage, where the vicar was quietly arrested and allowed to be driven to Belper in his own carriage. There, at the Occasional Court-house, Colonel Twyford, J.P. was waiting along with Captain Holland, Mr. Airey (the deputy chief constable), Supt. McDonald, and a few other persons from Crich. The general public had not ascertained what was about to take place, but later in the morning considerable numbers surrounded the Court-house and Police Station, anxious to obtain a view of the clergyman in the custody of the officers.

It was arranged the proceedings should commence at eleven o'clock. A short time was allowed for the accused to obtain a solicitor. Application was made to a Belper lawyer, who, however, did not attend the Court.

Shortly before noon Colonel Twyford proceeded to hear the evidence, on which a remand was to be asked for.

Mr. R.S. Clifford of Derby and Loughboro' conducted the prosecution.

The Rev. gentleman was called into a private room of the office of the Magistrate's Clerk. In the absence of the clerk, Mr. George Pym, the acting officer read the first charge.

The warrant charged William Acraman, of Crich, clerk in Holy Orders, on the fifth day of July 1899, with an unlawful offence with *child A*, a girl of the age of 13 years and not of the age of 16 years, and the said Wm. Acraman not having reasonable cause to believe that the said *child A* was of or above the age of 16 years.

The Prisoner: May I say one word?

The Magistrate: No, you had better wait.

Mr Clifford said he appeared in this case on behalf of the prosecution instructed by the chief constable. There were two charges against the prisoner. The facts he lay before the Court were shortly these: On the 5th of July the girl had occasion to go to the house of the prisoner, when certain liberties were taken with her.

The girl, *child A*, said she was 13 years of age and lived with her mother, a widow, at Crich. She had known the prisoner nearly all her life. She worked at a mill. After she got home from work, her mother told her to go to the Vicarage. She proceeded there and entered by the front door. The prisoner let her in.

Did you see anyone about the house? No, sir.

What room did he take you in? – The drawing-room.

Witness, in reply to further questions, said he put her on his knee and kissed her.

After other evidence as to what occurred, which cannot be repeated, she swore that prisoner told her she must not tell her mother.

Has anything occurred since that day? – No, sir.

Did it before? – Yes, twice before.

A similar thing? – Yes, sir.

The Magistrate: Was that in the drawing-room? – Yes, sir.

Mr. Clifford: You made a statement to your mother? – Yes.

The Magistrate: Do you want to ask the girl any questions?

Mr Clifford: If I may make a suggestion, I would say as the prisoner is not represented perhaps it would be advisable for him not to say much.

Prisoner: I only wanted to say one word.

The Magistrate: It will not be advisable to do so. I need not tell a man of your age what to do.

The Prisoner: I have simply one thing to say. I make out her age to be nearly 15 years. I want that summons to be amended. Here is

THE BAPTISMAL REGISTER

She was probably baptised by the curate who is coming next Sunday.

Mr Clifford: She is not 16, and that is quite sufficient for me.

The Prisoner: I believe that she is a year older than 13.

Mr Clifford: I have her certificate of birth; she was born 16th November 1885.

The Prisoner: I merely say I was led to think she was a year older.

The Chairman: I don't want to stop you or to put anything into your mouth.

The Prisoner: In common courtesy I wish the summons to be amended. He proceeded to make some further remarks on the age of the girl, and said he was sorry his solicitor was not present.

The Magistrate: You had better leave anything you have to say until later on.

P.c. Cosgrove, of Crich, deposed: I this morning received a warrant for the apprehension of the prisoner. I executed it.

Mr. Clifford: Did he say anything?

P.c. Cosgrove: I read the warrant to him, and in reply he said; "The girl is nearly 15 years old, I can certify that by the register."

Mr. Clifford: Was that all he said? – Yes, sir.

Mr. Clifford: That is all the evidence I offer on this charge. I think it is sufficient to justify a remand. I ask for a remand for eight days.

The Magistrate: Have you anything to say why you should not be remanded?

The Prisoner: I thought a remand was for seven days?

The Magistrate: You are remanded on this charge to this day week at eleven o'clock.

The Prisoner: I reserve my defence.

The second charge was then put to Revd Acraman.

THE SECOND CHARGE

Mr. Clifford proceeded with the second charge, which was that between the 20th May and 20th June, at Crich, being a male person, he unlawfully committed an act of gross indecency with another male person, *child B*. This, he need not say, was a misdemeanour.

The case, added Mr Clifford, was not before the Magistrates that day, but evidence would be offered. The boy was taken as far as the Darley Dale Institute in a four wheeled carriage, and on going home, at about eleven o'clock at night, prisoner took the boy along a lane, and there certain things transpired.

Child B, a boy, who said he was 12 years of age, and resided at home with his mother, at Crich, knew Mr Acraman, and remembered going to Darley with him. This would be about the end of May, or beginning of June. They drove in a carriage. They left Crich about three o'clock in the afternoon. Coming back they went into Birchwood Lane, Whatstandwell. It was dark when they got to the lane. The carriage lamps were lighted. Mr. Acraman blew the carriage lamps out. Witness described what took place. Witness had supper at the Vicarage then went home. There had been certain things since then, and also before.

Witness stated where the acts took place, but it was not possible to indicate further what was sworn to by the lad.

Mr. Clifford: I submit there is evidence to justify a remand.

The Clerk (to the Prisoner): Do you ask any questions?

Prisoner: No, I reserve my defence.

P.c. Cosgrove said: I received a warrant for the apprehension of the prisoner. I read the warrant to him and he said; "The boy, *child B*, has not been to the Vicarage for a year; I have not been in his company since that time."

Prisoner: I wish to say simply this: I have called to mind since, Mr Lee sent the boy with some charity paper to sign since then, but I don't believe I saw him. He came to the vicarage. I had no intercourse with him. He was sent to the vicarage with a paper, and was told to go away. I only want to say this in the interest of justice and truth. It is just possible he was seen against my wish. I could not help him coming; it was forced upon me. We would not have him upon the premises, he was so untruthful. He is well known to be most untruthful. The schoolmaster has justified that in writing. May I also say that the next day I called upon Mr Lee and told him he must never send the boy to the house again. Mr. Lee told me they were dismissing him because he was such a bad boy. I knew he was most untruthful; most unsatisfactory.

The Magistrate: That does not alter the facts.

The Prisoner: It is the truth.

Vicar remanded in gaol

Despite his appeals for bail – on any amount – he was committed to Derby Gaol as the Magistrates considered there was a case to answer.

The Magistrate: You will be reprimanded same as in the other case to the Public Hall at 11 o'clock next Thursday.

The Prisoner: I say I am the vicar of a large parish. I am alone, single handed. My curate is away, and I have not made arrangements with any other clergyman to carry out my duties. There are burials and baptisms and other work to be done. May I be allowed to go to Crich?

The Magistrate: I am afraid I cannot help you.

The Prisoner: I only want bail, substantial bail.

Mr. Clifford: On a serious charge like this I should certainly oppose bail of any kind.

The Magistrate: My own feeling is that I am bound to refuse bail. I have no objection to another magistrate taking it. I do not think this is a case for bail; I am very sorry to say so.

The Prisoner: I can find any amount of bail.

Mr Clifford: It is refused.

The Magistrate: I cannot admit you to bail. If other Magistrates took a different view –

Mr Clifford: There would have to be an application to a higher Court.

The Prisoner: May I say as a Christian man, I see reporters present – I don't want this case to be prejudiced by the Public press between now and next Thursday.

The Magistrate: I have no control over the Press.

The Prisoner: I ask this out of courtesy.

The Magistrate: This is a public Court and anyone may come in as he likes. I think the Press will confine itself to reporting the case.

The Prisoner: You are aware sometimes a case is prejudiced in a week. I ask them to say the least detail.

The Magistrate's Clerk: You are remanded eight days.

Again the prisoner appealed to be permitted to go to Crich, but it was declined.

As a last resource the prisoner asked that a policeman should accompany him to Derby gaol in private clothes so as not to attract attention.

Captain Holland replied that he would consult with Supt. McDonald as to this course.

The Prisoner: Fourteen years ago I was granted this privilege.

Captain Holland: I will refer to Supt. McDonald.

This closed the case.

Later in the day the prisoner was taken to the County prison in a private carriage. He was accompanied by Supt. McDonald.

The Rev. Wm. Acraman was ordained deacon in 1865 and priest in 1866 by the Bishop of Peterborough. He was appointed vicar of Crich in 1875 receiving the gift of the living from the trustees.

Chapter 41
Vicar's court hearing

After being refused bail at the preliminary hearing the vicar was taken to Derby Gaol to await the case that would take place in a week's time, again at Belper. He was allowed to travel to gaol in plain clothes, in a carriage with a superintendent. Other prisoners had to travel to Derby by rail in the company of uniformed police officers. He was spared this shame.

At the five-hour hearing in Belper the public were excluded and the press advised to exercise constraint in their reporting. This banning of the public caused quite an upset. Many of those wishing to attend expressed their dissatisfaction most strongly. A heavy police presence was needed to prevent things getting out of hand.

From the reporting of the evidence it could be inferred that *child A* might have been groomed by the vicar for his own ends. He tried to set her up in lodgings in Eastbourne with the promise of attending his daughter's school and becoming educated. When *child A*'s mother discovered the arrangement she did not like it and stopped her going. She had been under the impression that her daughter would be at a boarding school with the vicar's daughter Essie.

The gifts that were given to *child A* on each occasion she was assaulted seem rather peculiar. There was a pencil case that "became misplaced" and was not received. Flowers and blue ribbon were received, but the shilling he gave her was to be passed onto the church band.

The vicar had proposed to *child A*, the fourteen-year-old friend of his daughter's, even though he was sixty-two. This seemed very odd to the court. However, the history of Mr Acraman suggests that this could actually be true. Both his first wife, who died in childbirth, and his second wife, whom he married some years after his prison sentence, were both in their early twenties when he married them. He did have a preference for marrying young women.

After the hearing it was decided that the evidence was such that he should stand trial at the assizes. He was granted bail at £1000 (£500 from himself and £250 from two sureties) – today's equivalent amount would be well over £80,000. Again the newspapers reported the case very widely.

Derbyshire Times 9 September 1899

THE VICAR OF CRICH IN THE DOCK

FOUR SERIOUS CHARGES

"Desired to Educate and Marry a Young Girl"

AT THE BELPER POLICE COURT

Extraordinary and Sensational Evidence

Much excitement prevailed in Belper on Thursday morning, when it was known the Rev. William Acraman was to be charged at the Belper Police Court, with having committed serious offences against a young lad and girl, children of parishioners of his at Crich. Hundreds congregated near the Public Hall, where the Court is held, for the purpose of obtaining a view of the rev. gentleman when he was brought from Derby gaol, and the Court-room was crowded directly the doors were opened. The Bench, however, intimated that the Press alone would be admitted during the hearing of the case, and the Court was cleared. There were many objections to this, and one individual loudly protested, but in vain. There was a large staff of policemen present and the person in question was assisted in quickly retiring.

It was between one and two o'clock when the prisoner was driven up to the Court in a hansom. He was accompanied by Police sergeant Marshall, who was attired in private clothes. There was much groaning and hissing as he was taken into the Hall, where he was accommodated in a room adjoining the Court. About 2 o'clock he was placed at the prisoner's table, and the charges read over.

There were on the Bench:- Sir J. G. N. Alleyne, Bart (Chairman), Col. Twyford, Mr F. W. Greave and Mr John Smedley, Mr J. Burrough, J.P., the Diocesan Registrar also occupied a seat on the Bench, but took no part in the proceedings. The Bishop of the Diocese was represented by his solicitor, and the Rev. Cousens, curate at Crich, was present in Court.

Mr Clifford, solicitor, of Derby, prosecuted on behalf of the police and the Rev. W. Acraman was represented by Mr Clarke Hall, of London, barrister, instructed by Mr Wheatcroft, solicitor of Belper.

Captain Holland, the chief constable of the county, was also present during the whole of the hearing, which lasted over five hours.

PUBLIC EXCLUDED – PRESS ADMITTED

Before the proceedings began an appeal was made to the representatives of the Press.

Sir J. G. N. Alleyne, the Chairman, said the judges had decided the public could be excluded in cases of this description; at the same time as the Press could be admitted. His request was that the reporters of the Press use their own discretion and not make a sensational case. When the case went before a Grand Jury, if it got there, it would be another matter.

The first charge was then read by the Clerk to the Magistrates (Mr Joseph Pym). It was on the information of Mr J. C. Aurey, deputy chief constable of the county, for unlawfully and indecently assaulting *child A* at Crich, on or about April 1st.

A second charge of like nature was fixed on April 11th.

A third accusation was for indecently assaulting the girl *child A*, being above the age of 13 years and under the age of 16 years, at Crich, on or about June 5th.

A fourth summons put a similar offence at a later date.

NO EVIDENCE OFFERED UPON ONE CHARGE

The charge against the prisoner relating to the boy was for committing a certain act of gross indecency with another male person, *child B*, at Crich, between May 20th and June 20th this year.

Mr Hall said he appeared for the defence. There were, he observed, four different charges in respect to the girl, and they were covered precisely by the same facts and differed only as to dates. If it was thought necessary to send any case to trial they could all be taken together.

Mr Clifford said he appeared for the prosecution, and as far as he had been able he had made certain investigations and was not in a position to go into the boy's case so far as related to the dates given on the information. He should offer no evidence.

SAME PUBLICITY ASKED FOR BY THE DEFENCE

Mr Hall: If my friend offers no evidence I ask you, sir, to charge the defendant formally, so that he may be formally discharged upon that charge. A great deal of publicity has been given to this very disgraceful case, and it is not right anything should be kept hanging over my client. I have a large amount of evidence to show that no offence could have been committed, and, therefore, I think he is entitled to be discharged and the same publicity be given to the fact that he is not guilty of that fact, and must be discharged at once.

Mr Clifford: I merely say I am not in a position to go on with the case. I offer no evidence, and technically there is an end of it.

Mr Hall: My friend ought to be more candid.

Mr Clifford: I offer no evidence.

The Clerk to the Magistrates: The case is dismissed.

Mr Hall: Mr Acraman pleads not guilty to all the charges.

The case for the prosecution, led by Mr Clifford, was well reported. He outlined what was alleged to have happened.

OPENING THE CASE

Mr Clifford, addressing the Bench, said that in this case they had heard the four charges which had been brought against the defendant. Two were for criminal offences against the girl, and two were under the Criminal Law Amendments Act. The prisoner was the vicar of Crich, in that county, and the girl, *child A*, who he was charged with assaulting, was a girl, 13 years of age last November, and lived with her mother, a widow woman, at Crich. The girl appeared to have been

THE COMPANION OF THE PRISONER'S DAUGHTER

who he was told was about the same age. They went to school together at Crich Carr, until this Spring, when the prisoner's daughter went to Eastbourne. Now the facts he has to lay before them, as far as the first charge was concerned, were these: The date would be fixed by a cantata which took place in Easter week at Crich. The girl, *child A*, would tell them that on

THE SATURDAY BEFORE EASTER SUNDAY

which was the first of April, after the practice was over at the schools for the cantata the prisoner asked her to go with him to the vicarage. She went to the vicarage, and he took her into the drawing room. When there he sat down in an easy chair himself, and pulled the girl onto his knee and kissed her.

Mr Clifford explained the details of the offence. Before the girl left, he said, he told her not to say anything to anyone, and he took her to the front door, gave her a kiss, and let her out. As far as that case was concerned, here was a child of 13 years of age, and here was a man, the prisoner, many years older who had a child of about the same age. The girl returned home, and being rather late gave an explanation to her mother. About a week after the first assault on or about the 11th of April, Mr Acraman, the vicar, called and saw the girl's mother, and

ASKED FOR THE GIRL TO BE SENT
UP TO THE VICARAGE

as he had got a pencil case for her. The girl was at work at Lea Mills, at a hosiery factory near Crich, and did not finish work until about half past five or six o'clock at night. The mother delivered the message to her daughter and the daughter went to the house at about half past seven. She went to the front door and rang the bell, and the door was answered by Mr Acraman. He took her into the drawing room, fastened the door, and drew blinds down. He took the girl's hands and pulled her on to his knee and kissed her. He said he had a pencil case for her, but he had mislaid it and could not find it. He told her that

WHILST SHE WAS ON HIS KNEE

Having committed the offence, he placed her on his knee, and kissed her again. He told her he would like to marry her some time, and asked her if she would consent. He pressed her so many times, and at last she said, "Yes." Having kissed her again he let her go. But he never mentioned marriage afterwards. These

were the two cases of indecent assault. Under the Criminal Law Amendments Act these proceedings must be commenced within three months of the committal of the offence. If it had been within the time he would have had no hesitation in charging him under section 5. Up to this time he seemed to have

DESIRED TO SEND THE GIRL AWAY
TO SCHOOL

He saw the mother about sending the child to Eastbourne, and he believed he saw her two or three times. He went away about the 8th June to Eastbourne. But before going to Eastbourne he saw the girl again. She went to the house under these circumstances. A boy who was in the employ of the defendant of the name Greenhough, met the girl, *child A*, as she was coming from work. The boy delivered a message from the rev. gentleman, and the girl went. Before going she told her mother that she had been sent for to the vicarage. He met the girl in the garden, and said he had been looking for her a long time. He told her to go into the drawing-room through the window from the garden. He then locked the door of the drawing-room, closed the windows, and drew down the blinds. He pulled the girl upon his knees, kissed her and said

HE WAS LONELY NOW

without Essie. He expressed the opinion that he would like her to come and keep him company. The same offence was committed. He then gave the girl a piece of blue ribbon. The girl took the ribbon home and gave it to her mother. The ribbon would be produced for their Worships. It was just possible that on this occasion, the boy Greenhough's memory would be bad. He was in the vicar's employ. There was not very great corroboration of the first instance, but there was of the second as he went and asked the girl's mother to send her up for a pencil case. As to the third instance there was the corroboration of the blue ribbon. He desired to

SEND THIS GIRL TO EASTBOURNE

and saw the mother about it. The mother partly consented, but the defendant, whilst he was at Eastbourne, wrote a letter to Mrs Slack. That letter had been destroyed. This Mrs Slack, who had been for some years in charge of the defendant's daughter, talked the matter over with *Mrs A*, and the result was that *Mrs A* absolutely refused to let the girl go to Eastbourne as the child was to be put in lodgings and not sent to school. The vicar returned in June, about the 10th or 11th. On the 5th July he saw *Mrs A*, the mother of the girl. He called at the house, and said he had not come to trouble her about Eastbourne, but he had a letter from his daughter Essie, and there was one for *child A*. He asked that the child might be sent up to the vicarage, so that she might answer the letter. After he had been gone from the house a few minutes, he returned and said, "Tell the girl to come to the front door, as the servant is rather deaf." The girl went up to the vicarage about quarter to eight at night.

Mr Acraman was in the garden and said

"HE WAS GLAD THAT SHE HAD COME"

He "had been afraid she was not coming, as she was rather late." He added that he was sorry she had not gone to Eastbourne. Then he took her through the window into the drawing-room, fastened the window, pulled down the blind and fastened the door. He repeated the conduct previously explained. That was the last occasion the girl was at the house. She had a message to go again, but would not go. When the girl left the house on the last occasion she did not go on the highway. She went across a field, and the defendant walked down with the girl to where there was a haystack, at the bottom of the garden leading into another field.

Mr Clifford explained, by an Ordnance Map, how far the girl went, and pointed out that she jumped into the highway known as Bullen Lane. When she jumped into the lane, there happened to be a witness, John Wetton, the parish clerk present. Wetton would tell them that it was after the Lea Mills trip, and he made a remark to the girl the next morning about it. He believed that after hearing the evidence, that the Bench would say that they were justified in sending the case for trial at the Assizes.

Child A was next to give her evidence.

THE GIRL'S EVIDENCE

Child A said: I reside with my mother, who is a widow, at Crich. I was 13 years of age on the 10th November last. I have known Mr Acraman ever since I can remember. He has a daughter Essie. I left Crich Carr School last November, at the same time as Essie, with whom I used to play. I don't know when Essie went to Eastbourne.

Mr Clifford: Do you remember preparing for a cantata at Easter? – Witness: Yes.

Was it held on Wednesday in Easter week? – Yes.

Do you remember being at the practice before it was held? – Yes.

Do you remember one night before the cantata was given Mr Acraman saying something to you? – Yes, on the Saturday night before the cantata was given. We had been practising, and Mr Acraman told me to go on, as he wanted me.

The Magistrate's Clerk: Where was the conversation? – In the Crich schoolyard.

By Mr Clifford – When he told me to go on. Mr Acraman followed me and took me into the drawing-room. I cannot say what time it would be, but it would be after seven. It was between 7 and 8 o'clock when we finished the practice for the cantata.

Mr Clifford: When you got to the vicarage, which way did you go in? – Through the front door. He told me to go into the drawing-room. I went into the drawing-room. Mr Acraman came with me, and we were both in the room. Mr Acraman closed the door when we got in.

Can you tell me whether it was locked or not? – Yes.

Why? – Because I saw him lock it.

How about the blinds when you got in? – He pulled them down.

Did he sit down anywhere? – Yes, in the armchair.

Did he say anything? – He told me to come on his knee.

Did you go on his knee? – Yes.

Did he do anything to you? – He kissed me.

Witness described other acts.

What did he do before you went away that night? – He told me I must not tell anybody.

Did he let you out? – Yes.

Before you parted, did he do anything? – He kissed me.

Where was that? – Going from the hall to the doorway in the garden.

You went straight home and told your mother where you had been? – Yes, sir.

HER MOTHER TOLD HER TO GO TO THE VICARAGE

Mr Clifford: Do you remember about a week after the cantata? – Yes.

Did your mother tell you anything? – Yes, to go to the vicarage.

Were you working at Lea Mills? – Yes.

You delivered a message, and did you the same night go to the vicarage? – Yes.

What door did you go in? – The front.

Who answered the door? – Mr Acraman.

Witness went on to say she was told to go into the drawing-room. He followed her in and fastened the door. The blinds were drawn. Mr Acraman sat on an armchair and placed her on his knee, by placing hold of her hands. He kissed her.

He told her he had a pencil case for her, but could not find it.

The girl continued her story and detailed what took place.

Witness continued her evidence, and said that when she left the vicarage that night he told her she must go again soon.

PROMISED HER SOME FLOWERS AND BLUE RIBBON

Mr Clifford: Now, with regard to June 5th, do you remember Mr Acraman going to Eastbourne? – Yes.

Did you see him that week before he went away on the Thursday? – No, sir.

What caused you to go to the vicarage a third time? – He promised me some flowers.

As you were coming home from work did you meet Greenhough? – Yes, sir.

He said something to you? – Yes.

And in consequence you went to the vicarage? – Yes, sir.

What time would it be? – About half-past seven.

Did you see Mr Acraman? – Yes, against the gate leading into his front garden.

Mr Hall interrupted and asked the Bench to confine Mr Clifford to a period of three months as he was bound by the Criminal Law Amendment Act.

Mr Clifford proceeded and asked the girl what was said to her on arrival.

Witness: He said he was lonely without me, as Essie was away.

Which way did you go into the house? – By the drawing-room.

Witness continued and said the door was fastened and the blinds pulled down, then the vicar pulled her on his knee and kissed her.

Other evidence having been tendered, witness said that on this occasion Mr Acraman told her she must go again, and he would send a message by Johnny Greenhough.

Did he give you anything? – Yes, a shilling and he told me I could give it to the church band.

Did he give you anything else? – Yes, a piece of blue ribbon.

Witness also added that he told her not to tell her mother. He gave her some flowers on this occasion. The ribbon and flowers were given to her mother the same night.

SHE AFTERWARDS PROMISED TO MARRY HIM

Mr Clifford: Did you again go to the vicarage? – Yes, sir.

Has there been a trip from Lea Mills this year? – Yes.

When was it? – First Saturday in July.

Witness remembered going to the vicarage on the Wednesday the week after the trip. She went in consequence of something her mother had told her. She saw Mr Acraman in the garden.

What did he say? – He told me to go with him through the window.

Into what room? – The drawing-room.

Witness said that the blinds were drawn. The door leading into the hall was shut, and he went to see if it was fastened. After that he put her on his knee as he sat in the arm-chair.

What did he do? – He told me he loved me.

Did he say anything else? – He asked me if I would marry him.

What did you say? – I did not say

anything then. He asked me a lot of times and then I said, "Yes."

Witness added that he gave two letters on this visit, one from the daughter Essie. The letters were taken home for the mother to see. That night he separated from her near a hay-stack down the fields. He had told her to go that way so that people could not see her. When she jumped over the wall into the lane she saw John Whetton, the parish clerk.

Have you been to the vicarage since then? – No, sir.

Have you seen Greenhough since? – Yes, sir.

Mr Clifford: I believe you made no complaint to your mother until she asked you? – No, sir.

Mr Hall then cross-examined child A. From what was reported she came over as a very trustworthy and credible witness.

CROSS-EXAMINATION OF THE GIRL

Mr Hall: Mr Acraman took you on his knee and kissed you the same as his own daughter? – Yes.

He often kissed you, and you sat on his knee when Essie was there? – Yes, sir.

Mr Cousens, the curate, lives in the house with the vicar? – Yes, sir.

And besides; there is the cook and the boy Greenhough? – Yes, sir.

Witness stated there was a practice of a cantata on the Saturday night.

Mr Hall: I am going to put it to you there never was a practice on the Saturday night? – Witness: There was.

Did you ever hear anyone at the door, when it was locked, and trying to open it? – No, sir.

Why did you not tell your mother? – I promised Mr Acraman I would not do so.

Was Essie at home for Easter holidays? – Yes.

And you went to the vicarage about every day? – Yes, I went often.

Witness did not decline to go into the drawing-room on any of the occasions. On the third occasion she told her mother she did not want to go to the vicarage.

You said Mr Acraman gave you a shilling for the band? – Yes.

The band was to go out on the Whit-Tuesday? – Yes, sir.

Mr Clarke Hall: That is very material. (To witness): On the third occasion were they not hay-making? – The hay was down in the field; they had been hay-making.

And he asked you to marry him? – Yes, he said he should like to, some time.

When did he say that? – When we were going home, once he said it, and he said it in the drawing-room.

When did you first say anything? – One Saturday night my mother asked me, as she had heard of it.

Mr Hall: Was it some time before the

charge was brought?

Mr Clifford: It was the 14th of August it came to the knowledge of the police.

Mr Hall: We will take it one Saturday in August. (To witness): Who did you tell? – My mother; she asked me two or three questions.

Do you know Annie Holmes? – Yes.

Is she a friend of yours? – Yes.

And do you know Martha Milward? – Yes.

Is she a friend of yours? – Yes, but she is a greater friend of Annie Holmes.

SHE TOLD HER FRIENDS A LIE

Did you tell these two something? – Yes, one morning as we were going to work Annie Holmes asked me if it was right I was going to get married to Mr Acraman. As they were saying it in the quarry, I said that it was not true.

Did you tell Annie Holmes and Martha Milward that you had nothing to fear because Mr Acraman had never done anything to you? – Yes, to Annie Holmes. She told me they were talking about it in the quarry and at the top of the town, and I told her it was not true.

When you told Annie Holmes Mr Acraman had done nothing to you, you meant that he had never acted improperly to you? – Yes.

THE GIRL'S TESTIMONY UNSHAKEN

I put it to you, that what you said to Annie Holmes was true – be careful now! – and that he has never done anything to you? – He has done something to me.

You say now that he has? – Yes.

The Magistrates' Clerk: What you told Annie Holmes then, was it a lie or true? – It was a lie.

And is the statement you made today the truth? – Yes, sir.

Mr Hall: Do you then tell lies? – No, but Mr Acraman made me promise to tell no-one.

Then why did you tell anyone? – Because Mr Wetton told my mother something about it, and she made me tell her.

Mr Clifford: You told a lie because the prisoner told you to tell no-one? – Yes.

The girl's evidence was then read over, and signed by her.

Next to be called was child A's mother, who gave her evidence.

THE GIRL'S MOTHER CALLED

Mrs A said: I am a widow and reside at Crich. The last witness, *child A*, is my daughter. She was born on the 10th November 1885. I have lived some years at Crich. I remember the cantata, which took place on Wednesday in Easter week. There was a practice the week before; on the Saturday previously. Her daughter was taking part in it.

Mr Clifford: Do you remember whether your daughter was late home that night?

Witness: Yes, sir, and I made enquiries as to where she had been and what caused her to be late. After the cantata Mr Acraman came to her house. It would be about a week after the cantata.

Did he say anything about *child A*? – He said he had a pencil case for *child A* and would I let her go on to the vicarage and fetch it. I said I would when she came from work. I gave her the message and she went to the vicarage that same night. She returned home but I did not see the pencil case.

Do you remember another occasion when your daughter went? – Yes, before Mr Acraman went to Eastbourne.

BLUE RIBBON AND FLOWERS

Mr Hall: Does she know that she went to the vicarage at all?

Mr Clifford: I am going to show that. When she came back did she give you anything? – Yes, the piece of blue ribbon produced. She also brought some flowers with her on this occasion.

Do you know Mr Acraman went to Eastbourne? – Yes, I remember him calling at my house before he went. He wanted to know whether I would allow *child A* to go to Eastbourne to be a companion to his daughter. He said, "I will educate her the same as my own child."

What did you say? – I would rather keep her at home. I don't wish her to go.

AGREED FOR *CHILD A* TO GO TO EASTBOURNE

Did he see you again about it? – Yes, and I gave in for her to go.

How was the girl to go? – By London, and the curate, Mr Cousens, was to take her there.

Who was to meet her at Eastbourne? – Mr Acraman.

How long after that interview did he go away? – On the Thursday following.

How do you know he went on the Thursday following? – Of course I know he went on the Thursday. I do know.

After he had gone did Mrs Slack send for you? – Yes, she is a neighbour and used to live in the vicarage.

ARRANGEMENTS MADE FOR DAUGHTER TO GO TO EASTBOURNE

Did she produce to you a letter she had received from Mr Acraman? – Yes, sir.

Mr Clifford: Another witness will tell us the contents. But you tell us to best of your recollection what was in it. – He had made arrangements, he said, for his daughter to be in a boarding school altogether; and my daughter had to stay with some ladies with whom he had arranged.

You discussed this with Mrs Slack and decided not to let *child A* go? – Yes, sir.

How long was he away? – He was away one Sunday.

Do you remember Mr Acraman coming to you? – Yes.

Was it after the Lea Mills trip? – Yes, on the Wednesday after.

When he came what did he say? – He said, "I am not going to trouble you about Eastbourne, *Mrs A*, I have a letter from my little girl, and there is one for *child A*; will you let *child A* go on and see the letter and answer it for herself." I said yes, when she comes from work.

After this message did the vicar go away and then come back to your door? – Yes.

What did he say? – "Tell *child A* to come to the front door", as either Clara or the servant was hard of hearing. I cannot say which he said.

Did you deliver that message? – Yes, sir.

Did your daughter return that night? – Yes, sir.

And give you anything? – Yes, a bunch of flowers and two letters, one from Essie.

Have you destroyed those letters? – Yes, sir.

Now, did you subsequently ask your daughter certain questions? – Yes, sir.

From what she said the vicar subsequently came and saw you? – He was coming but –

You went and met him? – Yes, at the bottom of the yard.

TOLD THE VICAR TO KEEP AWAY FROM HER HOUSE

What did you say to the vicar? – I told him what I thought about him.

Witness: I told him I never thought his wanting her to go away would lead to anything like this. I said I should not allow him to come to our house any more. He wanted to say something to me, but I would not listen to him.

Mr Clifford: I suppose you were in a temper? – Yes, I was.

WHY THE GIRL WAS TO GO INTO LODGINGS

Mr Hall: You don't remember the details of the letter? – No, sir.

Did it say Mrs Pennington was to take charge of the daughter? – I think that was the name.

Did it say the reason was that the school was too full? – It might have done.

Had you asked Mr Acraman to call and see you in your new house? He called sometimes, but I did not ask him to call.

Next to take the stand was the doctor who examined child A.

THE DOCTOR'S EVIDENCE

Maurice Gerard McElligott said: I am a physician and surgeon practising at Belper. On the 14th August I examined the girl *child A* at my surgery.

What was the result of your examination? – The result was purely negative. The girl was practically virgo intacta.

John Whetton the parish clerk also gave his account. His name was variously spelt with or without the "h".

THE PARISH CLERK AT CRICH

John Whetton deposed: I am the parish clerk at Crich. I remember the Lea Mills trip. I recollect being in Bulling Lane one night, near the vicarage, I could see the vicar's stack of hay in the field. There was a gate against the stack, I saw against the gate *child A* and Mr Acraman.

Did you see which way Mr Acraman went? – He went up to his own home.

Which way did the girl come? – Down the fields.

There is a stone wall? – Yes.

Did she jump over the wall? – Yes; a good jump of seven or eight feet.

You did not say anything to her? – No.

What time was it? – About eight o'clock.

Mary Slack's evidence confirmed that vicar had stated his desire to marry child A. Mrs Slack was the person who looked after the vicar's daughter, Essie, as she was growing up. She spoke up for the vicar.

THE VICAR SPEAKS OF THE GIRL AS HIS FUTURE WIFE

Mary Slack, wife of Edward Slack, said: My husband is grocer at Crich. I brought up Mr Acraman's little girl. I was formerly in the service of Mr Acraman. I was there ten years. I remember Mr Acraman going to Eastbourne. It was this year but I don't remember the date.

Did Mr Acraman see you? – Yes.

Did he say something to you? – Yes; he proposed to send *child A* to school and educate her as he had proposed to her.

And what else? – That she had accepted him.

Did you receive a letter? – Yes.

Has that letter been destroyed? – Yes, I expect so, by my husband.

Was it in the handwriting of Mr Acraman? – Yes.

Did you write to Mr Acraman and say that the girl could not go to school? – Yes.

After conversation with *Mrs A*? – Yes; I read the letter to *Mrs A* as she could not read it.

"ALWAYS BEEN A PERFECT GENTLEMAN"

Mr Hall: I have known Mr Acraman ever since he came to Crich. That is over 20 years since. I have never known an impropriety to take place. He has always been a perfect gentleman to everyone in the house.

Next to take the stand was Mary Lee. The prosecution wanted to treat her as an hostile witness.

Hostile witness?

VICAR WAS NOT AWARE OF ANY TROUBLE

Mary Lee, wife of John Lee, of Crich, said: I remember Monday, August 14th, having a conversation with the vicar about *child A*, at the Vicarage. A day or two afterwards I had a conversation with Police-constable Cosgrove.

What did Mr Acraman say? – Witness: I told the policeman I did not wish to make a statement.

What did you do at the Vicarage: tell us what he said. – He said he was not aware there was any trouble going on at Belper until that morning, when he was told. He did not know there was any ground for it.

Then I think you say he said something about *Mrs A* having been before the magistrates: – Yes.

What about? – He did not say what about.

Mr Clifford desired to treat the witness as hostile (To witness): Did he say anything about the girl *child A*? – Witness: He said they had been down to Belper to lay a complaint.

QUITE READY TO MARRY THE GIRL

Anything more? – He said he was quite ready to marry the girl. He said he was very sorry they had taken out the actions.

It was very young for a girl of 13 to be married? – I had thought it was exceedingly kind of the vicar to take the trouble to educate the girl.

The Magistrates' Clerk: That has nothing to do with it.

Witness: He had told me frequently how fond he was of her, and how fond she was of him, and that he had spoken to her about marrying him.

Can you remember anything else? – That he had taken advice from a friend near to.

We spoke about his little daughter, and I advised him to send her down to her aunt if there was likely to be any trouble.

Did he seem in any trouble? – Yes, he was naturally troubled.

Did he say anything else about the girl *child A*? – He said he had never meant anything but what was right about her.

Did he say anything more? – Not on that occasion.

Or on any occasion? (Hesitating): If you wish to ask me if Mr Acraman admitted an offence with the girl, he never did admit such a thing.

By Mr Hall: I have known him 15 or 16 years.

Mr Hall: Have you known him to be a decent respectable man? – As far as I have known him myself. He has always behaved properly to me at all times.

Mr Hall: And is a hard working clergyman?

The Magistrates' Clerk: That is not a question.

Mr Clifford: Personally you have seen nothing improper with him? – Not myself.

Mrs Slack was recalled as a witness and quizzed about the living arrangements made for child A when she was to go to Eastbourne. It had been thought she would be living with Essie in a boarding school. It transpired that this would not be the case. Child A would be in lodgings.

WHAT WAS IN THE LETTER

Mary Slack was recalled, and asked by Sir John Alleyne: Can't you remember anything that was in the letter. Was she going to these rooms as lodgings?

Witness: She was to go with a widow lady with two children to be educated.

But Miss Acraman was to be a boarder in the school? – Yes, sir.

Mr Clifford: You got this letter from Mr Acraman. Did it deal with other matters except *child A*? – Nothing.

Just tell us in your own way what it said; what was in the letter? – "Tell *Mrs A* I have made nice arrangements for *child A* with a widow lady with two children."

It said she was to go on the Friday.

Sir John Alleyne: Was there any reason why she could not go to be a boarder? – I don't remember.

Did it say his own daughter had gone on to be a boarder? – I don't remember whether it said so in the letter, but Mr Acraman told me.

Do you know whether his daughter Essie had been a boarder before then? Not before then, but it was about then.

By the Bench: The girl *child A* was not to be in the same house as the vicar's daughter.

P.c. Cosgrove gave evidence as to the arrest of the vicar and what led up to it.

WHAT THE POLICE CONSTABLE HAS TO SAY

P.c. Cosgrove, stationed at Crich, stated: I produce the birth certificate of *child A*. Mr Acraman was away on the 11th June; and was at home on June 4th and 13th. I received a letter from him dated the 13th June. It was from Eastbourne.

Can you tell us when it was the cantata took place? – Sometime about Easter week: I cannot tell the date.

When had you an interview with Mrs Lee? I believe on the 15th August.

You made a report the same day and sent to your superior officer? – I did, sir.

I believe you received a warrant for the apprehension of the vicar? – Yes, I arrested him a week today.

Did he say anything? – I gave the warrant to him after arresting him. He said, "The girl is 15 years old in November. I can prove that by the register book."

Was that all? – Yes.

You conveyed him to the lock-up? – Yes.

Mr Hall: Was an application made to the Magistrate's Clerk for a summons? – Yes.

And it was refused? – Yes.

It was a matter of common talk of what was going on? – Yes, and had been for weeks.

He was not surprised when you arrested him? – No.

Mr Clifford: That is my case; on the evidence, subject to what my learned friend may say, I ask you to commit him for trial at the Assizes.

It was time for Revd Acraman's QC to sum up his defence against the charges.

COUNSEL'S ABLE AND ELOQUENT DEFENCE

Mr Clarke Hall said, in rising to address the magistrates, on behalf of that clergyman, who could not but feel that he had a painful duty to fulfil. He could hardly understand how a painful charge of that kind should have been made at all. Now that one had heard the whole of the evidence that could be adduced by the prosecution he could not but feel that the nature of that evidence was so slight, that in spite of the seriousness and gravity of the charge, that the prosecution had failed to make a case, which they were bound to make out to them that day in order to justify them in taking the action to commit the man for trial at the Assizes. The girl in that case, a girl of 13 years of age, had given her evidence, and they had heard it, but if there was one thing which stood out clear from that evidence it was this: That she had never at any time resisted what she said was done to her. She never took any action in the matter until the complainant, in answer to her mother's questions in August, and that, as a matter of fact, if such a thing were done, as was said, she was practically a party to the doing of it. If that were the case, it was, of course, perfectly clear that no jury would accept the evidence that she had given, unless it was corroborated in a material particular. It was for them, in considering this case, to say in their own minds whether they thought that any jury would convict. Now, if it was necessary, as he submitted it was, that there should be corroboration of this girl's story, she having been in fact

AN ACCOMPLICE

to anything done to her, where had the prosecution been able to adduce it there that day? It was common ground that the girl was a frequent visitor at the house, it was common ground that whilst the vicar's daughter was at home she was going constantly day after day. It was common ground that the vicar was very fond of this child, that she sat on his knee many times, and that he kissed her many times. But where had the prosecution been able to show by one iota of evidence that any more than this took place, except by the child's own statement? It had been laid down that where corroboration was necessary to a story of a prosecutrix, it was necessary the corroboration should not be something merely to what was common ground between two parties, but the corroboration should be of such a nature that if evidence given in corroboration be true, then the suggestion made by the defendant cannot be true. That was the test that was laid down on regard to corroborative evidence. As far as he knew the witness had stated what was perfectly true, and he sequenced in everything that had been said except by the girl herself. Admitting it all, what was there to show even to suggest, suspicious

circumstances in anything said by the vicar implicating him? There was nothing at all. The case

RESTED SIMPLY AND SOLELY UPON THE STORY OF THIS GIRL

If that was the correct view, then it was clear that, under the direction of a judge, no jury could possibly convict in this case. If that were the case he submitted that this man ought not to be put in this most painful position of having this charge hanging over him for the next two or three months, if it were a fact that no jury could convict because there was no corroboration, not sufficient corroboration. If that were so, suspicion might have been aroused in their minds by the evidence and by the way the girl gave her evidence, but if they were convinced that no jury would convict they ought not put this man in the position of waiting until November or December for trial upon which he would be acquitted. He would like to leave it on that broad ground if the case for the prosecution broke down because they could not support it, but he thought it was his duty to his client to point out that there were other defences, though he did not suggest or admit that the story of the girl was true. Still there were other defences which

WOULD PREVENT CONVICTION

With regard to the charge of the 1st April, the defendant was brought there to answer one of indecent assault, and his friend had made some curious admission in his opening. He had said that he had wanted to avoid an Act of Parliament which laid down the three month limit, because the 1st April could not be brought within the three months as that had elapsed. Therefore, said his friend, he had brought that case although he admitted that it was an attempt at carnal knowledge under the Criminal Law Amendment Act. He would be sorry to make such a statement before a judge in a criminal court – attempting to get out of a serious offence by avoiding an Act of Parliament. Could it be maintained, admitting that all the girl and all the witnesses had said was true, that an indecent assault had been committed on the 1st April? An assault was a forcible act against the person and will of another, and it had been laid down in numbers of cases by judges, that an assault could not be proved where the girl was shown to acquiesce. Upon the first occasion she did not cry out or make any complaint, and, knowing what had happened, she allowed it to happen on a second occasion. She went willingly and made no resistance, and though the curate was in the house at the time, in all probability and the cook was certainly in the house, she never attracted the attention of either. That made an assault impossible in law. If these facts were true, the first two charges, even assuming the truth of all evidence of the prosecution, must necessarily fall to the ground. The girl was over 13 years of age and unless one requested in some way, the defendant could not be charged with a forcible act against her. Now let him say a word with regard to the other case, the case which was alleged to have happened on the 5th June. There

HAD NOT BEEN A TITTLE OF EVIDENCE

to show what had happened on the 5th June. The only evidence which fixed it in any way was the evidence of the girl herself, and when he put it to her and his friend put it to her also, she denied she had seen the vicar during the week in which he went to Eastbourne. It had been proved that he went to Eastbourne on the 8th June, and the date of the alleged assault was June 5th, the Monday in the same week. The girl said, "I did not see him at all in that week," and she stuck to it. He gave her opportunity of altering her mind and found that when he rose to cross-examine she said that she had received 1s from Mr Acraman to give to the band that played on Whit Tuesday. Whit Tuesday fell on the 21st May, therefore, if the girl's story was true, as to what occurred on this occasion, whatever did occur occurred before the 21st May. The warrant was not taken out until the 31st August so that case fell to the ground absolutely because it was not brought until after three months had elapsed. Then they had only one occasion left which had been alleged to have been the 5th July.

This date did not appear to be clearly proved. He must admit that the girl seemed to have given her evidence very well, so far as he could judge, and, of course, one had to face the difficulty as to why the girl, apparently fairly well brought up, should tell a story of this kind, that was not true. This was a difficulty one always had to face in cases of this kind. Unfortunately

GIRLS DID TELL THESE STORIES

when they were not true. It was difficult to understand why it should be, but it was one, over and over again, without motive. He ventured to think it was more easily understood in this case than in some other cases, because he could disguise from himself that the conduct of Mr Acraman towards the girl had been very strange. He felt that himself. They had been told, and he was not in a position to dispute it, because it had been told by three different witnesses, that something had been said by Mr Acraman to this girl about someday, when he had educated her,

HE WOULD MARRY HER

It seems to have been a very strange idea to have entered his mind. He must admit that, and face it, and he was instructed by Mr Acraman to deny it. No doubt it was so, but however foolish Mr Acraman might have been, however extraordinary this idea that had entered into his mind, it had been done before. It had entered the minds of men to take a humble girl, and have her educated, and then to marry her. If something had been said to this girl about eventually marrying her, and as Mr Acraman did not wish to deny that she had sat on his knee, and that he had kissed her – these circumstances, all taken together – it was easy to understand that this girl, not mixing in a high class of life, but being amongst factory girls – thoroughly respectable girls, no doubt – would hear matters denounced which were not entirely decent, and taking them and connecting them in her own mind, with what had been said to her, suggestions having been made as to marriage, that

THE POISON WOULD ENTER HER MIND

and induce her to make that charge. If this girl had been a right minded girl, and had felt the anger she said she felt, it was perfectly clear that the first thing she would have done, when there was any suggestion of impropriety made to her, would have been to go direct to her mother, with whom she was living, and to whom she returned on the night the impropriety took place, and would have told her mother what had happened. Not a single word was said about this from the first of April until the 14th August when she made a communication to her mother. The girl did not go voluntarily to her mother. It was only when the mother put questions to her – made suggestions to her in all probability – that something was put into the girl's mind, and she answered these questions, and the suggestions made in consequence of some gossip, in a manner which brought forth that charge. But did it not come to this that the whole case rested upon the girl's evidence? They could take it from her own lips that she was not to be relied upon, and that

SHE HAD LIED

in this matter. Surely if the evidence of one witness was sufficient to justify a jury in convicting such a man as Mr Acraman, that witness's evidence ought to be absolutely untainted and pure. It could not be suggested that the evidence was untainted. The girl had admitted that she had told falsehoods about this. She had admitted that she told her friend Annie Holmes, that nothing of the kind was ever done to her by Mr Acraman, and that any jury, in the face of such an admission, would not admit the evidence of an admitted liar, and say it sufficient to convict Mr Acraman. It must appear to the Bench, as much as it did to him that the prosecution had failed to make out their case, and, therefore, they would not let this case hang any longer over this man, who must be eventually discharged.

The Magistrates retired to consider whether to send the vicar to the Derby Assizes to stand trial on the charges. They did not take long to reach a decision. He was to stand trial, but this time he was granted bail.

THE DECISION

The Bench retired to consider their decision. After a few minutes absence, the Magistrates returned into Court when

Sir John Alleyne announced that the Bench considered that a prima facie case had been made against Mr Acraman, and they had decided to commit him to take his trial at the next Assizes.

Prisoner was then formally charged, and in reply he said he reserved his defence.

BAIL GRANTED

Mr Hall appealed for bail. There was no question of Mr Acraman not meeting this charge, and he hoped the Bench would grant his application.

Sir John Alleyne: If you can raise substantial bail as will satisfy the police.

Mr Hall: There is no doubt about Mr Acraman appearing.

Mr Clifford: I would ask for substantial bail, and for the police to be satisfied upon it.

Sir John Alleyne: Bail will be allowed, the prisoner in £500, and two sureties of £250 each.

Bail was obtained.

Hundreds of persons attended the conclusion of this case and to see Mr Acraman. He was however received without a serious demonstration.

The question was, what would the vicar do whilst he was on bail? Would he quietly hide away from the glare of publicity? Not a bit of it! He was to return to Crich and deliver a sermon.

Chapter 42
Vicar's last sermon

After his hearing it was something of a surprise to his parishioners that the vicar took part in the Sunday evening service. His loyal curate, the Revd Cousens, had been round the parish drumming up people to attend the service and the church was quite full, many apparently coming out of curiosity. When the vicar went into the pulpit to preach there was an orchestrated walkout by a section of the congregation. It was suggested that this might have been organised by the dissenters, but this was strongly denied by one of their spokesmen. Neither of the church wardens were present at the service, although they must have known he was going to speak.

The service was somewhat disrupted by rowdy youths and girls both inside and outside the church. During his final sermon the vicar protested his innocence and said it was all a plot against him by powerful people in Derby. He would be found not guilty of the charges.

As he left the church the newspaper reports of the times differ as to what happened. The *Derby Mercury* had the vicar running the gauntlet of youths (although they met him in silence), whilst the *Derbyshire Times* had him escaping through the rear of the church over a low stone wall.

His appearance in the church resulted in the Bishop banning him from church duties, the wardens having to ensure the ban was adhered to.

Such was the notoriety surrounding the case that there was even extensive coverage for the events surrounding the vicar's last sermon. The following extracts are all from the *Derbyshire Times* report.

Vicar's last sermon

Derbyshire Times: 16 September 1899

THE CRICH SENSATION

THE VICAR WENT BACK TO HIS PARISH

And took part in both services on Sunday

FROM THE PULPIT HE DECLARES HIS INNOCENCE

The Bishop of the Diocese Intervenes

Last week we had to record a Crich scandal. But this week it must be termed a Crich sensation. And the sensation has been created by the central figure in the proceedings of last week in the Belper Police Court – the Rev. W. Acraman, vicar of the parish – delivering a sermon based on the charges against him. Those charges are now a closed book, and nothing further can be published about them until they come before the higher tribunal when "twelve good men and true" will be called upon to declare "Guilty" or "Not Guilty".

CHURCHWARDENS' APPEAL IGNORED

But considering what had taken place, it was hardly thought that the vicar of Crich would return to his parish and as usual minister to the spiritual wants and requirements of his parishioners. No injunction had been issued to restrain him; he was perfectly within his legal rights. And it is only fair to add that he did exactly what one section earnestly desired him to do. Another, or the other section in the parish was highly indignant. There were people who did not fail to show that they on their part considered it the very worst taste, if nothing else. The vicar, however, had had time for reflection; he had communed with himself, and no doubt his curate, the Rev. R. W. Cousens who resides at the vicarage. The church wardens had had an interview with him, and a request was made by one that he should "take no part" in the services on the Sabbath.

AN INVITATION TO ATTEND CRICH CHURCH.

Much to the annoyance of the church wardens and many of his parishioners, the vicar made up his mind that he would undertake all the duties as usual. Moreover, several residents state that the curate came to them on Saturday, and particularly requested that they should be in their pews on Sunday evening, when the Rev. W. Acraman would himself preach. That the curate is zealous none locally will deny; that he is loyal to his vicar everyone is ready to assert, but whether the course he took on Saturday was wise is likely to be questioned. Still he did it, but until the service, few could believe that the Rev. W. Acraman would deliver the sermon.

There was only a very moderate congregation at the morning service. A few people were observed on the various roads leading from the vicarage to the church. About twenty minutes to 11 the vicar arrived in the company of his sister. They entered the vestry and a few moments later the service began. The vicar took the prayers and the lessons were read by Mr Griffiths, master of the

Crich Carr National School.

The curate, the Rev. R. W. Cousens preached from St Luke X, 36 and 37

"Which now of these three thinkest thou was neighbour unto him who fell among thieves.

And he said, He that showed mercy on him.

Then said Jesus unto him, go and do then likewise."

In the course of his remarks he said their duty was to help their neighbours in daily life. Those who were not troubled with any anxiety should extend loving kindness and tenderness to others and the Lord would grant them true happiness and comfort.

There was not the slightest unusual incident before, during or after the service.

"GRACE TO HELP IN TIMES OF NEED"

There was more than an average attendance at the evening service in the Parish Church. One of the hymns was "Further let me dedicate", four lines of the first verse reading,

In whatever worldly stage

Thou wilt have it be

Not from sorrow pain or care

Freedom do I claim

When the hymn was nearly concluded the vicar left his position in the chancel and ascended the pulpit steps. Some of the congregation left the church, and for a moment the vicar could not proceed with the reading of the text. When quiet prevailed the vicar announced he should preach from four or five verses found in the Revelations, and Hebrews, as follows:-

And I saw a great white throne, and Him that sat on it, from Whose face the earth and the heaven fled away: and there was found no place for them – Revelation xx 11

Let us therefore, come boldly to the throne of grace, that we may obtain mercy and find grace to help in time of need – Hebrews iv 16

And cried with a loud voice saying, Salvation to our God, Who sitteth upon the throne and unto the Lamb – Revelations vii 10

"THE UNFORTUNATE VICTIM OF A CONSPIRACY"

The Rev. W. Acraman in the course of a forcible address, observed that before dwelling upon the text he had just read, he desired to refer to a personal and even a parochial matter that had pervaded the atmosphere of the village for the past week or two. He thanked God that the prayers of His people had been heard and answered, and that God had delivered from prison an innocent prisoner, who now stood before them in his accustomed place. He desired to publicly thank his Heavenly Father for bringing him so far through tribulation.

He had been the unfortunate victim of a conspiracy in that place; a conspiracy which, by God's help, would not go unpunished. It was devil's work, and it made homes miserable, and the people unhappy. He could say that the poor in their cottage had suffered as much through this evil work as those who lived in better homes, and were more able to stand against such cruel charges.

He felt bound to add that this case against him was not at the instigation of those in his parish whom he loved and served, but was the doing of men in their county town, whom he well knew, and who spitefully desired his ruin and removal. He pleaded for the continued prayer of God's people that the black cloud still hanging as a pall might be scattered before the winds of truth and justice, and especially let their prayers ascend for the harmony and success of the work of the Church and of the Day and Sunday Schools.

"THE HUMBLE VICTIM BEFORE THEM"

The scandalous tales they had heard had been begun by foul suggestion, a tittle tattle, an adding here and a putting in there of demoniacal untruth until an infamous case had been manufactured.

He hoped that the church would not suffer, and that there would be no falling away. It was true that nowadays, there was much made of following the man; but they did not go to church to worship man, but God. The best way to silence an accusing tongue was to say that they all, whether they liked it or not, would have to appear before the great white throne of God on a day when all secrets would be known. The Heavenly Father would marshal all before Him and no faults, no secrets would be hidden. It was for that great day everyone had to prepare.

ESSENTIAL THEY SHOULD LEAD GOOD LIVES

To be fully prepared for that time, which all were approaching through death, was more important than the threatened war in Africa; was more important than the Dreyfus case; was more important than current gossip, and he hoped his hearers would not suffer themselves to be busybodies, would mind their own business and would be more attentive to God's great newspaper – the Book of Life. It was essential that they should lead good lives, so that when they appeared before the Throne of Grace they would be able to stand unabashed and without fear, not timorous nor afraid.

The conclusion of the sermon was based upon;

And I said unto Him, Sir, thou knowest. And He said to me, they are they which have come out of great tribulation, and have washed their robes, and made them white in the blood of the lamb.

Therefore are they before the Throne of God and serve Him day and night in His Temple; and he that sitteth on the throne shall dwell among them – Revelation viii 14 and 15.

The article went on to describe P.C. Cosgrove's report to his inspector.

SHORT CUT OVER THE CHURCHYARD WALL

Police-constable Cosgrove, who is situated at Crich, made a report to his superior officer, Supt. McDonald, of Belper, as to the proceedings during Sunday evening, and after the service. He said: – "In consequence of having to go on duty at six o'clock in the evening, instead of tea, on account of many strangers being in Crich, and through their showing a lot of ill-feeling to the vicar, who, on leaving the church at eight o'clock had to get over the churchyard wall, at the back of the church."

The officer added: "I had to keep the people moving on in front of the church while the service was going on."

The interview with Revd Acraman's loyal curate was covered. It was he who went round the parish to get people to attend church for the vicar's sermon

"SPIRIT OF GODLINESS FAITHFULLY UPHELD."

On Wednesday night the curate, the Rev. R. W. Cousens, was interviewed at the vicarage and in the course of a short conversation he stated:

"I preached in the morning and the vicar in the evening. There was a nice congregation in the evening, and the service was orderly, the people were most contented and perfect quiet prevailed. I can say from ten months residence at the vicarage that Mr Acraman has always been treated with the greatest respect, and the spirit of Godliness has been faithfully upheld the whole time. We have much sympathy from our friends in the parish. All things are quite quiet through the neighbourhood. The vicar has requested me to make that statement to you."

The curate may have been happy that the vicar had attended the Sunday service, but the Bishop, George Southwell, was less pleased. He wrote to the churchwardens, James Lee and Nathaniel Hawkes, to give instruction that this must not happen again. The vicar was banned from his church.

THE BISHOP ADDRESSES THE CHURCH WARDENS

The churchwardens of Crich (Messrs. N. I. Hawkes and J. T. Lee) received the following letter on Tuesday from the Lord Bishop of the Diocese, Dr Ridding, who is in the south of England

"September 11th
Blackmoor,
Petersfield,

"Dear sirs, – I write to inform you that I have desired Mr. Acraman not to take part in the Church services or other ministrations so long as the present scandal against him remains uncleared. It will be your duty to see that this injunction is observed. I have informed Mr. Borough, who will be able to advise you in case of difficulty. – Yours truly,
GEORGE SOUTHWELL."

Mr Borough, the gentleman named in the Bishop's communication, is the Registrar of the Diocese, and resides at Belper.

The next interview was with an unhappy Nathaniel Hawkes, who was the vicar's warden.

Revd Acraman had respect for him as he was later included in the vicar's will, dated 1916 – "*To my late dear churchwarden Nathaniel Irvine Hawkes of Crich near Matlock in the County of Derby the sum of three guineas.*"

THE VICAR'S WARDEN WILL OBEY THE BISHOP

Mr N. I. Hawkes, who resides at Whatstandwell, is the vicar's warden. In the course of a conversation with our representative on Wednesday, he said: –

"I am taking no part in the incidents associated with the parish, except as an official. Mr Lee, the people's warden, and myself have received instructions from the Bishop. The church wardens have had a letter from the local Bishop requesting us not to allow the vicar to take part in any Church services or ministrations in the parish, which I take to mean he must not officiate at burials, weddings, and other duties of a clergyman. It will be our duty to see that the Bishop's instructions are carried out."

"What about the contents of the letter; are they known to the vicar?"

The contents have been communicated to the vicar by the church wardens. This was done on Tuesday night. We were in Crich on Tuesday evening, and eventually saw Mr Acraman. We read the letter to him and he distinctly promised not to take any part in the Church services. He is, I believe, about to go away. The vicar has three National Schools to supervise, and I presume he will exercise his authority as a clergyman over them.

Were you at church on Sunday? – No, indeed I was not. I hear Mr Acraman preached to a crowded congregation in the evening.

Were you surprised? – Yes, when I took the Bible Class on Sunday afternoon, as usual, I never anticipated what was to follow in the evening.

Where was Mr Acraman on the Sunday afternoon? – He superintended and opened the Sunday School at Crich, and I did not expect he would take any more duty that day.

What if the injunction from the Bishop is disregarded? – If he attempts anything of the sort we shall stop him. We shall certainly interfere.

When did you first hear of the charges, or the arrest? Mr Acraman communicated with me immediately on arrival at the Derby gaol. He wanted me to go down and see him. I received the communication by telegram, and I refused to visit the prison.

What about the parish? – The parish seems to be going on all right and satisfactorily. There is a great amount of anxiety among the people on account of the situation, but this will subside immediately the case is settled. The parishioners are most anxious the vicar should clear himself.

What course shall you take if there is an attempt to preach? – I cannot quite say. We shall see Mr Borough, probably.

AN AWFUL PARISH TO BE IN

When did you receive the letter from the Bishop? – It was delivered on Tuesday morning and opened by Mr Lee, my fellow warden, I received the letter later in the day, in the presence of the vicar. There was an official interview with Mr Acraman at Mr Lee's house. The letter was read and confirmed by word of mouth that the vicar must not take any part in the Church service. I do not think he should go to the Sunday School. He promised to adhere to the terms of the letter. I have been church warden six years next Easter, but I am determined to give it up. I am also lay representative; I won't be any more. I shall give all up after this year. It is an awful parish to be in.

"Did you take any action prior to Sunday giving the vicar to understand it might be prudent if he took no part in the service? – Yes, I sent word by Miss Acraman, the sister of the vicar, that he should not preach. The sister came to my house after I had reached home from business, and I specially instructed her to tell her brother to take no part in the services, but to wait until after the case was decided at the Assizes.

THE HONOUR OF THE PARISH

"Some of the people," proceeded Mr Hawkes, "have come to me within the last day or two and asked what was to be done. I have had to tell them there could be no interference until after the proceedings at Derby. I know all church people, and many others, are extremely anxious to have matters cleared up for the honour of the parish as well as the Church in general.

James Lee had been the people's warden for eleven years. The Lee family had been closely connected to the church for a great many years. He was next to be interviewed for his opinions.

197

ELEVEN YEARS PEOPLE'S WARDEN

Mr James Thomas Lee, the people's warden, favoured our reporter with his opinions on certain aspects of the vicar's occupation of the pulpit, and the events subsequent to Sunday. He stated: –

"I have been people's warden eleven years last April, following my father, who was appointed to the same office in November 1852. We have held the position nearly half a century. All this time my father was, of course, closely connected with the ecclesiastical affairs of the parish, and I have followed him. I am accustomed to attending church regularly, but I did not go last Sunday, neither morning nor evening. I had no idea what was going to transpire either morning or night. I have seen the vicar since the proceedings at Belper. He has passed my business premises several times.

Can you give any expression of opinion on the conduct of the vicar in preaching on Sunday evening? – I would rather not; I decline to make any remark about it. I believe it has been common conversation that people went to church out of curiosity on Sunday night.

What action should you take if the letter from the Bishop were not obeyed? – I cannot say. The wardens would probably see Mr Borough, as advised by the Bishop.

Shall you attend church to see that the injunction of the Bishop is carried out? – I suppose I ought to. Mr Borough may be consulted tomorrow.

Mr Lee then added: I think with justice you might say that I very much regret some of the congregation have considered I have not been doing my duty in not acquainting the Bishop at once with the rumours circulated through the parish. Both the wardens were consulted and we did not see we had any right to interfere. I had an interview with Mr Hawkes on Tuesday night. Mr Acraman came to my place. It was an official meeting. I eventually met Mr Hawkes, and he, along with the vicar, were at my home.

WHY THE VICAR PREACHED

What was said? – I don't think I ought to tell you. I will say, however, I told Mr Acraman I was very much surprised he should have preached when there was a charge hanging over him. His reply was that he only did it to help Mr Cousens, who was tired.

What do the parishioners think? – I have heard that people in the parish are quite relieved that the authority has come from the Bishop to prevent the vicar preaching and taking ministration for a time. I understand Mr Acraman considers the Sunday School distinct from the Church. I should not like to express an opinion about what steps the wardens would take until we have seen Mr Borough.

What arrangements are made for Sunday? – Mr Drury, former curate here and now at Burton-on-Trent, has arranged to preach on Sunday.

Mr Lee, in conclusion, remarked, "There is a fearful bitter feeling between church and chapel here. I am sorry it is so."

Mrs Lee, who was present, parenthetically added, "The vicar is too forgiving; he should prosecute these people then go away."

The newspaper even managed a brief interview with the vicar himself. He was of the opinion that he never trod on "people's corns". He considered some of his difficulties were due to the various religious beliefs in Crich – a dig at the Nonconformists.

GIVEN THE BEST YEARS OF HIS LIFE TO THE PARISH

On Thursday morning our reporter met Mr Acraman near the village of Ambergate, and discussed with him some of the events which had occurred.

Our representative referred to a rumour that the vicar was going away for a short time, and asked for confirmation.

"Well," he replied. "I may go away on Sunday with a friend for rest. I can tell you I have the utmost sympathy from many parishioners."

The rev. gentleman added: During the twenty years I have been at Crich there had been erected a new day school and one enlarged. This has kept away a School Board. I believe in the axiom, fight with neither small nor great, but only with the King of Israel. Smith the shepherd and scatter the sheep. That has been the object of my life. Crich, I consider very difficult to manage. There are ten places of worship besides the Parish and Mission Churches. The parish is much divided in religious beliefs. I have worked very hard and given my best years to the parish. I am not a high churchman, as you know, and never tread on people's corns. The scale has gone down a little but will come back.

Of course, when the dissenters were interviewed they did not consider themselves to blame for the vicar's troubles. Robert Dawes spoke for them.

A PROMINENT DISSENTER'S OPINION

Mr Robert Dawes, a prominent Dissenter, of Crich, in answer to a question, observed:

The matter belongs entirely to the Church; it is their own business, it is for them to settle. I have nothing to do with the Sunday evening service; nor do I know anything of those who walked out before the sermon began. I do not think the Dissenters had anything to do with what happened. Mr Acraman never comes amongst us.

One of the congregation's opinion

The Derbyshire Times then found an "outsider" in Mr Rice, from Alfreton, who attended the vicar's last service. He explained what happened.

AN ALFRETON MAN'S VISIT TO CRICH:
WHAT HE SAW AND HEARD

Mr G. E. Rice, a visitor at Crich, and who is known in Alfreton, made an impartial statement to our representative. When seen on Thursday, at Parkhead, Crich, his temporary residence, he said: – "I am not a churchman. I am fortunately, in an independent position financially and have been living at Crich some weeks for a change of air in the salubrious mountain village here. I was formerly in business at Alfreton. I went to Crich Church on Sunday evening in the expectation of hearing the vicar preach or take part in the service. I had been informed that he was going to preach. The curate was in our neighbourhood asking parishioners to attend the church. This was a day or two previously.

"What did you deduce from that invitation?" our representative asked.

"Why," replied Mr Rice, "that the vicar knew he was going to make a statement relating to his position."

"Had the curate been at your house?"

"He was at Parkhead and district asking people to go to the church. I thought this rather queer, hence my decision to go. I did not know either the vicar or the curate but thought I would visit the church in the evening. I reached the edifice in good time and saw the people coming in. There would not be more than about fifteen adult men in the congregation when the service began. Perhaps some fifty grown-up people would comprise the adults. The remaining portion of the congregation, was a lot of boys and girls and young people. They had appeared to be in batches and had evidently come for a little fun. They were laughing and chatting with each other pretty well the whole time of the service. The vicar read most of the prayers, and then Mr Griffiths followed with the lessons.

Mr Rice then proceeded: – I was astonished to see the vicar go into the pulpit, it seemed to send

CONSTERNATION THROUGH THE WHOLE OF THE EDIFICE

A number of people rose at once and went out. The noise they made prevented the vicar proceeding with the reading of the text. He waited for a moment until all those who wished had left the building. There was the greater part of the congregation remaining. Those who retired were principally boys and girls. The vicar gave what I may call an animated discourse. He

DECLARED HE WAS AN INNOCENT VICTIM

and had been a prisoner through gossip. He trusted that the parishioners would pray God not to allow the religious work of the parish to be hindered, nor the Sunday School teaching to be interfered with. He felt he was the subject of their sincere prayers, and these prayers had been answered in his temporary release. "That is a resume of his observations."

Was there any demonstration at the close?

"There was no demonstration that

I saw or heard at the conclusion. There was a lot of youths and girls near the exit from the church. I passed through them, and neither saw nor heard anything in the nature of a hostile character. I must say I did not see the vicar leave the church or its precincts. There were sufficient people present to make a row if they had been determined. If I said the young men were teasing the girls, and that all were frivolous, it would not be far wrong. This was provoked by the subject uppermost in their mind. I should have thought, I may add in conclusion, that when the vicar instructed his curate to preach and ask for the sympathies of the people, he must have clearly understood what he was about to do on the day or day but one following. Had the curate not personally invited the parishioners to church on the Sunday evening, the whole proceedings might have assumed a different form.

Courtesy Beryl Calladine

An early photograph of Town End

Chapter 43
Vicar imprisoned

The vicar was tried at the Derby Assizes in the December of 1899. The case was only thought suitable for male adults, so all women and children were ordered from the Court. The only females allowed to attend were the witnesses.

The case was covered fully in the *Derbyshire Times* and also received coverage in most of the national newspapers. It was a sensational story at the time. A sixty-two-year-old vicar proposing marriage to a fourteen-year-old friend of his daughter; accusations of plots against the vicar; village rumours; and the implication of grooming for sex, all made for good headlines.

What is indisputable is that Revd Acraman behaved inappropriately with a young girl. Incredulity was expressed at his proposal of marriage to one so young. However, both his wives were in their early twenties when he married them, when he was aged fifty and seventy-seven respectively. It is not inconceivable that the proposal was genuine.

At the trial the vicar was found guilty as charged. The judge had little truck with his defence that he thought the girl was older than she was. He was sentenced to two years hard labour in Derby Gaol.

The following *Derbyshire Times* newspaper report is quite a long one, but it makes fascinating reading. Victorian reporting was quite wordy but had many interesting turns of phrase. On reading it you get a feeling of the tragedy that was happening, and cannot help but wonder at the state of mind of the vicar to allow this to happen. It was almost as if he hit the 'self destruct button.'

Derbyshire Times: 2 December 1899

TWO YEARS HARD LABOUR

For The

VICAR OF CRICH

Scathing remarks from the judge.

Witness told what to say

Sensational Incident at Close of Trial

The last act of the terrible drama which has been played at Crich, in this county, and in which the vicar of the parish was the chief contributor has sent a thrill of horror through the country. A vicar, well over sixty years of age, is condemned to hard labour for two years. And as if the decision of the judge and jury were not sufficient, the condemned man, when sentence had been passed, actually pleaded for mercy, and in the same breath admitted the crime with which he was charged, qualified only by the expression that he thought the girl was fifteen years of age. When the astounding admission, left upon those in court, the judge withered the accused with sarcasm.

The Derbyshire Winter Assizes opened on Tuesday morning at 10.30. Two minor cases were disposed of, and by 12.30, the Rev. William Acraman, vicar of Crich, stood in the prisoner dock. It was not expected the trial would begin before Wednesday and there was an absence of people from the locality who had anticipated hearing the prurient details of a sensational case. Among the parishioners of Crich, Dr McDonald, Mr J. T. Lee (people's warden), Mr T. G.

Iveson, and Mr Bower, the Chairman of the Parish Council, occupied seats in the gallery or body of the Court.

Mr Ransome, of Nottingham, the solicitor for the Bishop of Southwell, was present in his official capacity, and Mr J. Borough, JP, the Diocesan Registrar, sat near the judge during the whole proceedings. All women and children were ordered from the Court.

The accused, who was described in the calendar as 50 years of age, is considerably older, and on good authority we learn he is nearer 70 than 50. There were four charges. The first that he unlawfully and indecently did assault one *child A*, at Crich, on or about the 1st April 1899. The second was for a similar offence on the 11th April; the third was for attempting to have unlawful and carnal knowledge of *child A*, being above the age of 13, and under the age of 16, at Crich, on or about the 5th June last; and the fourth was that he "unlawfully and carnally attempted to have unlawful carnal knowledge of *child A*, he not having reasonable cause to believe that she was of the age of 16 years, at Crich on the 5th July last."

To the whole of the charges he pleaded not guilty.

Mr Dominic Daly (instructed by Mr R. S. Clifford, Derby and Loughborough) appeared to prosecute, and the defence was undertaken by Mr Stanger, Q.C. with whom was Mr Walker (instructed by Mr J. Wheatcroft, Belper).

OPENING THE CASE

Mr Daly said he appeared in the case for the prosecution, and defendant was represented by his learned friends Mr

Stanger and Mr Walker, they had heard the charges laid against the gentleman in the dock, and they contained very serious accusations, accusations which, to use a comprehensive term of indecent assault and carnally knowing the girl, *child A*, during periods covering several months. It was a very common place observation to say that this was a most important case. It was most important on two points, first because the defendant in the case was a gentleman of Holy Orders, the vicar of the parish of Crich, in this county, and the sort of man who, from his exalted position and professional standing, and secondly from the position that men of his person were not usually found in the place where he, unfortunately, was now. The charge of indecent assault on a little girl was bad enough in the ordinary sense of the term, and among those of the criminal class; it was far more serious for Mr Acraman who was a man of intelligence. The jury would make no mistake however in their justice. They would do their best to sift the real merits of the case, and not convict a man of an offence, when that conviction would mean ruin and disaster on every hand. They had to be careful not to allow a criminal to escape, if there were criminality, simply because the accused was a gentleman of position and character.

"A LITTLE GIRL TO CONSIDER"

On the one hand the jury had a little girl to consider. They were the guardians for the present time, and he put the question to them, how would they feel if it were their child that had been interfered with. They would give their judgement against anyone if they were satisfied with the evidence no matter whether the person charged were a vicar, a labourer, or anyone else. They would be careful for the sake of the girl, for the sake of the public morality, and for the sake of justice. It would not be agreeable to the jury and the Court generally to hear needless repetition about the case of indecency. But on several occasions, according to the charges, the defendant seduced the girl to go into his rectory or dwelling house, where the alleged acts were committed. Under the pretence of making the girl presents of one sort or another, she was induced to go to the house.

BAD OR DARK DEEDS REQUIRED SECRECY

Mr Daly pointed out the salient and substantial details of the accusation against the defendant. The girl, and her mother, who was a widow, were well known to the vicar. The girl was 14 years of age on November 10th, and was what was commonly called a factory hand. He went on to say the common experience in such cases was that there was no direct corroborative evidence to support the charges made by the girl. It was impossible there could be, because of the secrecy it was necessary to observe. When a person in a good position was concerned in a bad or dark deed, there always was secrecy. In cases of a sexual character it could never be expected they would be open to the eye of an observer. As much privacy as possible was secured.

Still there was what might be called direct corroborative evidence in this case. They could not very ready expect to find eye-witnesses of what took place; it could very very rarely be found in cases of that description. There was however, practical corroboration of the girl's statement. The defendant was careful to lock the doors and secure the windows from all observation when these things took place.

The jury would have to rely upon the girl's evidence as to what was actually done to her. No mortal being saw anything but themselves. They would see her in the box and see what sort of girl she was. They would hear what she had to say, and she would make an impression, favourable or unfavourable. From what she said they would form their own opinion; they would draw an inference in their own mind. If they thought she was not an idle little huzzy, apparently trustworthy and guileless, then such evidence would impress itself favourably on their minds.

THEY DID NOT TELL THEIR MOTHERS

There was another weakness inherent to prosecutions of that kind. It was this: The girl manifested a certain reserve; she was silent and showed a certain amount of reserve in telling those near her of what was going on. People like her, young people, who were committing, it was alleged, certain acts with the concurrence of the vicar of the parish, did not tell their mothers. But when the girl did speak to her mother, or was asked what certain things meant, the whole story came out.

The prisoner had known this girl from her birth; she had been a companion of his daughter; he had frequently made her little presents and shown a friendly disposition towards her. He desired to send her to school and educate her. All the way through this lamentable story the defendant appeared to take advantage of the familiarity with the girl.

Another reason for the girl's reserve was to be found in the fact that she, being largely under his influence, and knowing her from being a baby, she was enjoined by him to keep perfectly quiet. They would have to consider how far this told for or against her.

EXTRAORDINARY SUGGESTION OF MARRIAGE

Mr Daly next referred to the details of the charges on the specific dates, the presents made by the defendant, and the alleged bad feeling that was said to be in the district against him. Most of the people, he would say, wished the vicar well, and through the case. None of the witnesses were inspired by bad feeling and they were taken there to say what they knew about a transaction. The view of the prosecution about the proposed marriage was that it came about with an idea of closing up the scandal. To him it was a most extraordinary thing for a suggestion of marriage to be made at all.

Why could there be the interest manifested in the girl, the poor little child. She appeared to finally agree to marry the defendant. Surely he would never have seriously proposed marriage to a girl like this. It was incredible.

Mr Stanger: It was before any complaint had been made.

Mr Daly: Quite true! It is a very curious thing all the same. All these stories and others they would have to hear must decide them in giving their decision. Although he appeared for the prosecution, he

INVITED THEIR SYMPATHY FOR
THE UNFORTUNATE MAN

in his pitiable condition. The decision, should it be against him, was more to one in his position who moved in the society he had done, than it was to a common labourer, or some besotted individual. No matter what difference there was in the cloth a man wore, it made no difference there in the dock. They would administer justice in this case just as if the vicar was a labourer, a carpenter or smith. If they came to the conclusion those things imputed to him were true they would find him guilty. If on the other hand Mr Stanger and Mr Walker succeeded in satisfying them there was something like a conspiracy against the vicar to ruin him, or they succeeded in convincing them there was not sufficient in the evidence to warrant a conviction then their duty was plain.

After the opening address it was time for child A to give her testimony and be cross-examined. As at the hearing in Belper she was a very credible witness.

THE GIRL'S EVIDENCE

Child A, the girl, was placed in the box. She said she was 14 years of age this month. She had known Mr Acraman since the time she was a little child. He had a daughter, Essie, with whom she used to play, she was about the age of witness. They went to school together. Witness went on to refer to a cantata which was performed in the school in Easter week of this year. After the performance of this cantata the vicar asked her to go to his house as he wanted her. She went as requested and he met her at the front door. They went into the drawing room and he fastened the door and drew down the blinds. Witness described certain actions which related to the first charge. When she left the house that night he kissed her.

She went straight home but did not tell her mother anything. The second visit was described and the date was fixed through the annual trip from Lea Mills, which was on the first Saturday in July. On this occasion the blinds were drawn as before. When she left he kissed her. She was given a shilling and told by the defendant she could give some of it to the band. She did not say anything to her mother, as Mr Acraman told her she must not.

On the occasion of the third visit she was told the vicar wanted to see her. The time of this visit was fixed by a journey made to Eastbourne by Mr Acraman. Her mother knew where she was going. Mr Acraman told her he was lonely now that Essie was away. He also said he had no-one to love him now Essie was away.

On this occasion he asked her if she would marry him. After being asked a lot of times she said she would marry him. He presented her with a piece of blue ribbon. When she left the house he told her he would send Johnny Greenhough when he wanted her to go again. She said nothing to her mother. Prior to the fourth visit Mr Acraman saw her mother and gave her a letter from Essie, which witness was to read. When she left the vicarage she went through the drawing room and into the garden and home through the fields. Mr Acraman accompanied her to a hay stack in the field and there left her. On her way home she saw Mr Wetton.

At this juncture the Court adjourned for luncheon.

CROSS EXAMINATION

On resuming Mr Stanger proceeded to cross-examine the girl.

You say there were four occasions on which there was impropriety? – Yes.

You say he took you by the wrist on each occasion? – Yes, sir.

Was it exactly the same on each occasion? – Yes, sir.

Did you on any of these occasions go home and say anything to your mother? – No, sir.

Were you alone with your mother after going home after these visits to Mr Acraman's house? – There were other people in the house.

Why did you not tell your mother? – Because Mr Acraman told me I must not tell anyone.

But you knew it was very wrong? – Yes, sir.

When did you tell your mother? – It was some little time afterwards.

Did your mother say something to you first? – Yes.

What did she say? – She told me she would give me a good hiding.

What was it for? – Because I had not told her before.

Did you see P.c. Cosgrove? – Yes, sir.

And did he tell you some of the words you had to say? – No, sir.

Did he tell you some of the words you had to say? – No, he told me I must speak the truth.

Did your grandfather speak to you? – Yes, sir.

After you had told your mother did you not say something quite different to the mill girls, some of your companions? – Yes, I told one.

Who was it? – Annie Holmes.

Were there other people there when you told Annie Holmes? – No, sir.

Did you say anything to another girl Martha Millward? – No, we are not very great friends, and never have been.

Then you say you were alone when you told Annie Holmes? – Yes.

Now tell me exactly what you said to her. – She told me they had heard about it at the quarry, and I said it was not true. Nothing more was said then.

Was that after you had told your mother? – I don't know whether it was before or after my mother asked me.

You did not tell anyone before you told your mother? – I don't think so, but I am not quite sure.

You told Annie Holmes it was not true? – Yes, sir.

What do you mean by that? – I meant her to believe that he never did anything wrong to me.

You put it in another way before the Magistrates. It was not true what you said to Annie Holmes? – No, sir.

Are you an untruthful girl? – No, sir.

You have been in the habit of going to the vicarage for years and playing with Mr Acraman's daughter? – Yes.

Did he kiss you the same as his own girl? – Yes, sir.

Were there people in the house besides the vicar and the servants? – Yes, there was Mr Cousens.

Was there a housekeeper? – Yes.

Did Greenhough, the boy, live in the house? – I don't know.

And you say Mr Acraman locked the door? – Yes, sir.

Precisely the same on every occasion? – Yes, sir.

Child A's mother was the next to take the stand and give evidence.

THE VICAR'S PRESENTS

Mrs A the mother of the girl, was the next witness. She said that she was a widow living at Crich. She spoke of the preparations for the cantata about Easter and her daughter going home late. When an explanation was desired the girl said she had been at the vicarage. The vicar told her he had a pencil case for *child A* and asked that she might fetch it. *Child A* went to the vicarage after she had come home from work, and returned about nine in the evening with some blue ribbon and flowers. The vicar came to witness's house one day and asked her consent to send *child A* to Eastbourne to be a companion to his daughter. He said he would educate her the same as his own child. He pressed her so much that she consented and it was arranged that the curate would take her to London where she would be met by Mr Acraman who was at the time visiting Eastbourne. Mrs Slack afterwards showed witness a letter which she had received from Mr Acraman and after reading it decided not to let girl go to Eastbourne. Mrs Slack had been for nine years Mr Acraman's

housekeeper. Witness threatened to give her daughter "a good hiding" because of what had happened. A few days later the vicar came to her house and asked if he might enter. She replied, "No, I shall not allow you to come to our house any more." She was in a bit of a temper owing to what she had been informed regarding his conduct with her daughter.

WHY THE CHILD DID NOT GO TO EASTBOURNE

Cross-examined by Mr Stanger: With regard to the letter Mrs Slack showed you, did it say one of the children was to be sent to boarding school and the other was to stay with some ladies? – Yes.

Did you not approve of that? – No, sir.

Did the letter not say there was not enough room at the boarding school for two, and one would have to board out? – I cannot say.

I am not in the least blaming you. You did not like the proposal and you did not comment to it? – No.

The proposal that your daughter should be educated the same as his own child? – Yes.

Mr Acraman's housekeeper was next in the witness box. The prosecutor wanted to treat her in the spirit of a "hostile witness". This would have allowed him to question the witness as if in cross-examination, thus permitting the use of leading questions. The judge was having none of it.

TOLD HIS HOUSEKEEPER WHAT HE PROPOSED

Mary Slack, wife of Edward Slack, of Crich, stated that for ten years she was Mr Acraman's housekeeper. Before Mr Acraman went to Eastbourne he told her he was going to send *child A* to be a companion to his daughter and to have her educated. He also mentioned that he had proposed marriage to *child A* and she had accepted him. She showed *Mrs A* a letter that Mr Acraman had sent to her, and witness wrote one back for *Mrs A*. She had spoken to Mr Acraman since he was committed but not regarding the case. Mr Acraman had spoken to her husband about it, but she could not remember what was said.

Mr Daly: Did Mr Acraman say anything about *child A*? – Not to me.

To anyone in your hearing? – To my husband.

His Lordship: In your presence? – Yes my Lord.

Mr Daly: Tell us what was said? – I do not remember what was said.

Mr Daly asked to be allowed to continue the examination in the spirit of a hostile witness.

His Lordship: There is no reason for it

Cross-examined by Mr Stanger: There was some talk about the two girls being educated at Eastbourne? – Yes, sir.

It was after the talk about education that he spoke to you about marrying *child A*? – Yes, sir.

She would be a more suitable person to marry after education? – Yes, sir.

A little light relief was offered when John Wetton, parish clerk at Crich, gave his testimony. It is unlikely that he intended it to cause amusement.

FROM ONE GENERATION TO ANOTHER

John Wetton, parish clerk of Crich, said he recollected the Lea Mills trip. About the same time he saw *child A* returning from the vicarage one night. She came by a roundabout way into Bulling Lane, and he saw her jump over a wall close to where he stood.

His Lordship: Where were they? – Near a gate at the corner of the field.

Did you look at them? – I did.

Mr Daly: Did you see them part company? – I did.

Which way did the vicar go? – Towards his own home.

Which way did *child A* go? – She came down the field, jumped over the wall into the lane.

Cross-examined by Mr Stanger: Has Mr Acraman been vicar of Crich since 1876? – Yes I dare say he has.

And how long have you been parish clerk? – Forty years; it has been in my family about 300 years. (Laughter)

And since he came has he taken great interest in the schools and parish work? – Yes; I believe he has.

Witness: But that has nothing to do with the case. (Laughter)

His Lordship: You and I shall hear a great deal more about the case before we have finished with it. (Laughter)

Mr Daly (to witness): You will, perhaps, be a judge presently. (Much laughter)

Mr Stanger: And perhaps that may be in the family another 300 years. (Renewed laughter)

Mr Daly: Has there been some trouble in the parish about some people wanting a School Board? – There may have been.

Do you know the policeman, Cosgrove? – Yes.

Are you a particular friend of his? – Well not particular. (Laughter)

Mr Stanger: You are a wet-ton I see (Laughter) Have you met him at the Rising Sun Inn and tried to get evidence in this case? – No.

There are a few you don't know. Do you go to the public house? – Sometimes I go, sometimes I don't.

Who spoke to you first about this evidence? – Mr Clifford.

How long ago? – Before the case went to Belper.

That was a good many weeks after this happened. – I cannot say.

Come you can, now? – I cannot; you do not want me to tell untruths.

Would you do it if I did? – No.

I want to know when your recollection was brushed up? How long was it before you gave evidence spoken to? – I was told I should have to go.

You have had some trouble with Mr Acraman? – No.

He has complained about your going to the public houses? – No.

Has there been some trouble about the parish fees? – That has been sealed and settled.

Re-examined by Mr Daly: You have no ill-feeling towards Mr Acraman? – I have never had an angry word with him.

What side are you in the school disputes? – I have never taken on any side. I let them do as they like and have nothing to do with them. (Laughter)

Mary Lee acted as a sort of go-between for the vicar and *Mrs A*. There was some suggestion that the vicar had primed her what to say in the witness box.

SAW THE GIRL GOING TO THE VICARAGE

Mary Lee, wife of John Lee, of Crich, was the next witness. She knew the prisoner and the girl. She recollected the cantata at the school, and also the day of a practice.

Where were you on the Saturday evening? – I was locking up and looking into the buildings.

His Lordship: You were not locking up this cantata? – No, my Lord.

Mr Daly: Did you see anyone? – I saw the vicar and *child A*.

Where were they going? – Down the lane towards the Vicarage.

And you saw them later? – I saw *child A* later.

Where did you see her? – I saw her pass up the lane.

Witness spoke to another evening when she saw *child A* going into the vicarage.

Was the vicar in the garden? – Yes.

Did they meet? – Yes, at the front gate.

From the front gate did you see where they went? – They went into the house.

You remember the ugly rumours going about in Crich concerning the vicar and *child A*? – Yes.

You remember proceedings against the vicar? – Yes.

Before these proceedings did the vicar call on you? – Yes.

What brought him to your house? – He frequently came on business.

Did he speak to you on certain matters? – He told me there were rumours of which he had heard.

What did he say he had heard? – He told me he had heard proceedings were likely to be taken by *Mrs A* against himself.

What about? – Things which had been said about her daughter.

SHE THOUGHT IT VERY QUEER

Did he make any request to you? – He asked me to tell *Mrs A* it would be very serious if it went on. He was willing to marry her, and would educate her.

Did you make any remark about that? – I thought it very queer at the time that he wished to marry a girl.

Anything else? – He asked me to tell *Mrs A*.

Did you comply with his request? – Yes, I saw her.

Did he talk to you more than once about marrying *child A*? – Yes.

Did you give any advice as to what he had better do? – I told him she was too young to marry.

That is practically what you told him all along? – Yes.

When the police were making enquiries did he call on you? – Yes.

How did you receive him? – I was very poorly and not fit to see anyone.

I believe you gave evidence at Belper in September? – Yes.

On the previous day did you receive a communication? – Yes.

Who was it from? – The postman.

Who was the letter from? – From the vicar.

You can speak to his handwriting? – Yes.

Have you got the letter? – Yes.

The letter was handed in. It was dated the day before the trial at Belper, and came from the prison at Derby.

TELLING THE WITNESS WHAT TO SAY

There were portions of the letter read, and the vicar regretted to hear from his sister she (Mrs Lee) had been subpoenaed by the other side. She would do them no good but the other way. It only showed up how hard up they were for witnesses. All she could say was that he took an interest in *child A* and wanted to have her educated; she was only his child's former monitress. He had never spoken on any incorrect subject, nor had he seen the girl at the vicarage in the year. The letter added that it might be best to tell the magistrates how annoyed she had been by P.c. Cosgrove calling when she (Mrs Lee) was ill.

Mr Daly said there were references to other matters in the letter.

Mr Daly, continuing the examination: That letter you received from the vicar?

– Yes.

Have you seen him since he was on bail? – Yes.

Has he spoken to you and said he still wished to marry the girl? – Yes.

And what about the mother? – He has asked me to go and see *Mrs A* and say he would marry the girl at once.

Did you see *Mrs A*? – No, not again.

I think your husband was ill during this time? – Yes.

Did you speak to him about this? – Yes.

Cross-examined by Mr Stanger: Can you tell me about when it was he first spoke to you about educating and marrying the girl? – About July.

But she might have been away some years before that? – Yes.

At the end of that time she would be old enough to marry? – Yes.

That was what you understood? – Yes.

She would be old enough to marry some person? – Yes.

My friend asked you about many conversations. Mr Owen lodged at your house? – Yes.

That was why the vicar came? – Yes.

As far as you know the behaviour of the vicar has been of the best? – Yes.

How is it you have given this fresh evidence? – I told Mr Clifford.

Next up was newly promoted Police sergeant Cosgrove. At this time Crich would have had two policemen based in the village. The police station was in the Market Place – where the butcher is presently situated. It was not until 1901 that the new police station, with its lock-up, was built on the Common.

THE FIRST DEFENCE

Police Sergeant Cosgrove spoke to making a report to his superior officer at Belper and receiving a warrant for the arrest of the accused. The vicar was arrested at his house, and in reply to the charge he said; "The girl is 15 years old in November, I can certify that from the register book."

Cross-examined by Mr Stanger: Before you arrested him it had been a matter of common talk about the case? – It had.

He must have been aware that he was likely to be arrested? – Yes.

There had been a previous application to the magistrates? – Not to my knowledge.

Had you been engaged in working up the case? – Yes.

Had you to meet with Mr Hinton? – I had.

Did you meet at the Rising Sun with Hinton and others to get evidence? – No.

My question was to whether you went to the Rising Sun Inn about this case? – I never went to the Rising Sun Inn about this case.

You had had disputes with Mr Acraman? – No never.

Did you say you would get his cassock off as he had tried to get your jacket off? – No, I never even thought of it.

Once the village police station, now a butcher's shop.
Unknown date.

213

Prosecution sums up

Mr Daly then summed up for the prosecution.

Mr Daly then addressed the court, and said he had not much to add to what he said at the opening. The witnesses had given evidence without ill-feeling towards the unfortunate defendant. Had there been anything done to disturb the minds of the jury on the effect of the case? He admitted there was nothing. There was nothing in what the girl had said to make them think she was a liar. Substantially they might accept what she said. Mrs Lee's evidence must have favourably impressed them. The prisoner spoke to her about extremely private affairs when he told her he was going to marry the girl. Then there was the letter which the prisoner wrote from his cell. This was

A VERY SIGNIFICANT LETTER

It was a letter, he suggested, telling Mrs Lee what she would say in the witness box for his protection. One could easily see through Mr Acraman writing such a letter. Was it the letter of an innocent or guilty man? He submitted the prosecution had made out their case as far as any could hope in human affairs. Did they think the girl had gone into the box to commit perjury; had she invented a story which had no existence? Was it a conspiracy on the part of the Parish Clerk, Mrs Lee, Mrs Slack and others to pull the Vicar down because he was a respectable man? If they did not believe the evidence the prisoner should have to go free. But he did not think they would take this view. If they thought he took advantage of the infantile mind and overcame her it was quite enough for a trial of the character. Although they might sympathise with the man that had fallen, they must not allow sympathy to go before justice. They could have sympathy for a man in the place only fitted for the common criminal, but they must not neglect their duty, but treat him just the same as they would any Tom, Dick or Harry. If they were of opinion that what he did, if they did believe these things were done, then they must return a verdict of guilty of indecent assault.

It was then time for Mr Stanger to speak for the defence.

LAW AND JUSTICE ALONE TO OPERATE.

Mr Stanger rose to speak for the defence. He said when his learned friend opened the case he was surprised at the friendly attitude he assumed toward the defendant. That soon faded away. His learned friend was careful to speak about the evidence of direct corroboration, and pointed out that these things had been going on for months before there was any complaint. He was there to ask them to come to a very different conclusion from what his friend invited them. His learned friend had asked whether Mr Walker and himself liked their position.

To that there was no objection, because what was before them was whether this man, whether he was the vicar or rich or the

POOREST PRISONER OR PERSON

in the world, they must deal with him according to the evidence, to law and justice. His learned friend also spoke about the Vicar receiving greater consideration than another kind of person. They in this country knew only one law which was administered in a spirit of fairness and equality. He was not sure whether they did not trust people in the position of the defendant with greater harshness than they would some people. They had to deal with him whether he Dick, Tom or Harry. If they had any feeling or prejudice in their minds before the story of this girl was sifted he beseeched them to expel it from their minds. He was going to ask them to picture two lines of thought. He was going to ask them whether the prosecution had made out their case. Because there

MUST NOT BE ONE ATOM OF
DOUBT

if they accepted what the prosecution laid before them. There had been failure, so far as any prejudice was concerned, he would ask them to dispel it from their mind. They were told there could not be direct corroboration in a case of this kind. What did they look for in all such cases? They looked for corroboration and it was a very salutary principal there must be corroboration. He proceeded to define the law as to its application in this case, and referred to the medical evidence which was conclusive. There

had been nothing said by the mother to confirm the story of the girl, and this was naturally expected. As to the proposal of marriage, it had been put before them with an air of great importance. There was nothing in it. The witness Wetton had been brought before them to say

HOW GREAT AND GRAND WERE
HIS ANCESTORS.

It was not corroborative evidence. Then they must consider there were people in the house. Were it possible to say that because two people were in the house together for ten minutes or a quarter of an hour there was impropriety? Corroboration was wanted in every sense. The question of education and marriage of which so much had been made was mooted long before there was any charge against the defendant. It was the last day of August before proceedings were taken, and the conversation between the vicar and Mrs Lee was in July. Mr Acraman had never denied what he had said. It was the first time a scheme of this kind had

ENTERED INTO THE BRAIN

of a man in years. His learned friend talked about a marriage with a girl of 13. This was made perfectly right by Mrs Lee who told that the girl was to go away and be educated. Then when she was 17 or 18 she would be near the time when she would be of marriageable age. This girl had admitted to them

SHE TOLD A LIE

to Annie Holmes. Why was that? Because she said Mr Acraman told her she must not say anything to any one. That would not do. When there was talk about prosecution how preposterous it was to say "I denied it to Annie Holmes because Mr Acraman told me". If anything were done in the nature the prosecution suggested it was with consent. Here was a girl whom his learned friend characterised as guileless, simple-minded, honest, trustworthy and truthful. What do they find in her admission about Annie Holmes? What would a modest girl like this have done had there been truth in what was alleged to be done to her? She would have rushed out of doors, burst into tears and asked her mother for protection. She would have asked her mother not to send her to the vicarage. Not a word escaped her until the mother is suspicious. Had the girl made out in her evidence an offence which was punishable by law?

ANOTHER TRIAL AWAITING

If the defendant escaped that day he would be before his spiritual superiors.

What they were dealing with was with a criminal offence. It was with the utmost possible importance that they should scrutinise most carefully the evidence laid before them. When they had scrutinised all that evidence and dealt with it fairly they would be bound to come to the conclusion that the prosecution had failed to make out a criminal case. If they accepted every word the girl had said, there was this to remember; there was not the least resistance. They had in their hands a very solemn duty to perform. He begged with them not to be led away with sentiment, but to do an act of simple justice, bearing well in mind their verdict could not be reversed, and if it were against Mr Acraman then a very awful future they would be dooming him to.

Finally the judge summed up for the jury.

THE JUDGE SUMS UP

His Lordship said he had already expressed his opinion on one part of the case. There was no evidence of carnal knowledge of the girl, because if that had been attempted much more would have been done than the prosecution alleged. All that remained was the indecent assault. He proceeded to define the law and observed that if it were proved to the satisfaction of the jury that a girl of 13 or under had been thus assaulted, it would not matter whether she consented or not. They had to decide whether they thought

the girl was telling the truth and if there had been any impropriety. If they came to the conclusion that she consented to it, he would be entitled to be acquitted, because there would be no assault if they came to that decision.

They had to say, did this man do what was alleged to this girl? Clearly if he did there was an end of the whole case, and if he did they would have to find on the further questions: did he do it with the consent of the girl, or was it merely submission? If he did it with her consent no crime was committed which could be punished in that court. If she merely submitted to it as a girl would submit to her spiritual counsel, they would find differently.

The facts of the case were very short. It was quite true the greater part of the case rested upon the evidence of the girl herself. And if the case did rest entirely upon the girl, however much they might be inclined to believe her, they would rightly say they must have some corroborative evidence of some sort. The difficulty about corroboration always arises about young children. When a woman complained about assault it was not expected the matter would rest entirely with the story told in the witness box. There would be screams, perhaps bruises and something from the doctor in the way of corroboration.

The difficulty before them always arose in the case of young girls who were unable to protest the same way as grown-up persons. His Lordship alluded to the evidence of the girl and the question of marriage. He did not know what impression it would make on their mind. It depended on how they were constituted. After there was a talk of being had up before the magistrates it was stated he had said: "I will marry the girl and there will be an end to all this". Mrs Lee told him he could not marry her for several years. He supposed they could not have married then with anything like decency. Was there anything in the story of the girl to lead them to the conclusion she was telling the truth or not? They had to say whether the story of the parish clerk and Mrs Lee led them to any conclusion or not.

To him it seemed rather wide to accuse a Vicar of conduct like this because some people could not get a Board School at Crich. In conclusion His Lordship commented upon the letter sent to Mrs Lee. In that letter the statement was made by the vicar that he had not seen the girl at the vicarage during the year. On the other hand three persons told them they had seen the girl either at the vicarage or coming away from it. They had to decide whether an offence was committed, if so was it with her consent or without it. If she submitted and did not consent, they could not expect the girl to do what a woman would do. If they came to the conclusion that he did commit an indecency with the girl, and that the girl consented in the sense of submission only, and did not comment, then it would be an assault on the girl.

The jury retired to consider the case and come to a verdict. It took them all of twenty-three minutes to decide his fate.

The jury retired at 5.37. At six o'clock they returned and the foreman, in answer to the Clerk, answered:

"We find the defendant guilty and the submission was under his influence."

His Lordship: Did she consent? I told you submission was not consent.

The foreman: Submission but not consent.

The judge then passed sentence on Revd Acraman. It was to be the longest sentence in prison that the law allowed. This clearly came as a great shock to the vicar.

THE SENTENCE

His Lordship, in passing sentence, said William Acraman, the jury have found you guilty of this charge and I am not in least degree disposed to differ from the view they have arrived at. It is quite true in the one sense there is but little corroboration, but what there was told, in my judgement, and no doubt in the judgement of the jury heavily against you. Your letter to Mrs Lee, I am speaking for myself and do not know what ran through the minds of the jury and your constant talk about marrying a girl of 13 years shows more than anything what had passed between you and the girl. You were placed in a position over her. As a clergyman she was one of your school children and you availed yourself of that position to commit this assault upon her. It was your duty to have taught her what was right and good and proper. Instead of that you take advantage of her. I should be wanting in my duty if I did not pass upon you a very severe sentence. I have before me ignorant men, men who give way to drink, and who are led into temptations of one sort or another, and who are punished, and punished very severely of offences of this kind. When a man of education, a minister of the gospel, stands charged with such an offence the

CRIME BECOMES A HUNDRED TIMES WORSE

My duty is to pass upon you the longest sentence which the law permits me. It is that you be imprisoned and kept to hard labour for two years.

The sentence caused a profound sensation in the court, and it appeared the prisoner did not exactly realise the decision. He was staggered by the concluding words of the Judge. In a moment he recovered, and Mr Stanger turned towards him in the dock. His counsel intimated the prisoner wished to say something.

The vicar asked for and was given permission to address the Court. He restated that he considered the girl to be slightly older than she had been given. It obviously still angered him that she was reported as being thirteen when the offences occurred, but she had been fourteen. He also made a plea for mitigation as he was in poor health and feared that the "hard labour" would injure his health even more.

The judge was of the opinion that he would be well looked after in prison and should have nothing to fear. His comments regarding the girl's age caused the judge to pass somewhat acid remarks. He considered the Vicar had made his case ten times worse.

The Judge listened most attentively, as everyone else in the court did.

The prisoner, resting his arms on the front of the dock after he had snatched a sheet of paper from his pocket, read or partly read a statement which had been prepared previously. The purport of this was that he believed every prisoner before being sentenced had the privilege of speaking.

He wished to say to the learned judge, and to all present, that he fully believed, and was supported by the baptismal register, which he produced when he was arrested, that the girl was 15, and was now in her 16th year, and he was lead to think so not only by the book, but by the girl's and her mother's own statements, because she was removed from Crich Carr School more than a year ago, and it was said that she was of an age to go to the mill. Her mother removed her, and she stated that age, which agreed with the girl's statement and the baptismal register. He thought she was in her 16th year and proposed to educate and ultimately to marry her, though not now of course. With regard to the calendar there was a mistake in his age.

He was older than he was stated to be, his health was broken and the doctors had ordered him a total rest for the two months during which this matter had been hanging over his head. He gave up everything, very good prospects, to become a clergyman, and now he had lost them all, and everything in this life. He had one motherless child, his wife having died tragically when it was born. He put forward these reasons in the hope that the judge might make some mitigation of the sentence especially so far as hard labour was concerned.

His Lordship: Every care of you will be taken in prison; your health will be carefully watched by the prison doctor, and you will have nothing more to do than you can properly be called upon to perform. With regard to what you said about the child's age, it makes it ten times worse. It seems as if you were waiting for some age when you thought you could with impunity do these things to the girl. I do not understand your point. From a moral point of view it makes it ten times worse.

Prisoner was then removed.

The hearing occupied five hours.

Much was made of the girl's age. For six hundred years, between 1275 and 1875, the age of consent (which only applied to girls) was twelve. In 1875 it was raised to thirteen. It was not until 1885 that it was raised to sixteen. Had the assault occurred a few years earlier the vicar would not have committed a criminal offence and would have been spared gaol.

219

Chapter 44
A kind offer

A Lincolnshire vicar, unrelated and unknown to the Acraman family, wrote to the churchwardens offering a home to the disgraced vicar's daughter.

Derby Mercury: Wed 6 December 1899

CRICH.

THE AFFAIRS OF THE PARISH CHURCH. A GENEROUS OFFER. – We understand that on Saturday afternoon the churchwardens of the parish church (Messrs. N. I. Hawkes and James T. Lee) met Mr John Borough officially, and in future all accounts must be paid directly to them. The stipend of the ex-vicar ceased to be paid a week ago. – In an interview with Mr. Hawkes, we are informed that the gentleman has received the following letter from a Lincolnshire vicar: "It is with great sorrow that I read in the papers of your vicar's fall, and the sad consequences to his family. I am not acquainted with Mr. Acraman or any one connected with him, but my wife and myself feel deeply for the daughter, and we have come to the conclusion to offer her a home with us, if she is in need and if her guardians are willing to allow her to come and stay with us until her father's release. Would you therefore kindly give this offer to those who may have charge of the girl, and let them know of our willingness to receive her as our guest, so that they may act as they think best. I am sorry to trouble you, but you are the only source through whom I can make my intention known, I trust you will excuse the trouble I am putting you to."

So, Revd William Acraman's twenty-five year tenure at Crich ended in a most ignominious way. He certainly was a troubled and troublesome vicar who saw the most significant changes occur in his parish – most notably the rise of nonconformist religion and the development of National Schools in the parish. Whatever his faults, his labours to keep School Boards out of Crich and to promote church schooling were successful. Part of his legacy continues today.

Chapter 45
Vicar deprived of Holy Orders

Derby Mercury: Wed 21 February 1900

THE VICARAGE OF CRICH.

A solemn and impressive, though happily rare ceremony, took place on Tuesday in Southwell Minster, where the Bishop of the Diocese, acting under the provisions of the Clergy Discipline Act, 1892, declared the living of Crich vacant – in consequence of the late incumbent, Mr. Acraman, having been convicted at the last Derbyshire Assizes of serious misdemeanours and sentenced to two years' imprisonment with hard labour – and also formally deposed and degraded Mr. Acraman from Holy Orders. The Court was held in the Chapter House of the Cathedral. The Bishop presided, having on his right the Chancellor of the Diocese, the Worshipful Alfred Bray Kemp, M.A. F.R.S. There were also present the Bishop Suffragan of Derby, the Archdeacons of Derby and Nottingham, and several of the Honorary Canons of the Cathedral, all attired in Canonical habit. The Bishop was attended by his domestic chaplain. The Registrar of the Diocese, Mr. J. Borough, having certified to his Lordship that all the legal preliminaries had been complied with, the Chancellor read the opening recitals of the "declaration of vacancy," which the Bishop completed by declaring "that the preferment of the vicarage of Crich, in the county of Derby and our Diocese of Southwell, held by Wm. Acraman is vacant and destitute of an incumbent by the deprivation thereof of the said William Acraman." His Lordship then signed the declaration and handed it to the Registrar with a direction to record it in the Registry of the Diocese. The Bishop, with the Canons and other dignitaries the Chancellor and Registrar, then proceeded to the choir of the Cathedral and took his place within the altar rails. Having offered prayer, his Lordship handed a document to the Chancellor, who, as before, read the formal recitals. This was the sentence of deposition from Holy Orders, and included the statement that "the said William Acraman by his said offences, has grievously sinned against Almighty God and has caused grave scandal to the Church and to his Holy Orders." The Bishop, seated in his chair, read the operative part of the sentence, concluding as follows: "And we do hereby, by the authority committed to us by Almighty God, the Father, the Son, and the Holy Ghost, remove, depose and degrade him, the said William Acraman, from all clerical offices and Orders of Priest and Deacon respectively, by this our definitive sentence and final decree which we give and promulgate by these present." The Bishop then signed the sentence and the Chancellor, Bishop Suffragan, Archdeacons, and certain of the Canons also signed it, in accordance with Canon 122 and the whole was attested by the Registrar. The proceedings closed with the Benediction.

We understand this is only the second instance of a clergyman being deprived of Holy Orders since the passing of the Act of 1892.

Chapter 46
Postscript on the Revd Acraman

The census of 1901 showed William Acraman in Derby Gaol.

When he left gaol he changed his name to William Monteagle, announcing the change in the personal columns of the Times. He was of the opinion that his family were descendants of Lord Monteagle, who was involved in the 1605 Gunpowder Plot. It was Lord Monteagle who "shopped" all the plotters.

THE TIMES

Saturday Jul 27, 1901
PERSONAL, &c.
I WILLIAM ACRAMAN, hereby notify that I have this day TAKEN the SURNAME of my ancestor, MONTEAGLE, by which I desire henceforth to be called.
Liverpool July 22 1901

After prison he moved away from Crich and lived on the south coast. Did he opt for a quiet uneventful retirement? That was not his style. On the 30th September 1914 in Deal, Kent, William Acraman Monteagle, aged seventy-seven, married his second wife, twenty-three-year-old Maud Lilian Dawson. They had one son, born in Eastbourne seven months after the marriage. William was described as a "Retired Christian Minister (Clergyman)".

Even though he was a new father he continued to write cantatas. One such, called "The Rose of June – A Military Cantata", was particularly well received and reviewed.

William Acraman's life was packed with strange, unusual and dramatic happenings. His death was also somewhat unusual. It was not as dramatic as that of another defrocked vicar, Harold Davidson, who was eaten by a lion. Our ex-vicar was knocked down by a Hastings tram in January 1917 and later died of his injuries. William Acraman Monteagle died in Hastings hospital on the 8th February 1917 aged nearly eighty years, leaving a young widow and a twenty-one-month-old son.

Hastings tram in the early 1900s.

Even William's will raised some fascinating questions. Why was his new wife not mentioned? What did he have against the town of Deal to make him stipulate that his son was not live or be educated there?

"... that my said infant son shall if possible be brought up and educated in Hastings or else in London but not in Deal"

Land he still owned in Whatstandwell was to pass on to his son. His daughter Essie had married and was now Mrs Harold Ivimey. In his will she was asked to –

"take a kindly interest in her "little step brother"

Actually he was her half-brother.

And so ended the life of William Acraman, later William Acraman Monteagle, one-time vicar of Crich. However, his legacy is still evident in the parish, in the shape of four thriving schools; Crich Infants, Crich Carr Primary, Fritchley Primary and Crich Junior.

He may have been accused of many things, but being boring certainly wasn't one of them!

Thanks to Alan Howe for this postscript and the following cantata information.

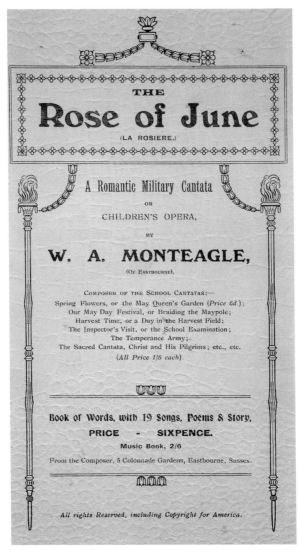

Cover of canata written by William Acraman Monteagle in about 1914.

24

—·· PRESS NOTICES. ··—

———————

"SPRING FLOWERS" or "THE MAY QUEEN'S GARDEN" (10,000 sold)

"A charming Cantata."—*Eastbourne Society.*

"The music of 'Spring Flowers' is simple and tuneful, and the words above the average. We are sure that many clergymen and teachers will be glad to know of this Cantata, which has already been successfully performed on several occasions."—*School Guardian.*

"HARVEST TIME."

"There are a number of pretty action songs for seniors and junior scholars, a prologue, and a school-boys' Song and March. This was loudly encored. The music exceedingly bright and melodious."—*Eastbourne Chronicle.*

"THE INSPECTOR'S VISIT."

Mr. Monteagle is a really clever composer. His latest work, a humorous piece called 'The Inspector's Visit" treats of the event of a school examination, and was the attraction last evening."—*Sussex Daily News.*

"This is the third time Mr. Monteagle has favoured an Eastbourne audience with a charming original composition."—*Eastbourne Society.*

"THE ROSE OF JUNE."

"The Rev. W. A. Monteagle has made a mark as a composer of School Cantatas, and his delightful Cantata, 'The Rose of June,' was presented for the first time last Wednesday."—*Eastbourne Gazette.*

"The Cantata is bound to become popular on account of its melodies, which appeal direct to the heart, as well as the graceful words and pure sentiment, its teaching being thoroughly sound, and its thoughts far above the average, with a definite and interesting story."—*Eastbourne Chronicle.*

"The Cantata written and composed by the Rev. W. A. Monteagle, of Eastbourne, was produced last night at the Queen's Gate Hall. It is a fanciful representation of country life, in which the author claims with some justice to revive the style of Balfe. The music shows facility in writing graceful melody, and is simple in design."—*Morning Post.*

"THE TEMPERANCE ARMY," or "THE BAND OF HOPE BOY."

"The Cantata includes some bright and enlivening music, and was productive of considerable pleasure to the audience."—*Eastbourne Gazette.*

"Performed with complete success before a crowded audience."—
Band of Hope Chronicle.

"OUR MAY DAY FESTIVAL," or "BRAIDING THE MAYPOLE."

"This picturesque and melodious composition, (the chief attraction on the programme), was rendered with great success, to the entire satisfaction of those present."—*Eastbourne Chronicle.*

Review of the cantata.

Appendices

Crich Cross, date unknown

Crich Market Place, date unknown

APPENDIX 1a
Florence Nightingale's shipwreck letter

Lea Hurst
Cromford: Derby
Aug 16/78

Dear Sir

Four of our trained Nurses have been wrecked
on their way home from Canada, where they
had been nursing for us at the Montreal
General Hospital & were returning for
further Nursing employment under us.
The steamer was wrecked upon a reef two
days out from Canada: on July 21.
All night she was beaten about & in danger
of going to pieces. At day-break the Captain
lowered his passengers into a life-boat:
but she drifted out to sea & again they were
with difficulty saved. For a whole week till
the 28th they were on an island, whence an
Officer made his way to the nearest light-house,
swimming two rivers, (which the crew would
not cross): or battened down in the hold of
a small fish-schooner, without food or air, in a
terrific storm: On July 28 they were rescued
by the Erl King, Capt. Ed. Scott, whose kindness
we can never forget, bound for Glasgow where
they landed safe on Aug 9.

Would you allow me to return thanks for ~~them~~
our four Nurses in your Church next Sunday?
Their names are: Nurse Styring
                    Nurse Wilson
                      "   Cross
                      "   Webb:

Might I say, in any terms you would be good
enough to use:

✝ ――――Florence Nightingale desires to return
~~the~~ most humble & hearty thanks to Almighty
God for four trained Nurses returning home
(on duty) from Canada   Who were wrecked
on July 21, were saved three times from a
watery grave, & after severe sufferings for a

week from exposure & hardships, were
rescued on the 28th by a vessel bound for
Glasgow & safely landed on August 9. thro'
a merciful Providence

                    Pray believe me, Sir,
                        Ever your faithful servt
                            Florence Nightingale

The Revd
    W. Acraman

228

APPENDIX 1b
Florence Nightingale's temperance letter

Lea Hurst
Nov 26 1881

Dear Sir
I beg your acceptance of £3.3 for any
of your works that require it most: Temperance
or Bible or Day School.
I wish it were more, but the claims
upon me are far beyond my means.
I trust that your fight in favour of
Temperance will be crowned with success.
as I am sure you also pray for ours —
Drink & dress seem to be the great
barriers against a higher civilization,
against God's work in these parts.
The people do not even understand
their own interests: they will live in
wretched quarters, perhaps 7 in family
and a lodger in two miserable
bed-rooms — happy too if grown up sons
& daughters are not in the same bed
room & even (up into the teens) in the
same bed — While they spend
more on eating & drinking & dressing
(with no mending) than we do —
& mend their clothes less than we do.

229

These are people earning (Parents,
Sons & daughters included) considerably
more than a London Government clerk,
who has to appear like a Gentleman.
What wonder if immorality is rampant!
I have to thank you for a Sermon
preached the Sunday before last
against profession, & against drinking,
repeated to me, as far as I could judge,
almost word for word, by my Maid.

I always make them tell me the Sermons
they hear.
I pray God to bless your work.
  Excuse pencil
    I pray believe me
      ever your faithful Serv.t
        Florence Nightingale

Rev.d W. Acraman

APPENDIX 2a
Mr Wheatcroft's letter to the vicar

Mr Wheatcroft was secretary to the Parochial School Managers and also, for a time, Revd Acraman's solicitor.

The letter was part of the story surrounding the sacking of Mr Kent, headmaster at the Parochial School for three days.

J. WHEATCROFT,
SOLICITOR.

29th October 1897

Rev W Acraman
Dear Sir

With reference to our late conference Yesterday, and having fully considered the matter I have finally decided to withdraw from the business. I have no wish to add to your difficulties or cause you any pain by assigning my reasons & I therefore refrain from doing so. The course I have decided to adopt will leave you ample time to entrust the business to other hands and leave you free to allow the charge against Mr Nevile to go undefended

I send you copy of Mr Potter's letter received yesterday which will put you in possession of the position of the business up

Appendix 2a: Mr Wheatcroft's letter

to date. I am returning to Mr
Neville by this post the summons
served upon him.

I shall be pleased to reply
to any letter from you, but you
must excuse me in declining to
lose any more of my time in
useless discussions of worthless
lay opinions and gossip upon
legal matters.

Yours faithfully
Jno. Wheatcroft

APPENDIX 2b
Mr Wilson's letter to the vicar

FIRM,
WILSON & SON.

PARTNERS,
JOS⁹ GEO. WILSON.
W. MORTIMER WILSON M.A.

TELEGRAMS,
"WILSONS, SOL⁹⁹, ALFRETON."

Alfreton.

11ᵗʰ Nov: 1897

Dear Sir

Yourself ats Kent
—————"—————

Herewith we send you copy of a letter
received by us this morning from Mr Potter
of Matlock Mr Kent's Solicitor which we
enclose for your consideration. As things now
stand no action can be commenced before
the January Court so that you have a little
time to consider the matter. From what you
have informed us Mr Kent ~~~ gave great
provocation to the managers and you would have

a reasonable ground upon which to convince
the Judge that you had just cause for summarily
dismissing him and should this be established
he could not recover anything. On the other
hand there is no doubt that the if the matte
comes to trial there will be a great deal of
publicity given to it and the ill-feeling which
already exists in the Parish will be much increase

You have already offered a Quarter's Salary
"without prejudice" and considering that M:
Kent has now got another berth a month's salary
viz £7.10.0 with something for his expenses say to
a £12 altogether would be a fair thing to offer should
you be disposed to settle at all. Kindly let us know your
views at an early date. We regret very much that the
Belper Bench took the view they did of the Assault Case

Rev? E.m. acraman.   Yours faithfully

APPENDIX 3
What the National Newspapers wrote

Many of the escapades of our vicar were of such notoriety that they were widely reported across the country. Scandals involving vicars, then as now, made for good copy.

What follows are snippets of news about Revd Acraman's troubles as reported in various newspapers and magazines.

Daily Post: 10 February 1883

Gleanings

The *Sheffield Independent* says a memorial to the Bishop of Lichfield asking his lordship to recommend the Rev. W. Acraman, vicar of Crich, to resign his living, is being signed in the Crich district. This action is the outcome of the school scandal in the village. The memorial sets forth that the rev. gentleman has lost all spiritual influence in the parish, and that his residence amongst his parishioners is wanting in influence for good.

John Bull: 17 February 1883

The vicar of Crich summoned before the Belper magistrates on Thursday, two of his parishioners for assaulting him at a public meeting. There was great excitement at the meeting, and it was admitted that one of the defendants accidently touched the Vicar. After hearing ample evidence on both sides the magistrates dismissed the summonses.

Bristol Mercury and Daily Post:
17 February 1883

News of the Day

CHARGE OF ASSAULT – Sir John Alleyne and other Derbyshire Magistrates were engaged at the Belper Petty Session for several hours on Thursday on hearing a charge of assault on the vicar of Crich by two of his parishioners, Elijah Kirk and Samuel Bennett. The Rev. William Acraman, it would appear from the evidence, had caused some ill-feeling by the dismissal of the village schoolmaster. This action brought about a public meeting of ratepayers, at which the vicar's conduct was protested against. The proceedings were of an uproarious character and Kirk was alleged to have called the vicar a "tyrant" and other epithets, and to have put his fist into his face. The other defendant, it was stated, endeavoured by rough usage to push Mr. Acraman out of the room. In cross-examination the complainant said he went to the meeting uninvited and twice interrupted the speakers. The magistrates decided to dismiss the case.

Leeds Mercury: 13 April 1883

ASSAULT BY A DERBYSHIRE VICAR – At Belper yesterday the Rev. Wm. Acraman, vicar of Crich, was fined 1s and costs for assaulting his curate, the Rev. Andrew Blair, on the 28th March. Recently there has been a good deal of agitation and bad feeling against the Vicar in the parish.

Lloyd's Weekly: Sunday 22 April 1883

A VICAR ASSAULTING HIS CURATE – At Belper Petty Sessions on Thursday, the Rev. Wm. Acraman, vicar of Crich, was fined 1s and 16s 6d costs for having assaulted the Rev. Andrew Blair, his curate.

Northern Echo: 14 April 1883

ANOTHER CLERICAL SCANDAL

At Belper Petty Sessions on Thursday, the Rev. William Acraman, vicar of Crich, was fined 1s and 16s 6d costs for having unlawfully assaulted the Rev. Andrew Blair, his curate. Much painful scandal has been caused in the parish by dissensions between the vicar, his curate, the schoolmaster and the people generally, the assault in question arising out of the vicar ejecting the curate from his house with personal violence. There were several unseemly scenes in court, personalities being freely indulged in.

Manchester Times: Saturday 14 April 1883

A VICAR CHARGED BY HIS CURATE WITH ASSAULT
EXTRAORDINARY CASE

The Rev. William Acraman, vicar of Crich, Derbyshire was on Thursday summoned before the Belper magistrates by his curate, the Rev. Andrew Blair, for an assault alleged to have been committed on him on the 28th March. Mr. Jackson (Belper) appeared for the complainant, and Mr. Brown (Stockport) for the defendant. There had been a great deal of disagreement and disturbance in the parish of late, mainly in connection with the management of the parochial schools. Meetings have been held in opposition to the vicar, and a few weeks since he summoned one of the parishioners for attacking him at a meeting, but the case was dismissed. The vicar and curate then appeared to be on the most cordial terms. The assault with which Mr. Acraman was now charged took place at a meeting of the school managers which was held at the vicarage, and at which complainant, the defendant, Mr. A.F. Hurt (a magistrate), Dr. Dunn, and Mr. Saxton were present.

The complainant, who was till recently curate at St. Alban's, Leeds said he came to Crich about Christmas, and for some time he loyally supported the vicar in his disputes with the parishioner but he gradually saw through him, and found he had a propensity to injure the innocent. He, therefore, refused to assist in putting up memorials on his behalf, and then he found that the vicar was doing what he could by privately communicating with the Bishop to ruin him. On the 26th March he received a letter from the Bishop, enclosing a letter which Mr. Acraman had written to him, headed "The Curate at Crich and his stipend," and containing various accusations against him. He wrote a reply, and on the 28th he attended the meeting of school managers at the vicarage. He there attempted to read the vicar's letter to the Bishop, but the vicar objected to its being read, stating that it had nothing to do with school matters. He replied that it had and, on the vicar again stating that it had not, he (the curate) said it was a lie. He was proceeding to read the letter when the vicar rushed at him and seized him by the collar. A scuffle ensued, in which he (the curate) was thrown to the ground, and the chair was broken, he was seriously injured on the left hip, and he put his feet up to protect himself from the vicar. Mr. Hurt however, took hold of the vicar round the body and prevented further violence. He was picked up by Dr. Dunn.

Mr. Brown: Did you call the vicar a liar?

Complainant: I don't remember, but I used the word "lie."– But did you use the word "liar?" I don't know, but it is all the same whether I did or not. – But are you in the habit of calling people liars? If I called him a liar it would be perfect truth. – Then you admit that you called him a liar? I don't admit that I called him one but he is one. – And do you consider that is a proper tone in which to speak to your vicar in his own house? Far worse conversation has passed in his own house from him. He has said most dastardly and filthy things in his own house. I ask you, as a clergyman, do you consider that it is a proper phrase to use to a person in his own house? And I tell you, as a man, that he has used worse.

Sir John Alleyne (one of the magistrates): Take the advice of the Bench and say yes or no.

Mr. Brown (to the complainant.): You are showing yourself in your true colours now. You are being photographed as you are at Crich. Now, do you consider that it is a proper phrase to use to your vicar in his own home?

Complainant: Under the circumstances, yes.

The Chairman (Mr. A.P. Heywood) several times protested against the manner in which the cross-examination was conducted, and remarked that he thought any advocate would have kept the Court from having to listen to such real absolute idiotcy.

Mr. Hurt stated that several times in the course of the meeting at the Vicarage Mr. Blair interrupted the vicar with the remark "That's a lie," but he was not sure whether the term "liar" was used. Whether the vicar seized Mr. Blair, it was evidently with the intention of either taking the letter from him or putting him out of the house, which he had previously threatened to do. He thought Mr. Blair threw himself on his back purposely, and he then kicked about a good deal to keep the vicar off. His (Mr. Hurt's) finger was kicked as he had hold of the vicar. In his opinion a technical assault had been committed, but it was under great provocation.

Eventually the Bench convicted the defendant of a technical assault, and fined him 1s and costs.

Newspaper reports from round the country

Liverpool Mercury: Monday 21 May 1883

THE VICAR OF CRICH — Dissensions having existed for some time between the Rev. W. Acraman, vicar of Crich, Derbyshire, and his parishioners, respecting his recent conviction for assaulting his curate, an enquiry has been made by the Bishop of Lichfield, who has forwarded the following reply to the memorialists: – "As the result of the inquiry I have to intimate to you that, although the commissioners were far from satisfied with the state of the parish as revealed by the witnesses whom they examined, they could find no sufficient reason to take any further steps with a view to remove the incumbent. I am bound to admit that events that have recently occurred were sufficient to have produced a feeling of distrust and uneasiness on the part of the parishioners, and I cannot deem unreasonable the application which you made to me with a view to inquiries being initiated."

Manchester Times: 15 September 1899

DERBYSHIRE CLERICAL SCANDAL
SERIOUS ALLEGATIONS AGAINST A VICAR.

Yesterday week the Belper magistrates were occupied, for five hours in hearing the charges against the Rev. Acraman, Vicar of Crich, Derbyshire, as already briefly reported. The accused was brought from the County Gaol in a private conveyance; During the whole of the proceedings hundreds of people congregated near the Court, which was cleared of the general public. There were two charges against the prisoner of having indecently assaulted a girl named *child A*, aged 13 years.

Mr. Clifford opened the case for the prosecution, and mentioned that the defendant was the Vicar of Crich, and the girl, *child A*, whom the defendant was charged with assaulting, was 13 years of age last November, and lived with her mother, a widow, at Crich. The girl had been a companion of the prisoner's daughter, who was about the same age. They had gone to school together, and had been frequently in each other's company. At the end of last year the two girls left Crich Carr School, and *child A* went to work at Lea Mills. The Vicar's daughter early in this year was sent to a boarding school at Eastbourne. About Easter some of the young people at Crich were being taught a cantata, and it was after one of the practices in the school that the defendant asked the girl to go to the Vicarage. She was taken into the house by the defendant and into the drawing-room. Whilst there, counsel stated, the defendant locked the door, pulled down the blinds, and took the girl upon his knee, kissed her, and committed the offence with which he was charged. This was repeated on three subsequent occasions. The defendant asked her if she would marry him at some future time. At last the girl agreed to marry him, and the Vicar commenced to make arrangements for her to be sent to Eastbourne to be suitably educated. He saw the girl's mother, and told her he wished the girl to go to Eastbourne as a companion to his daughter and to be educated at the same school. Though she objected to this arrangement at first, she ultimately consented. On the 8th of June the defendant went to Eastbourne, and a few days later wrote to Mrs. Slack, a neighbour, telling her to inform *Mrs. A* that he had made suitable arrangements, that the girl was to reside with a widow lady with two children, and was to be sent on to Eastbourne on the following Friday. The curate was deputed to take her as far as London. After discussing the matter with Mrs. Slack, *Mrs. A* refused to allow her daughter to go.

Evidence was given by the girl as to the four alleged assaults. She was examined at considerable length, and admitted that she informed two of her friends, who worked at Lea Mills, that nothing had taken place between Mr. Acraman and herself.

Mr. Hall: Then you told a lie?

Witness: Yes, I did, because I had promised him not to say anything.

Mr. Clifford: You told a lie because the parson told you to do so? – Yes sir.

The mother of the girl, Mary Slack, Mrs. John Lee, Police-constable Cosgrove, and Dr. McElligott gave evidence, the latter stating that the girl was virgo intacta. Mrs. Lee recounted a conversation she had had with the Vicar, who had informed her that, he was very fond of *child A*, and *child A* was very fond of him, and that when he had properly educated her he should marry her.

Mr. Hall, for the defence, argued that the magistrates should not allow such a serious charge to hang over the head of the defendant until the Assizes, unless they were perfectly convinced that a jury would be likely to convict. The defendant's conduct had certainly been strange, but men in his position had before now taken it into their heads to educate a girl of humble birth, and, having educated her, to make her a wife. He had no instructions from Mr. Acraman to deny that this was his intention, but he maintained that they had no right to send him for trial on the very grave charge put forward, unless there was some corroboration of material facts.

The Bench retired, and in a few minutes returned. The Chairman (Sir John Alleyne, Bart) then stated that in their opinion a prima facie case had been made out, and the prisoner must take his trial at the next Derbyshire Assizes.

Mr. Hall asked for bail, which was allowed, the prisoner in £500, and two sureties of £250 each. These were forthcoming.

Newspaper reports from round the country

Derby Mercury: Wed 6 September 1899

SERIOUS CHARGE AGAINST THE VICAR OF CRICH

At the Magistrates' Clerk's Office, Belper, on Thursday morning, the Rev. W. Acraman, Vicar of Crich was brought up before Col. Twyford on warrants charged with criminal assault on *child A*, of Crich, she being under the age of 16. – Mr. Clifford, Derby, prosecuted on behalf of the Chief Constable, who was present.

Mr. Clifford, in stating his case, said that it was taken under Section 16 of the Criminal Amendment Act, and he should produce such evidence that would justify a remand.

Child A said that she was 13 years old, and lived with her widowed mother at Crich. She had known Mr. Acraman all her life. After leaving her work on the 5th July her mother sent her on an errand to the vicarage. She went in the front door; there was no one in the drawing room, and the prisoner there committed the assault complained of. He asked her not to tell her mother; the same thing had occurred twice before. When questioned by her mother she told her what had taken place.

The prisoner here produced the baptismal record to show that she was nearly 15.

When arrested, in answer to Police-constable Cosgrove, he said he could certify that the girl was nearly 15.

The second charge was preferred of assault on a boy of the name of *child B*, aged 12 years, living with his father at Crich.

Mr. Clifford said the assault took place one day when the prisoner had taken the boy to the Darley Dale Institute, and on returning committed the alleged assault in a dark lane. When they got back to Crich Vicarage he gave the boy his supper. It had occurred four times previously, and once since.

When arrested, the prisoner said that the boy had not been to the Vicarage for one year, and he had not been in his company since that time. He now qualified his statement that the boy had been once to the Vicarage on an errand from the churchwarden. The boy was not allowed on the Vicarage premises, as he was so untruthful.

The prisoner was remanded for seven days, bail being refused, the case being so very serious. The prisoner pressed hard for bail on account of his church duties.

Derby Mercury: Wed 13 September 1899

THE SERIOUS CHARGES AGAINST THE VICAR, OF CRICH.

At Belper on Thursday the Rev. William Acraman, vicar of Crich, was brought up on remand on four charges of indecent assault upon a girl named *child A*, whose age is about 13 years.

The charges were taken under section 5 of the Criminal Law Amendment Act. Some time before the prisoner arrived at the Belper Public Hall the Court was crowded, but the Magistrates decided to clear the Court, and the case was proceeded with in the presence of the representatives of the Press. –

Sir John Alleyne, the chairman of the Bench, appealed to the Press to exercise discretion, and not to indulge in sensational reports. Besides Sir John Alleyne, Colonel Twyford, Mr. F. W. Greaves, and Mr. J. Smedley were the other magistrates present. The prosecution was conducted by Mr. R. S. Clifford (of Derby), and the prisoner was represented by Mr. Clarke Hall (who was instructed by Mr. J. Wheatcroft, of Belper). – Captain Holland, the chief constable was present, as also was Mr. J. Borough, the diocesan registrar, a representative of the Bishop of the diocese was also present. – Mr. Clifford opened the case, and intimated that with regard to the alleged offence upon the boy *child B* no evidence would be offered. – Mr. Clarke Hall asked the magistrates to dismiss this case, which was done. – Mr. Clarke Hall further appealed for the same publicity to be given to the dismissal as was given to the charge.

Mr. Clifford, in opening the case of the girl *child A*, said that it involved two charges of indecent assault, and two under the Criminal Law Amendment Act. The defendant was the Vicar of Crich, and the girl, *child A*, whom he was charged with assaulting, was thirteen years of age last November, and lived with her mother, a widow, at Crich. She appeared to have been a companion for the defendant's daughter, Essie, who was about the same age. They had been to school together until the latter part of last year, when Essie went to Eastbourne. *Child A* would tell them that on the Saturday before Easter Sunday she had been practising, with others, a cantata, and at the close the defendant asked her to go with him to the vicarage. She did so, and he took her into the drawing-room, and was there alleged to have

committed the offence complained of. Some days after this the defendant called on the girl's mother and asked for the girl to be sent to the house, as he had got a pencil case for her. The girl worked at Lea Mills, a hosiery factory, and upon her return the message was delivered to her, and she went to the vicarage, where she was admitted by the defendant, who subsequently, committed certain actions which would be detailed. Afterwards he told her that he would like to marry her, and after he had pressed her for some time she said that she would marry him. In June the defendant went away to Eastbourne, and there was some negotiation as to the girl *child A* going there to school with his daughter Essie, but ultimately *Mrs. A* declined to allow her to go. Upon the defendant's return he again sent for the girl to come to the vicarage and met her in the garden. Again he took her to the drawing-room, and similar occurrences were alleged to have taken place. Upon this occasion he gave the child a piece of blue ribbon. On July 5th defendant asked *Mrs. A* to send the girl up to the vicarage to the front door, and she went, Acraman meeting her in the garden. The offence was repeated, and the child was seen coming out of a field on to the highway, on her way from the vicarage, by the parish clerk.

Child A was then called, and bore out the opening statement in the main, though she said that nothing was said about marrying on the second occasion. On July 5th she deposed that the defendant told her in the drawing room that he loved her and asked her if she would marry him. She said nothing at first, but he asked her a lot of times, and eventually she said "Yes." When she left that evening he took her through the garden and a field, and told her to go that way so that "folks" should not see her. She went on and got over a wall into Bulling Lane, where she saw John Wetton, the parish clerk. She made no complaint of these occurrences to her mother until she was asked about it. – Cross-examined: When Essie was at home she (witness) was constantly at the vicarage playing. Mr. Cousens, the curate, the cook and a boy named Greenhough, all lived at the vicarage. She used to see Mr. Cousens frequently about the house when she was with Essie. She was angry with the defendant, but she promised him not to say anything, and she did not. She denied to one of her girl friends that the defendant had assaulted her, but she said that because of her promise to the defendant. She was telling the truth that day.

Mr. Clifford: You told a lie because the parson told you to tell one? – Yes.

Mrs A, mother of the last witness, said that her daughter was born on November 10th, 1885, and spoke to the occasions upon which the accused came to ask her to send *child A* up to the vicarage. The first time he said he had a pencil case for *child A* at the vicarage, and asked if she could go and fetch it, and witness said "Yes." On another occasion the girl brought home a piece of blue ribbon and some flowers. Subsequently defendant asked witness if she would let *child A* go to Eastbourne to be a companion for his daughter, and promised that he would educate her, "the same as his own child." Witness declined the offer at first, but on a later occasion she agreed, and arrangements were accordingly made. The accused then went to Eastbourne, but in a letter he wrote from there he said that his daughter was to be at the boarding school, while *child A* would stay

with some friends, and upon that witness decided not to let her daughter go. Upon the defendant's return he called and asked her to let *child A* call for a letter at the vicarage from his daughter, and *child A* accordingly went, bringing back two letters, which were now destroyed. Some time afterwards she put questions to her daughter, and meeting the defendant, she told him she would not allow him to come to her house any more. Acraman wanted to say something to her, but she left him. – Cross-examined: She thought the name of Mrs. Pennington was mentioned as the lady at Eastbourne who would take charge of *child A*.

Mr. M. G. McElligott, physician and surgeon, practising at Belper, gave the result of an examination of the child. It was purely negative.

John Wetton, parish clerk at Crich, gave evidence of seeing the girl *child A* in Bulling Lane one evening, when she came over the wall near the vicarage, a drop of some seven feet. Just previously he had seen her in company with the accused.

Mary Slack, of Crich, corroborated *Mrs. A's* evidence as to the receipt of the letter from Eastbourne, and added that the defendant had told her that he was going to have *child A* educated with his little girl, because he had proposed to her, and she had accepted him. Witness was, prior to her marriage, for ten years in the defendant's employ. – Cross-examined: She had known the defendant ever since he came to Crich, over 20 years ago. During that time she had never known any impropriety to go on in the house. He had always been a perfect gentleman to her and to everyone else in the house.

Mary Lee, of Crich, said that she had a conversation with the defendant about *child A*. He said that he was not aware that there was any trouble going on at Belper until he was told of it in the town that morning. He understood that *Mrs. A* had been to the magistrates to make a complaint, and added that he was quite ready to marry the girl when she was educated. He was fond of her, he said, and she was fond of him. He seemed a great deal troubled, but said that he had never meant anything except what was right to her. He never made anything in the nature of an admission to witness.

Mrs. Slack, recalled, gave, as far as she could remember, the contents of the letter from Eastbourne.

Police-constable Cosgrove, stationed at Crich, said that on August 31st he arrested the defendant on a warrant and in reply to the charge he said, "The girl is 15 years old in November; I can prove that by the register book". – Cross-examined: It was a matter of common talk in Crich for weeks before the defendant's arrest.

This closed the case for the prosecution.

Mr. Hall, addressing the magistrates in defence, said that he had a very painful duty to perform. It was exceedingly painful that a charge of this kind should have been made at all, but now that one had heard the whole of the evidence that could be adduced by the prosecution, he could not but feel that the nature of that evidence was so slight that, in spite of the gravity of the charge, the prosecution had failed at every point to make out a case which would justify the Bench in committing the accused for trial. The girl had given her evidence, but if there was one thing that stood out clearer than another it was that she never at any time resisted what she said had been done, and, as a matter of fact, if such things ever were done, she was practically a party to the doing of them. If that was the case, it was perfectly clear that no jury would accept her evidence unless it was corroborated in some material particular, and it was for the Bench to consider whether it was at all likely that a jury would convict. If it was necessary that there should be corroboration, where had the prosecution been able to adduce it? It was common ground that the girl was frequently in his house, and that he was very fond of her, but the prosecution had not produced a single iota of evidence, except hers, to substantiate the charges. He (Mr. Hall) could perfectly acquiesce in, and agree with, everything that all the witnesses had said, with the exception of the girl. It was all so far as he knew, perfectly true, and he had not disputed any of it. From their evidence there was not even the suggestion of more suspicion, and the case rested solely upon the story of the girl. He submitted that it was perfectly certain that under those circumstances no jury could possibly convict. If that was the case, he urged that the accused should not be placed in the painful position of having this charge hanging over his head for two or three months, if it was a fact that when he came for trial no jury could convict because there was no corroboration. He would have liked to leave the matter with the Bench simply on the broad ground that the prosecution had not been able in any single particular to support the girl's story, but there were other defences, even if her tale was admitted. There was a defence to, at any rate, three of the charges which would prevent a conviction. With regard to the alleged offences of April 1st and 11th, the accused was charged with indecent assault, but the whole of the girl's conduct was indicative of that acquiescence which made it utterly impossible in law to prove an assault. With regard to the incident on the 5th of June, the girl had sworn that she had not seen the accused at all that week, and upon Whitsuntide being put to her she had admitted that the alleged offence was committed before Whit-Sunday, which was May 21st. As the warrant was not issued until August 31st, the three mouths' limitation imposed by the Act within which information could be laid came into force, and this charge must also fall to the ground. As to the occurrence on July 5th, the girl's story was entirely uncorroborated. It was, of course, difficult to explain why the girl should tell a story of this kind if it were not true; but, unfortunately, girls did tell these stories sometimes. It was more easily understood, perhaps, in this case than in some others, and he could not disguise from himself the fact that the conduct of the defendant towards this girl had been very strange. They had been told – he (Mr. Hall) was not in a position to dispute it – that something had been said to her about marriage. It seemed a very strange idea to have entered into Mr. Acraman's mind, but it must be remembered that many men had done similar things before. If this were the case, and something was said to this girl about marrying her, it was not difficult to understand that the girl, having mixed among a certain class of girls, should have got the poison into her mind which had induced her to make the charge. If she had been a right-minded girl surely she would have complained at the outset to her mother. Everything rested upon her, and they had it from her own mouth that she was not to be relied upon, and had already lied in the matter. Surely, if the evidence of one person was to be sufficient to justify a jury in convicting a man that evidence should be untainted, and it could not be suggested that the girl's evidence was untainted in this case. He affirmed, without hesitation, that no jury would convict under such circumstances, and that no Judge on the Bench of the High Court would allow a jury to convict a man on the evidence of one girl, who admitted telling a lie. The prosecution had failed to make out the case, and he begged, therefore, that they would not allow the charges to hang any longer over this man when he must be acquitted before a jury.

The magistrates, after a brief retirement, said that in their opinion there was a very strong prima facie case against the defendant, and they were bound to send him to take his trial at the Assizes.

The defendant reserved his defence, and Mr. Hall applied for bail.

Mr. Clifford asked that it might be substantial.

The magistrates granted bail, the prisoner in £500, and two sureties of £250 each. The hearing lasted close upon five hours.

Derby Mercury: 20 September 1899

THE CRICH SCANDALS.
LETTER FROM THE BISHOP.

A letter has been received by the two churchwardens of Crich, from the Bishop of Southwell, in reference to the Vicar of the parish, the Rev. W Acraman, who, it will be remembered, was recently committed for trial at Belper on a charge of indecent assault. The communication was made known on Friday, and the contents are as follow:

"Blackmoor, Petersfield, September 11th

"Dear sirs, – I write to inform you that I have desired Mr. Acraman not to take part in the Church services or other ministrations so long as the present scandal against him remains uncleared. It will be your duty to see that this injunction is observed. I have informed Mr. Borough, who will be able to advise you in case of difficulty. – Yours truly,

GEORGE SOUTHWELL."

Messrs. N. I. Hawkes and J. T. Lee, the wardens, have made the contents of the letter known to the vicar, and it is understood he is to go away for a short time. Mr. Acraman preached last Sunday. The vicar took part in both services on that day, and in the evening made reference to his position, and the charge against him. Arrangements have been made for a former curate, the Rev. Mr. Drury to preach on Sunday. It is stated the churchwardens are in communication with Mr. Borough, the gentleman mentioned in the bishop's letter. Mr. Borough is the diocesan registrar, and lives in Belper.

The 'Belper and Alfreton Journal' says that on Sunday evening last the Rev. W. Acraman preached at Crich Church. There was a very small attendance, and as the vicar ascended the pulpit and began to announce his text a number of adults, mostly ladies, rose and left, followed by batches of boys and girls, the noise being sufficient, the rev. gentleman paused for silence. Mr. Acraman said that, before dwelling upon the text he had just read, he desired to refer to a personal, and even a parochial, matter that had pervaded the atmosphere of the village for the past, week or two. He thanked God that the prayers of his people had been heard and answered, and that God had delivered from prison the innocent individual who now stood before them in his accustomed place. He felt bound to say that this case against him was not instigated by those in his parish whom he loved and served, but was the doing of men in the county town whom he well knew, and who spitefully desired his ruin and removal. He pleaded for the continued prayers of God's people that the black cloud which still hung over him as a pall might be scattered before the wind of truth and justice; and especially let their prayers ascend for the harmony and success of the work of the Church and of the Day and Sunday Schools. The scandalous tales which they had heard had been begun by foul suggestions, a tittle-tattle, an adding here and a putting in there of demoniacal untruth, until an infamous – complete it was called – case had been manufactured. To all this he could only give his emphatic denial, and time would tell in his favour. He urged all who loved truth to suspend their judgment, to judge only as they themselves would be judged, to say only as they would be spoken of themselves, and the Almighty Judge of All would vindicate the innocence of the humble victim before them. After the service a crowd of rough and noisy youths and young women assembled outside the church door, but as the vicar passed out none ventured to raise a sound.

Distant view of Crich Stand, date unknown.

Fritchley view, date unknown.

246

APPENDIX 4
A brief background to Board Schools

Elementary Education Act 1870

The Elementary Education Act 1870, commonly known as *Forster's Education Act*, set the framework for schooling of all children over the age of five and under thirteen in England and Wales. It was drafted by William Forster, a Liberal MP, and it was introduced on the 17th February 1870 after campaigning by the National Education League.

Need

A driving force behind the Act was a need for Britain to remain competitive in the world by being at the forefront of manufacture and improvement.

There were objections to the concept of universal education. One was that many people remained hostile to the idea of mass education. They claimed it would make labouring classes 'think' and that these classes would realise their lives were dissatisfying and possibly be encouraged to revolt. Others feared that handing children to a central authority could lead to indoctrination. Another reason was the vested interests of the Church and other social groups; the churches were funded by the state, through public money, to provide education for the poor, and they did not want to lose that power.

The Act laid the foundations of English elementary education. After 1880 attendance was made compulsory for children until they were twelve years old.

Principles

The 1870 Education Act declared that:

The ratepayers of each Poor Law Union (in the county districts) or borough could petition the Board of Education to investigate educational provision in their area. This was done by comparing the results of a census of existing school places with the number of children of school age recorded in the Census. If there was a substantial shortfall, a ***School Board*** would be created.

Board Schools

These Boards were to provide elementary education for children aged five to twelve (inclusive)

Board Members were elected by the ratepayers. (The number of Board Members was determined by the size of the population of the district.) Each voter could choose three (or more) Board Members from a list of candidates, and those with the highest number of votes were chosen for the existing number of seats available. It should be noted that a voter could cast all their votes for one person. This was known as 'plumping' and ensured that religious (and, later, political) minorities could ensure some representation on the Board. This franchise was different from national elections, since female householders could vote and stand for office.

The Boards financed themselves by a precept (a requisition) added to either the local poor rate or the municipal rate. They were also eligible to apply for capital funding in the form of a government loan.

Parents still had to pay fees for their children to attend schools. Boards would pay the fees of children who were poor, even if they attended Church schools.

The Boards could make grants to existing Church Schools and erect their own Board Schools or elementary schools. Boards could, if they deemed it necessary, create a by-law and table it before Parliament to make attendance compulsory (unless there was an excuse, for example, sickness, or living more than one mile from a school, or child having been certified as reaching a certain standard of education). In 1873, 40% of the population lived in compulsory attendance districts.

Religious teaching in Board Schools was restricted to nondenominational instruction, or none at all. Parents had the right to withdraw their children from religious education. This applied even to church schools.

All schools would be inspected, making use of the existing regime. The individual schools continued to be eligible for an annual government grant calculated on the basis of the inspection ('payment by results').

Effects of the Act

Between 1870 and 1880 there were between three and four thousand schools started or taken over by school boards. Rural boards run by parishes had only one or two schools to manage, but industrial town and city boards had very many. Rural boards favoured economy and the release of children for agricultural labour. Town boards tended to be more rigorous in their provisions, and by 1890 some had special facilities for gymnastics, art and crafts, and domestic science.

There were ongoing political clashes between the vested interests of the Church, private schools, and the National Education League followers. In some districts the creation of boards was delayed by local vote. In others, church leaders managed to be voted onto boards and restrict the building of Board Schools, or divert the school rate funds into church schools.

Education was not made compulsory until 1880 since many factory owners feared the removal of children as a source of cheap labour. However, with the simple mathematics and English they were acquiring, factory owners now had workers who could read and make measurements.

Following continued campaigning by the National Education League, in 1880 attendance to age ten became compulsory everywhere in England and Wales. In 1891 elementary schooling became free in both Board and voluntary (church) schools.

The school boards were abolished by the Balfour Education Act of 1902, which replaced them with around three hundred Local Education Authorities, by which time there were 5,700 Board Schools (2.6m pupils) and 14,000 voluntary schools (3m pupils). The LEAs' remit included secondary education for the first time.

Text taken from http://en.wikipedia.org/wiki/Elementary_Education_Act_1870

APPENDIX 5
Standards of education

In areas served by School Boards which had implemented by-laws requiring attendance, compulsory attendance until the thirteenth birthday was exempted if a child (being over ten) had been certified by the inspector as satisfying the required standard for that board. These children could start work.

The following are the six Standards of Education contained in the 1872 Revised code of Regulations.

STANDARD I

Reading   One of the narratives next in order after monosyllables in an elementary reading book used in the school.

Writing   Copy in manuscript character a line of print, and write from dictation a few common words.

Arithmetic   Simple addition and subtraction of numbers of not more than four figures, and the multiplication table to multiplication by six.

STANDARD II

Reading   A short paragraph from an elementary reading book.

Writing   A sentence from the same book, slowly read once, and then dictated in single words.

Arithmetic   The multiplication table, and any simple rule as far as short division (inclusive).

STANDARD III

Reading   A short paragraph from a more advanced reading book.

Writing   A sentence slowly dictated once by a few words at a time, from the same book.

Arithmetic   Long division and compound rules (money).

STANDARD IV

Reading   A few lines of poetry or prose, at the choice of the inspector.

Writing   A sentence slowly dictated once, by a few words at a time, from a reading book, such as is used in the first class of the school.

Arithmetic   Compound rules (common weights and measures).

STANDARD V

Reading	A short ordinary paragraph in a newspaper, or other modern narrative.
Writing	Another short ordinary paragraph in a newspaper, or other modern narrative, slowly dictated once by a few words at a time.
Arithmetic	Practice and bills of parcels.

STANDARD VI

Reading	To read with fluency and expression.
Writing	A short theme or letter, or an easy paraphrase.
Arithmetic	Proportion and fractions (vulgar and decimal).

From the Parochial School Logbook 1894:

OBJECT LESSONS

Animals – elephant, singing birds, sheep, tiger, fish, owl

Trades – baker, pottery, shoemaker, butcher, grocer, post office

Common Objects – leather, iron, cotton, salt, rain, coal, butter, tea, books, sponge, knife, stone quarrying, fire, wild flowers, train, making a bed, laying the table

REPETITION

I	Signs of rain
II	Keeping his word
III	Keeping his word
IV-VII	Horatio
IV-VII	Geography of Europe; maps of the Rhine, Spain and Yorkshire

Sale map of 1892

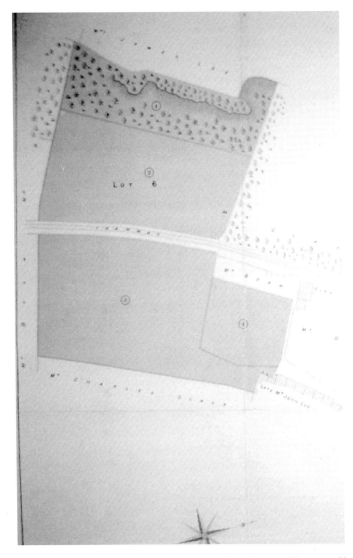

An estate for sale in 1892. These lots are where New Road is now. The row of houses belonging to the late Mr John Lee was originally Workhouse Row – now called Chapel Row.

The other lots were around the Wesleyan Chapel, just off the Common.
Notice the tramway which ran from the Clay Cross Company Quarry at Town End.

Map courtesy of Rosemary Hall

Crich Carr view

Anonymous family album

View from Crich Carr towards Holloway
about 1900.